LESSONS FROM IRAQ

LESSONS FROM IRAQ

MEMOIR OF A MARINE

MIKE KUBISTA

Lessons from Iraq
Copyright © 2023 by Mike Kubista. All rights reserved.

All rights reserved. No part of this publication may be reproduced, distributed, or transmitted in any form or by any means, including photocopying, recording, or other electronic or mechanical methods, without the prior written permission of the publisher, except in the case of brief quotations embodied in critical reviews and certain other noncommercial uses permitted by copyright law.

ISBN: 979-8-88759-737-9 - paperback
ISBN: 979-8-88759-738-6 - ebook

CONTENTS

Author's Note 7
Further Reading 9
Rapid Fire 13
Thank You for Your Service 20
Information War 23
"Grab Your Gear!" 28
Lessons From Iraq 31
Wild Dogs (1) 33
GAS! GAS! GAS! 39
Weapons of Mass Destruction 1: It Begins 47
MOASS 51
"Good, Good, USA!" 57
Weapons of Mass Destruction 2: Sanctions 63
Remnants 66
If You're _____, Leave the City 72
Exit Soul 75
Weapons of Mass Destruction 3: The International
    Cash Pipeline 81
Women 85
Wild Dogs (2) 94
Marine Corps 98
Fucking Reservists 101
Choke 106
Unknown Iraqi Man 117

Unknown Iraqi Girl...119
Bush's War (1) 122
Iraqi Pastoral...126
Morning Piss..131
Sweaty Balls and Dysentery 137
Wild Dogs (3)..150
Matilda 152
Guard Shift 164
Weapons of Mass Destruction 4: Smuggling Victory....169
Cereal Aisle 174
Wild Dogs (4)...179
Napalm Ditty-Bop 183
The Walls of Abu Ghraib 190
Luck..195
Transition 199
Desert Chapel..213
Bush's War (2) 216
Crash..219
2/4..224
Weapons of Mass Destruction 5: Iraqi Resurgence 231
Wild Dogs (5)..239
Ramadi Detention Facility 246
Shadow Man 260
Last Ride 263
The Death of Saddam 265
American Barbecue Flies.................................272
PTSD 275
Obama's War 306
Weapons of Mass Destruction 6: Failures 311
Dark-Bright..318

AUTHOR'S NOTE

Iraq was a strange war in that so few members of the American population were actually affected by it. Soldiers went to war while kids back home played video games of the same wars those men were fighting. Many Americans knew people who served, but it was a relative few who went back again and again while society rapidly moved ahead back home like nothing was happening. War, like all trauma, creates gaps between those who have experienced it and those who haven't. I want to close some of those gaps, let people experience some of the war for themselves.

I served with a lot of different Marines in Iraq, guys who taught me many things, most good, some bad. For the purposes of this book, I decided to change the names of the men I served with. I don't want small moments recorded from my memory to be used to represent the characters of those men. They are complete people on their own, not my memories, and even the guys I didn't like were brave in ways far beyond anything I've seen since. A few Marines named in my memoir represent multiple people. For example, I mention Peters several times, but he's not always the same guy. I remember many events from Iraq, but not always which Marines were involved, this is how I chose to solve that problem. There are also things that are impossible to write from memory, like exact words from conversations. I did my best to retain the general ideas and feelings of conversations, but very rarely could I remember a conversation word for word.

If I wrote about anyone in a negative way, it's because they were important to my life at the time, and their actions clarified something to me about what I wanted to be as a man or Marine, nothing more.

(To see pictures of the Iraq War in '03 and '04, check out mikekubista.com or https://www.facebook.com/Lessons.from.Iraq. A special thanks to Nate Blevins, Bob Pederson, Dave Shopp, and Brett Murton for the pictures.)

FURTHER READING

I've spent a lot of time since my deployments researching the history, politics, and people of Iraq from the last 40 years. I did this because I needed to make sense of things for myself. Here are a few resources that were helpful or interesting to me in my search. These are a good place to start for anyone curious to learn more.

The Unraveling, by Emma Sky

Emma Sky was a British operative working alongside US Military leadership in Iraq. She worked with all the key players, both Iraqi and American, and was in country when key political decisions were made that ultimately destroyed any chance of peacefully rebuilding the country.

Hide and Seek, by Charles Duelfer

This book has many interesting insights on the failings of US intelligence under the Bush administration. Duelfer has a lot of experience with Iraqis from the old regime and with the bureaucratic systems in Washington and the UN. That firsthand knowledge of both worlds gives his assessments an interesting level of clarity.

The Iraq Survey Group Report, assembled by Charles Duelfer and his team in Iraq

This is a thousand-page government report on weapon's programs and WMD in Iraq. It's arduous technical reading, but it gives a rich analysis of Iraq's internal politics, weapon's programs, and international political machinations. If you're okay with a difficult read and want something deeper than headlines and the wildly over-simplistic analysis given by the media about weapons of mass destruction in Iraq, this is a fantastic resource.

I Was Saddam's Son, by Latif Yahia

This is a disturbing look at the life of Uday Hussein as told by his body double Latif Yahia. It does a great job of showing the stratification of Iraq under the old regime, how guys like Uday Hussein could commit really any crime they wanted to, and no one would dare say a word against them.

The Hangman of Abu Ghraib, by Latif Yahia

This is a brutal book, a biography of a man who started as a low-level enforcer for Saddam and became his chief executioner at Abu Ghraib Prison, hanging thousands of people for the regime. This book does a good job of giving a glimpse into the lives of the underclass of people in Iraq before and during Saddam's regime.

The Invisible War, by Joy Gordon

After the Gulf War in 1991, the US and international community implemented heavy sanctions on Iraq to make sure they couldn't attempt to rebuild their weapon's programs. The result was a bureaucratic nightmare of arbitrary rules that devasted the Iraqi people and turned Iraq into a smuggling state. Saddam Hussein's regime survived, but the people of Iraq grew poorer and more brutalized by their own government. This book has a lot of bias, so some of its conclusions are superficial, but the data about the arbitrariness of the sanctions is really interesting and disturbing.

The Reckoning, by Sandra Mackey

There are a lot of books about Iraq's history up through Saddam's regime. I like this one because it's a clear and easy read and hits a lot of the main points. Mackey spent a lot of her life in the region, and her interpretations of the political situation in Iraq and what would likely happen in a US invasion turned out to be almost completely correct. It's a shame US government officials didn't listen to people like her.

Saddam: King of Terror, by Con Coughlin

I'm generally uncomfortable recommending books from journalists who were capitalizing on current world affairs, but this book gives a lot of good background information on Saddam and his regime and has several first-person accounts from interesting sources who knew Saddam personally.

The Prisoner in His Palace, by Will Bardenwerper

This book shows Saddam in a different light. Most books portray him as some version of the devil. And while I don't disagree with those assessments, Saddam was still just a man. Great evil is done by real people with recognizable characteristics. Mythologizing evil makes it seem like it can never happen to you.

The Marsh Arabs, by Wilfred Thesiger

I wasn't going to include this book because it seems somewhat irrelevant. But it's something I don't think a lot of people are aware of. I didn't even know the Marsh Arabs existed until I went to Iraq. I never would have expected that a civilization thousands of years old and a vibrant marshland ecosystem existed in those areas just a couple decades earlier until Saddam eradicated them.

RAPID FIRE

In the spring of 2003, out front of an abandoned bank a few miles south of Baghdad, Sergeant Stanley sat down to have breakfast in the passenger's seat of his Humvee. Stanley was a short, thick-muscled black man who always wore a smile, treated everyone with dignity, and was quick to give his friendship. While Stanley was eating, an Iraqi man walked up to his Humvee, said "Good morning, mister," drew a pistol, and shot him in the face.

Stanley should have died that day in front of the bank. The shot was point blank and he wasn't wearing his Kevlar helmet. The bullet should have smashed straight through the spongy bone between his eyes. Instead, it ricocheted off his Oakley sunglasses and careened up his forehead, leaving only a graze wound and a muzzle burn the size of a quarter from the discharge of the round. After the shot, Stanley sprang out of his seat and shoved the Iraqi man, shouting, "Shoot him, shoot him, shoot him!"

In the short time it took the Marines in Stanley's team to respond, the man cycled through his clip. The second shot hit Stanley in the chest, but his flak vest absorbed most of the blow. The third shot zipped through the open door of the Humvee, passing inches behind the neck of the driver and smashing through the window on the other side. The fourth shot bounced off the rifle hand guards of a Marine running from his post on the street to respond. The shots were good, and the Iraqi man was willing to die for what he believed, but he didn't accomplish his purpose. Seconds after the man began firing, seven bullets passed through his body, fracturing and tearing as they went. The man fell to his knees and swayed. A corporal from Stanley's team stalked up behind him, leveled his muzzle at the back of the man's head and squeezed the trigger, painting the street with brains and bits of skull fragment.

Stanley re-gathered himself and went back to work.

Sometimes I close my eyes and see bodies of men strewn along the street, bodies shredded by bullets and ground to mush under the treads of armored personnel carriers. Sometimes I hear a wail in my mind that transcends everything I thought I knew.

I've been in Iraq about a month, and a bear of a man approaches me. I'm working crowd control, turning away Iraqi civilians who want to get home past our roadblock. Heavy attacks are raging a few miles ahead and we don't want civilians there. We don't want dead civilians. As the man gets closer, he makes me feel small, frail. He's full-grown, thick-chested and heavy through the gut with a jet-black beard and fury in his eyes. I'm just a kid, nineteen, not knowing exactly why I'm here or what I believe but wanting to do the best I can.

The man frantically points at an exploded blue hatchback just past our checkpoint. I can't understand him, but he's insistent, so I get our translator. The man says the blue hatchback is his brother's car, and his brother has been missing for a couple days, so we allow him through the checkpoint. When the man gets to the car, his fears are confirmed. His brother is in two pieces, blown in half just above the hip. His torso lies face down and would be choking on sand if his lungs could still draw breath. His lower spine and blood-crusted legs are still plastered to the driver's seat.

There are also two skeletons in the car, picked so clean by fire they look almost as if they've never been anything but bone, one in the passenger's seat, and one in the back. A layer of glossy fat fused to the seat backs confirms that they were once something more substantial. The two skeletons are the man's mom and dad.

When the bear-man realizes his entire family is gone, his howls come deep and guttural. His sounds are otherworldly, a kind of grieving I've never heard before. He lifts his heavy-muscled arms to the sky and seems to rave at God. I can't understand his words, but his agony pierces the limitations of language. I watch the massive man crumble, feel myself crumble. I want to lend him comfort, to extend my hand and let him feel that he is not alone. We stand meters apart, but there is a wide gulf between us. I'm just a teenager in a strange land wearing the uniform of a foreign invader. It was likely at the hands of my people that his family was destroyed. Duty pulls me one direction, compassion another. Half of my heart goes with my body as I deal with the swelling crowd—we can't lose control, can't add violence to violence—half stays with the man as he scoops his family into a wooden box.

My team drives up to the bank in time to see the remains of Stanley's attacker on the road. From the turret, I peer down on this ruined man, shattered bones jutting out at irregular angles, fragments of skull and grey matter in the concrete gutter, puddle of blood coagulating underneath him. I scan the crowd of Iraqis walking by for threats. We're on a busy street in the middle of town, dozens of men and women skirting by. I'm always uneasy in crowds. I know that enemy gunmen use them as shields, make us choose whether or not to fire back. But even with that in the back of my mind, I'm fascinated by the men and women walking by. I watch their eyes, see how they respond to the mutilated man next to me on the ground. Most pretend he doesn't exist. A few let their eyes flicker toward the body but quickly force themselves to look straight ahead again. They're curious, but also highly aware I'm watching them over my machine gun. I watch one woman pass with two small children, each no more than five or six years old. She's cloaked from head to toe in black, her eyes the only visible part of her face. I remember the franticness in her eyes, how they bulged wide and white as she looked anywhere but at the corpse and gore, hurrying her children past me and the body, pushing their little faces forward every time their eyes began to wander.

Two Marines pick up the body and throw it inside a wall around the bank. Another Marine grabs a bucketful of water and sloshes it across the pavement where the body was, rinsing away the brains and blood and pieces of skull. It's all so matter of fact, like washing away drippings from a torn sack of garbage. The callousness claws at my insides. I want to double over, wrap my arms around my chest and shield myself from feeling what I'm feeling, but there's nothing for it. I put my eyes back on the passing crowd and scan for threats.

I'm on night watch, leaning against the cool steel rim of my turret, one hand resting on the butt stock of my M240G. The wind blows softly at my face, refreshing me after many hours in the desert sun. This is early in the war, and we expect chemical attacks, so we spend every minute of every day in charcoal-lined chemical suits. The suits are heavy and oppressive. They're meant to keep things out, not let air in, and in our full combat gear in the sun we sweat and sweat until the sun goes down and the desert chill gives us a few hours reprieve.

The night is quiet. We're at a crossroads in a small town with a row of locked up automotive shops behind us. Stacks of unattended tires bracket us on each side. We haven't seen a soul, Iraqi or American for hours. The rustle of sleeping Marines kicking at their Bivy sacks in the dirt is the only sound interrupting the night.

I've been on watch about an hour when an infantry operation begins several miles from our position. A nearby battery of artillery joins in, thumping along in deep rhythmic support. The concussion blast from each round cuts through the stillness, cuts through me. My chest pounds in unison with every round launched into the deep black sky, rocket-assists trailing fire until they get too high to see. I listen to the expectant pause in the night waiting for impact. This is my first time around artillery. I'm used to machine guns and rifles. I'm used to seeing my rounds impact almost immediately. Waiting for artillery is intolerable. At ten seconds, I wonder if something went wrong. At twenty seconds, I wonder if the rounds shoot so far I can't hear them land. Then rolling thunder cascades across the desert, and I know the rounds found their mark.

Shortly after the artillery starts, a squad of Cobras swoops in—attack helicopters, invisible in the night, but distinct in sound. Their blades make them sound angry as they whip through the air. In the daylight, Cobras are intimidating, the way they angle forward, scanning the ground for something to kill. At night they are devastating, streaking barrages of hellfire missiles erupting out of the dark, punishing into submission whatever lives and breathes on the other end.

The attack continues into the night. I'm too far away to see the ground fighting but I continue to feel the explosions. I swing my legs over the side of the turret and onto the roof of the Humvee. The cold metal presses against the backs of my legs as I slide off the roof onto the ground and gently shake awake my replacement. After he throws on his boots, I lay down on my bag in the dirt, close my eyes, and let the explosions wash over me. I feel so calm, so at peace as the assault rages into the night.

There is so much firepower around me I feel like nothing can touch me, while a few miles away, a terror is being unleashed in the lives of other human beings that at the time I can't much understand.

The dead body in the bank becomes a part of daily life. When no one comes to claim it, we leave it festering in the sun. Whenever a Marine goes inside the abandoned bank to piss or find a safer place to eat, they walk past the body. A few guys decide to stop walking past and just piss on the corpse instead. This disturbs me in a way I can't explain. I wasn't a religious guy at the time, but moments like those made me wonder if God might be watching. Pissing on a guy's corpse was a little more irreverence than I could bear.

Eventually the dead man's brother musters the courage to approach us and claim the body. Before he returns with a box to scoop up the remains, I walk past the dead man one last time. It's quiet inside the bank wall, and I'm totally alone. I wonder when again I'll have the chance to look so openly at violent death and ponder it without distraction, so I stand over the corpse, let my eyes pass over the unnatural angles, blackened blood, and fractures. I scan the gaping hole where the right eye once was, observe the bloating and putrefying skin, the hundreds of charcoal flies buzzing around in a gorging frenzy. Standing above the wreckage of this single human life, I watch a fly crawl out from inside the man's skull. It leaps off the corpse, flies at my face, and lands on my lower lip.

THANK YOU FOR YOUR SERVICE

I'm walking down the cereal aisle of a grocery store, throwing a football in the park, cashing a check at the bank, ordering a beer at the bar, greeting people at church, cutting into a chicken fried steak at Cracker Barrel, when a well-meaning man, woman, grandma, grandpa, bartender, waitress, friend, cousin, acquaintance, stranger says "Thank you for your service." I drop my fork, beer, bible, football, two-dollar tip and say, "You're welcome. I'm just glad to be home. Absolutely. Just doing my job. Happy to be alive. It was an honor to serve. Just glad to have my bits and pieces." And then, after an awkward pause, each of us wanting to end the interaction with positive feelings but having nothing to say to the other, we smile and go our separate ways.

Every time this happens, I say the same things, because the people approaching me are nice, and nice people saying "Thank you. I'm grateful to you guys. I appreciate all you do for us," is a lot better than self-important dirtbags saying "Fuck you. Fuck your service and the military industrial complex you're a part of." Nice people saying thank you is also better than being ignored, like the war was some inconsequential blip that should just be forgotten while I put the blinders back on and assimilate into my old life. But all the same, every time someone says, "Thank you for your service," I wonder, "What exactly are you thanking me for?"

Do you mean wondering if I'm going to trigger a land mine every time I step off the road to take a piss or praying no one shoots me with my pants down while I crap in the hole I dug on the side of the highway? Do you mean guarding an empty desert camp in Kuwait for months, so bored that guys have masturbation contests to see who can rub the most out during a shift in their guard towers? Do you mean shoving the muzzle of my rifle in peoples' faces, barking, "Get the fuck back!" knowing that they don't understand the words coming out of my mouth, but they understand the rifle and the crazed horse look in my eyes? Do you mean playing cards on pigeon shit-covered floors or eating nothing but beef jerky and potato chips once the mail quits getting blown up, and we start getting care packages from home? Do you mean watching Marines give pork MRE's to prisoners as a joke, then me switching them with beef or chicken when no one's looking because the idea of making someone violate their religion stings me in a way I can't dismiss, but I don't want anyone to know that? Do you mean straining my eyes over every piece of roadside garbage—old tires, rusted engine blocks, empty tin cans, rotting dog carcasses—scanning for IEDs but missing them anyway, hearing my failure as explosions rip the back half of our convoy? Do you mean the end of my last deployment when I'm happy to be stuck on base listening to gunfire pop across the river, happy that it's over there, happy that it's not me? Do you mean shootings, dead civilians, detaining men for months in squalid, steaming cells? Do you mean seeing faces of Iraqis in my mind ten years after my last deployment and wondering which of these men, women, or children has been dismembered, sold, or burned alive? Or maybe you mean me choking back my hatred when I get home and watch people gorge themselves on more food and drink then I've seen in months, pausing just long enough to say things like, "Those people just don't appreciate freedom."

It's usually around here I need to stop myself and say in my head, "Breathe, you crazy asshole. You're here now. This is what people are. They don't mean anything by it. She's a middle-aged mom with two boys who served like you. He's a Vietnam vet who remembers how soldiers were treated when he returned and doesn't want to repeat the same mistakes. And what about the other things? What about standing on the side of the highway watching lines of American tanks head toward Baghdad while men and women ask you if Saddam is really gone? What about the old Iraqi man sobbing into your hand when he realized after all these years, he was finally free to grieve? What about smiling kids, laughing and waving, chasing your convoy barefoot through the muddy streets, or that little boy, the one who spoke such remarkable English, who walked out to your Humvee with a steaming cup of the most delicious tea you've ever tasted and said, 'The tea is from my father. He wishes to say thank you."

INFORMATION WAR

During the first Battle of Fallujah in 2004, my team was running convoy security on the roads between Ramadi and Fallujah. One night after a mission, we had a couple hours free and stopped at the Ramadi chow hall to get some food. Inside, I noticed a haggard-looking soldier, probably nineteen or twenty like me, sitting alone at a table, so I sat down next to him, and we got to talking. He had just come from Fallujah. His unit was in the middle of the city and a few of them had come to Ramadi to grab a shower, some hot food, and a few hours R and R.

I was curious about what was happening in Fallujah. I knew what I was told in briefings, that a large group of insurgents had come to Fallujah to make a stand, and Marines and soldiers were going house to house killing some and funneling the rest toward areas more advantageous to our forces. When we drove through the outskirts a few days earlier, I saw Humvees cordoning off the city and American helicopters patrolling the skies. But I was interested to hear from someone on the ground. The soldier and I talked for about twenty minutes. He told me about troop movements, enemy fortifications, and an enemy tank his unit unexpectedly found dug in in the city. He looked worn out as he spoke about what he was going through and even more worn out when the guys from his unit showed up and told him it was time to go back.

A few minutes after my conversation with the soldier I watched a news broadcast from a major American network. The anchorwoman came on with the words "Battle of Fallujah" written at the bottom of the screen in big letters. It was a high-level production—official looking maps, quality graphics, smooth cuts to live action sequences taken somewhere in Iraq. But as the anchorwoman spoke, not a word of what she said was even close to what the young soldier had just told me. Not a word of what she said matched what we'd been briefed on or what I saw driving through the city a few days earlier. I always wondered after that what the American people back home were even seeing.

Over the years, I've been surprised at how little people actually know about what happened in Iraq. It's disturbing to me how information gets shaped to make people think certain things. A few chapters of this book are dedicated to addressing that issue. People need some context.

To begin to understand what happened in 2003, you have to understand America's relationship with Saddam Hussein. When the Baath Party first came to power in Iraq, America saw them as potential allies against the spread of the Soviet Union. The Communists in Iraq were the main challenger to the Baath Party for power, so US intelligence supplied Saddam Hussein with information on Iraqi communists, knowing that he'd likely use it to hunt them down and kill them, which he did. Later, when Saddam took control of Iraq and made the monumental mistake of invading Iran, the US stepped in and provided his forces with satellite surveillance of Iranian troop movements. Iraq was on the verge of being overrun, and even though the US knew Saddam would use the information to disperse tens of thousands of chemical weapons on Iranian forces, we helped him anyway. Iran was our enemy, and we were worried about Iran gaining power in the region.

The thing that most changed America's relationship with Saddam Hussein was the collapse of the Soviet Union. Saddam's main value to the US was his rabid hatred of communists, and once the Soviet Union was no longer a threat, the US no longer needed Saddam as a bulwark against the spread of communism in the Middle East. Only then did his human rights abuses and expansionism become an "affront" to American values.

The Iran-Iraq War was grotesque. One side sent children walking across minefields to clear paths for human wave attacks. The other side gassed human beings at a level not seen on a battlefield since World War 1. Roughly a million people were killed during the Iran-Iraq War, and millions more were savagely injured. It was a war that left deep scars on both countries. It also led to the US invasion of Iraq in 2003.

After the war with Iran, Iraq was bankrupt, its infrastructure was devastated, and the country was tens of billions of dollars in debt. This was a major problem for Saddam Hussein. With no money left to pay the security forces that kept him in power, he was in real danger of being overthrown, so he decided to strongarm his small, oil rich neighbor, Kuwait.

Saddam claimed that Iraq had valiantly repelled Persian aggression during the Iran-Iraq War to spare Kuwait and other Arab nations that pain. Because of this service, he argued, it was only fair that Kuwait should forgive Iraq its debts and finance its rebuilding. When Kuwait refused, Saddam switched to propaganda and threats. He accused Kuwait of illegally slant drilling in the Rumaila oil field to steal oil from underneath Iraq and intentionally over-selling Kuwaiti oil to destroy Iraq's economy. When Saddam moved his army to the border, Kuwaiti leaders thought he was just posturing to get them to make a deal. They didn't understand how much he needed the money.

Saddam's forces ravaged Kuwait. Stories of gang rape, murder, torture, and imprisonment were common. Many Kuwaitis were lined up against walls and shot. Others were tortured with power drills or lowered into acids baths. The invasion went so quick, some women went to work in the city in the morning and by night were imprisoned in their offices as sex workers for Iraqi soldiers. And during all the chaos and atrocities, Saddam took anything of value and shipped it back to Baghdad, including substantial cash reserves.

When Saddam started threatening Saudi Arabia, the US brought force. While political speeches were made in America about freeing the people of Kuwait from tyranny, the reality was, Saddam put the US in a precarious economic position. Iraq had one of the largest tank forces in the world and more than enough military to continue into Saudi Arabia. If he was allowed to take both Kuwait's and Saudi Arabia's oil fields, he would've controlled by far the largest oil reserves on the planet. That would've made the US economy beholden to the whims of a Middle Eastern dictator. That was never going to be allowed. The US sent 400,000 troops to Saudi Arabia and told Saddam to leave. When he refused, the war was a slaughter. Iraqi forces simply had no way to deal with US tanks and airpower. The war was over in hours, and whoever didn't surrender was quickly killed.

What happened next is the main reason the US invaded Iraq in 2003. The US let Saddam Hussein live.

"GRAB YOUR GEAR!"

The Kuwaiti desert is bleak and lifeless, nothing around for miles and miles but a sea of Soldiers and Jarheads flooding in for the invasion. It's February 2003. We freeze at night and train during the day under a sun that blisters our ears and noses. There's an urgency in Kuwait. All of us feel it. We've got a few days, maybe a few weeks. None of us knows when the order will come. We just know we'll be the ones to carry it out when it does, so we fix vehicles, dig fighting holes, run in flak vests, set up and take down communication towers, run observation posts, practice camouflaging positions, dig comm wire trenches, call in pretend medivacs and artillery fire, disassemble and reassemble weapons, patrol, practice ambushes, practice night movements, practice vehicle tactics. We configure our gear, then reconfigure our gear, then reconfigure our gear, then one night, Staff Sergeant Chilcott walks in the tent and says, "Grab your gear! We won't be coming back."

It's almost a relief when the order comes. I'm tired of running scenarios in my head, tired of imagined snipers, ambushes, and chemical attacks, tired of this unavoidable thing we all know we have to do. The only way through is forward. So, let's go do it.

Marines fly in and out of the open flap of our canvas tent. Our Humvees have been mostly prepped for days: water, ammo, rations, and other essential equipment already packed in designated locations. All that's left is to throw in our sleeping bags and go.

It's a chilly night as we roll out of camp, full desert moon high overhead, almost bright enough to read by. I lean against the steel rim of my turret as we bounce across the desert, hands pressed on the buttstock my M240G to keep it firmly in place. My fingers are numb beneath my thin leather gloves, and I wonder how well my hands will function if we have to fight in the cold.

A few miles out, when camp is no longer visible, our unit contacts 1st Marine Division, about 20,000 strong, rolling toward the Iraqi border. The column breaks, allows our line of Humvees to fold into the movement. The magnitude of fire power rolling forward seems surreal. Armored vehicles stretch from horizon to horizon and continue on beyond sight: Humvees, Abrams tanks, Amphibious Assault Vehicles, Light Armored Reconnaissance Vehicles, Seven-ton troop transport trucks pulling 155mm Howitzers; all carrying armored men, heavy weapons, and thousands of rounds of a dozen types of ammunition.

The convoy crawls forward at barely more than idle speed, quiet except for the low growl of creeping diesel engines, no headlights, no taillights, no flashlights looking at maps. Like a vast metallic snake, it slides through the night, powerful beyond comprehension, but choosing, for now, not to draw attention. Watching this division of Marines cross the desert is sobering. I can't imagine being on the other side of what's about to happen. But I can't help the thrill I feel. It's like I'm watching a natural disaster unleash on the world, a roving column of meat shields and machines with the destructive capacity to level cities, and somehow, I'm a component part, this dumb kid with numb fingers and a runny nose.

LESSONS FROM IRAQ

* Baby wipes work just as well on grown men's asses.
* Two-day field scruff is a rite of passage. Never trust a clean and pressed Marine.
* One dog tag goes around your neck, one goes in your right boot. This is in case your foot and body lose each other, and no one can find your body.
* Feet can smell like cheese puffs taste.
* Spiders should not be that size.
* Chickens don't do well in sandstorms. You can breathe in sand for hours before your body shuts down.
* A rocket that doesn't explode will lodge itself in the center of a tree trunk.
* Sometimes you need a cigarette.
* When driving down the highway, a pillar of fire might shoot hundreds of feet up into the sky.
* Sometimes you need twelve cigarettes.
* Rigor mortised cattle legs look like rockets, straight out, readying for launch, carcass inflated with gas, cow balloon nearing explosion.
* Given enough time and sweat, any part of the body can smell like a jock strap.

- It's not just a saying. Dogs literally eat other dogs.
- A cat in Iraq has no chance.
- A cigarette tastes better when a stranger offers.
- When no other option, men in fancy suits wash themselves in ditch water.
- Kids are kids everywhere, except some kids can bleed and butcher goats.
- A warm cup of goat stew is better than you'd think.
- Dysentery and dried-out moist-towelettes make an anus bleed.
- Sometimes the ground blows up and almost knocks you on your ass.
- Sometimes it knocks you on your ass.
- A cigarette tastes best when you realize you're not going to die that day.
- Flies crawling out of human eye sockets stay with you a long time.
- You can handle more than you think. Until you can't.
- Kids in bare feet running through mud and human shit still grin and wave.
- Even people blockaded by Humvees and machine guns show strangers pictures of their kids.
- No tea will ever compare to the cup of chai that little boy handed you with his father's gratitude.

WILD DOGS (1)

The first day of the invasion, after crossing the fifteen-kilometer no man's land with two million landmines that separates Kuwait and Iraq, we find ourselves rolling through an Iraqi border town called Safwan City. The city is falling apart, one-story mudbrick houses battered from years of unrelenting sun and sandstorms, rusty sliding garage doors, half-starved people with hollow cheeks in groups all over the street. I've never seen people that look like this before, not happy to see us, not angry, not even scared. They just look worn out, like they're waiting to endure whatever fresh horror is coming their way. The only things new and bright in the city are murals of Saddam Hussein, which are everywhere. Saddam the general. Saddam the pilot. Saddam the benevolent Sheik. Saddam the great Arab leader on his white horse. Every direction you look, you see his thick moustache and bright grinning eyes, the all-knowing, omnipresent, ever-punishing "Father" of Iraq. I wonder what this must be like for the people of Safwan, for decades watching your people butchered every time they fight back, your sons hung from lampposts, your daughters, wives, and mothers raped in front of you, people you care about tortured and murdered, disappeared by the order of the man always peering down at you from every corner of the city, the man who has stolen anything you've ever valued, the man who has starved your children, sometimes for punishment, sometimes for leverage, always out of total indifference for their lives, and you dare not say a word against him, dare not even speak his name or give a cross look because his spies are everywhere, even amongst your friends. And the price of speaking the President's name is your tongue, or the blood of your family, or your decomposing body in an unmarked pit in the desert with thousands of others.

As we drive down the road, groups of men gather together whispering in front of buildings. I watch these men over my machine gun. They watch me back with unflinching eyes. I'm definitely not the scariest thing they've seen.

A couple years after my second deployment, I was a missionary in Holland, and a university professor invited me to talk to her students about the war. I was perplexed by how sure these students were of what they knew. None of them had ever set foot in Iraq or knew any part of its history. None of them had ever looked into an Iraqi man or woman's eyes as they told their stories of people they loved who disappeared. None of them knew the stories of people being treated like cattle, girls being branded as property, soldiers having their hamstrings cut by their own officers so they couldn't run away, boys having their ears sliced off by state surgeons to send a message, because mutilated boys send a more powerful message than dead boys. Mutilated boys are breathing billboards. For the rest of their lives, they'll remind the population of who is in charge and what he's willing to do.

The students didn't know any of this, but they were so sure of the fact that I was a fool in an evil cause, and I was just too stupid to see it. In some ways, they might have been right. But while they were in college, I was in Iraq. I saw with my eyes, smelled with my nose, heard with my ears, and felt with my hands and soul things I couldn't unsee, unsmell, unhear, or unfeel. I spent three years of my life preparing for Iraq, deploying to Iraq, and redeploying to Iraq. I spent many years after thinking about Iraq and reading everything I could get my hands on to better understand it, and I still don't know enough to say I know the truth. All I can do is be honest. People will think what they think.

It's impossible to understand modern Iraq without understanding a little about Saddam Hussein, a man both fascinating and terrible, a man who used rape as a weapon against countless people, but who also loved his mother with an almost religious fervor, a man sometimes moved to great bouts of generosity who was just as likely to put a gun to your head and leave parts of your body in a duffel bag for your wife to find. An uncompromising man who fiercely believed in his own destiny, who believed force of will was always enough, even when faced with the most technologically advanced army in the world, twice. A true believer in the cause of Iraq, but completely corrupted by his own hubris until he believed he and Iraq were synonymous and that all Iraqi people and property existed to serve his ends.

Saddam Hussein was a bastard, and picked on by other kids for not having a father, he grew up a barefoot thug in one of the poorest most violent regions of Iraq, fighting with an iron rod for survival and whatever dignity he could earn through violence. When the Baathist revolution came in 1968, he saw opportunity. Laughed at and belittled by his fellow revolutionaries for being backward and crude, he forged his way by doing whatever dirty job needed to be done, threatening, extorting, murdering, torturing. He was efficient, merciless, and a tireless worker, and soon became the man the party called on to hunt down its enemies. The more people he killed, the more power he gained, power which he then used to hunt down his personal rivals from the shadows.

By 1979, Saddam was the most powerful man in Iraq, and the elite members of the Baath Party who had dismissed him were no longer laughing. Trying to save themselves from Saddam's growing power, a few members of the Revolutionary Command Council, Iraq's governing body, made agreements with Syrian President Hafez al-Assad, attempting to unite Iraq and Syria in one nation under Assad's rule. On July 20, 1979, Saddam made his counter move at a gathering of hundreds of high-ranking Ba'ath Party officials:

At the beginning of the proceedings Saddam brings out Muhyi Abdel-Hussein, a high ranking official and co-conspirator in the coup. Muhyi walks on stage a broken man. He's been tortured for weeks. His family has been kidnapped, and he's been promised if he doesn't perform well today, he'll watch the women of his family raped and murdered before it's his turn to die. As Muhyi speaks, he stumbles over his words, constantly looking at Saddam for his approval. Saddam leans back, relaxed, smoking a cigar. Muhyi finishes his tale, admits his guilt, and is led away by guards.

Panic erupts in the assembly hall, men rising to their feet in terror shouting crazed praises of "Long live Saddam Hussein!" Men shriek, almost weep as they shout, their pathetic voices thinly veiled pleas for their lives.

When Saddam takes the podium, he's in complete control. The crowd cowers before him.

"There are faithless among us," he says, "How must we deal with these men? You all know the answer."

Some men shout, "Execute them! These men must be executed no matter their number!" Other men hold their faces in their hands, wiping sweat from their foreheads or tears from their eyes.

"If I call your name," Saddam says, "Stand up and leave the room," He begins reading a list. The people named stand and are escorted from the room by armed guards.

One man stands and shouts, "But, I didn't do anything!"

Saddam looks through him and repeats, "If I read your name, stand and leave the room." The man looks down and submits.

More scattered chants of "Long Live Saddam!" erupt. The assembly breaks into panicked songs of praise, tightening the noose around their own necks.

In his final move to cement control, Saddam forms firing squads out of top ministers and party leaders. They are the ones who execute their former colleagues. They are now complicit in the crime, and Iraq falls firmly into the hands of Saddam Hussein.

GAS! GAS! GAS!

"VX gas is a nerve agent," the Intelligence officer begins, my platoon sitting in a half circle in the sand at his feet. "It's odorless, tasteless, and heavier than air. If you breathe it in, it'll settle in your lungs and attack your nerve centers. Your muscles will seize, and you'll fall to the ground, spasming until you snap your own spine. If your unit gets hit, go to MOPP level 4, and move to higher ground. Do not remove your mask or protective gear for any reason."

This is a common briefing on the Iraq-Kuwait border in early 2003.

"Sarin gas is a lot like VX. It's odorless and tasteless and attacks your nerves, causing paralysis of the muscles. Saddam used this shit in the 80's on the Kurds, so don't be surprised if he uses it on us."

The last few weeks have been a blur. In mid-January, my MP unit got activated in Minnesota. After a flurry of dropping classes, cancelling leases, packing gear, and saying goodbyes, I'm on a plane to North Carolina, a plane to Germany, a plane to Kuwait. By early February, I'm in a desert camp preparing for the invasion of Iraq. Three weeks ago, I sat in a Midwestern college classroom listening to a sociology professor give another speech about men being selfish pigs who do nothing but hold women down. Now I'm in a desert with an Intelligence officer telling me that in a few days I might puke up my lungs or snap my own spine.

"Mustard gas is a blister agent," he continues. "It smells like garlic and onions. If it contacts your skin, your skin will bubble, and if you don't die, you will be severely scarred. If mustard gas gets in your eyes, your eyes will swell in your head, and you'll go blind. If you breathe it in, your lungs will blister, and you will vomit and cough up blood. Saddam used mustard gas on the Iranians in the Iran/Iraq war, and he used it on the Kurds in the 80's. Don't be surprised if he uses it on us."

"Fuck, man," Romero says, "I hope my dumb ass gets shot. This shit ain't no way to die."

"Nice clean shot to the head," Baker says, "That's the way to go. Not flopping around on the ground with my goddamn skin melting."

"Phosgene gas and chlorine gas are both choking agents. Phosgene smells like fresh cut grass. Chlorine smells like bleach. Both attack your lung tissue. If you breathe them in, your chest will tighten, and you will hack and choke until you run out of air. Chlorine gas is cheap and easy to produce. Don't be surprised if Saddam uses it on us."

"At least we've got chemical detecting chickens," I say. Romero and Baker snicker. A truck load of farm chickens arrived in camp the other day. They were supposed to be another line of defense, a gas detection system like canaries in coal mines. If gas was present, especially nerve agents we couldn't see or smell, the chickens would die first and let us know to mask up and get the fuck out of there. Two days after the chickens arrived at camp, they were all dead. Apparently farm chickens don't just die from chemical weapons. They also die from heat exposure and sandstorms.

MOPP levels tell us how much protective gear we should be wearing based on imminence of chemical attacks. Most of the time in Kuwait we are at MOPP level 1. At MOPP 1, you wear a charcoal-lined chemical suit instead of desert utilities. The charcoal suits are heavy and don't breathe like the light fabric of our normal desert uniforms. They also aren't the right colors. Instead of deserts browns, they are forest greens. We look ridiculous dressed in green camouflage in a desert where nothing green grows, but it probably doesn't matter. The slogan for the campaign is "Bringing Peace through Superior Fire Power." I don't think we plan on hiding much.

At MOPP level 1, you also have a gas mask strapped to your hip in an awkward pouch bulging out at your side. The rule is nine seconds. You have nine seconds after hearing the dull thud of an impacting chemical weapon to put on your mask, clear it of contaminated air, and cinch it tight. If you fail to do this in nine seconds, your buddies watch you do the funky chicken on the ground until you die. This is why the mask is always on your hip, even if you're in PT shorts and flip-flops going to the shitter.

MOPP 2 is the same as MOPP 1, except you also strap rubber coverings on your boots. The boot coverings take too long to put on in an emergency, so when we cross the border, we cross at MOPP 2. My feet always sweat in my boots anyway, but with the rubber coverings, I feel like I've got sneakers on in a swimming pool. My feet slosh every time I plant my feet on the metal grated Humvee floor to rotate the turret. I can feel the stink trapped inside my boots, the funky cheese smell waiting to be released.

At MOPP 3, you've got the chem suit and boot coverings, but now your mask is cinched tight on your face, and a chemical hood is drawn over the top of your head. MOPP 3 is the level that's going to save your life, so we practice going to MOPP 3 over and over. The gas drills become a sort of game, guys yelling out "GAS! GAS! GAS!" usually after someone put a fresh wad of chew in their lip. This forces the Marine to make a choice. Tobacco is precious. No one knows when or if we'll be able to get more. So, when the gas call comes, the Marine has to either spit out his tobacco or mask up anyway and gut the spit. Most guys gut the spit.

MOPP 4 is the same as MOPP 3 but with rubber gloves. MOPP 4 is the highest level of protection, and at this point every inch of your body is covered with protective equipment. We only go to MOPP 4 one time, and it's before we cross the border. It's a ball-scorching sunny day in Kuwait when we get the call for incoming SCUDs—missiles potentially used as delivery systems for chemical agents. Even though we are several kilometers away from the impact, we go to MOPP 4 and take cover behind a dirt berm in case there are more.

It's still early spring in the Kuwaiti desert, but the temperature is around ninety degrees, and you can't pray for a cloud. With our hands, feet, and faces covered in rubber, and our bodies draped in thick suits and fifty pounds of combat gear, we're pouring sweat. No matter how tight I cinch my mask, I can't get a good seal as it slips and slides over my face. The eye holes fog up from the heat my head is generating, and my hands involuntarily move toward my mask so I can pull it off and wipe the lenses clean. Just as my fingers touch the straps, I stop myself. You can't unmask during a gas attack, dumbass.

"This is fucked," I say to Romero or Baker or whoever is next to me on the ground. "How the hell can anyone fight in this? I can't see twenty feet in front of my face."

A passing field reporter sees us lined up on the ground at MOPP 4 and jumps out of her truck, thinking she stumbled on a story. She crouches next to me while her camera man shoves his camera in my face.

"What's the situation?" the reporter asks me, clearly excited. I really have no idea what the situation is. At this point, I don't even know there was a SCUD attack. I figure we're rolling around in the dirt because our CO is kind of a dick. I mumble something unintelligible to the reporter about identifying targets, and she promptly stands up to look for someone who's not a moron.

A few days into the invasion, my unit camps outside of An Nasiriyah during the first big gunfight of the war. I'm on night watch, and there are so many flashes from discharging weapons and explosives in the city, it looks like a lightning storm coming from the streets. As I watch the city, a lone high-back Humvee rolls up the dark road behind me. When it turns toward where my platoon is camped, I walk out to meet it. There is one Marine inside, and he looks equal parts embarrassed and anxious. "Hi, um, I got separated from my unit, and my radio's not working. You haven't seen them come through here, have you?"

"You lost your unit?" I say, "Shit, no one has come past here in a couple hours."

The Marine, probably nineteen or twenty like me, looks down at his steering wheel, unsure of what to do.

"Whatever you do," I say, "You should quit going the direction you're going. There's a huge fight in the city right now, and you're heading right for it."

"Oh," the Marine says. "You think I could stay here with you guys tonight?"

"Yeah, I think that's fine. Just park next to my truck, and I'll let the next guy know why you're here."

When my shift is over, I shake awake my replacement in his sleeping bag. After he gets on his boots and takes my place, I tell him why the extra Humvee is there and walk to my sleeping bag. Wow. Driving toward Nasiriyah alone in the dark. What the fuck?

When I get to my sleeping bag, I take off my boots and pull off my chem suit. I usually sleep with it on, but I want one good night's sleep without the crusty thing stuck to my body. Once I'm in my skivvies, I slide into my sleeping bag with my rifle nestled against my right hip and gas mask carrying case cradled on my chest. When everything I need is where I need it, I slide easily to sleep.

"GAS! GAS! GAS!" I don't know who calls this out, but I jerk awake to a sitting position. In the moonlight, I see a Marine from a neighboring unit running toward our position across a field. He's at MOPP level 4 and is frantically giving the arm signal for a chemical attack, hands over head, two thumbs extended but pointing downward, arms waving up and down. I'm losing my mind with panic now. I've just been snapped out of sleep with the gas call, and I don't know where or when the chemical round impacted. I don't know if it's already too late, if my next breath will be a lung full of VX, and I'm going to spend the rest of my short life thrashing around in contorted agony on the ground. Nine seconds. I grab at my chest where my mask should be. My mask case is gone.

What the fuck?! I get on my hands and knees and grope around in the dark. With every wasted second, I expect a lung full of poison. I finally find my mask on the ground several feet from where I was sleeping. I must have flung it off my chest when I jerked awake. I've wasted too much time and expect my next breath to kill me, so after I exhale, I don't breathe in again.

I pull my mask out of the case, slip it on over my face and half-tighten it. Before I can tighten it all the way, I need to clear it of contaminated air by forcefully blowing any unfiltered air out the bottom flap. I have no air left in my lungs, because I quit breathing, but I try to forcefully exhale anyway. My little sigh isn't close to enough to clear my mask. I have to take a breath. This is it. This is how I die.

I breathe in quick but deep. When pain doesn't explode in my chest, I blow out hard, clear my mask, and cinch it tight. It was clean air, and after a couple shallow breaths inside my mask, I'm fine. My panic subsides.

Now that I'm masked up and breathing okay, I think about the exposed skin on most of my body. What a night to not wear my chem suit. If this is a blister agent, it'll burn me badly. I don't have time to find my chem suit and put it on, so I slide into my sleeping bag and pull it over my head, hoping it'll offer some protection and that the nylon won't just fuse to my bubbling skin.

In my cocoon, I'm alone with the sounds of my breathing. I don't think about the other guys in my unit or what's going on outside. All I think about is the air going in and out of my lungs, and some sign, some pain or hitch in my chest, to let me know that I didn't get my mask on in time or that my mask is malfunctioning. While there's no pain or discomfort in my breathing, every breath is getting more and more difficult. Something must be wrong with my filter. Soon I'm laboring to pull in any air at all. I can't believe this is happening. In the middle of a gas attack, my mask is malfunctioning. When the air stops coming altogether, I have no choice. I'm going to have to peel the sleeping bag off of my head, unmask, and breath in whatever air is outside. I delay as long as I can, but if I don't get this mask off soon, I'm going to die anyway.

This is it. You have no choice. Do it now.

I rip the sleeping bag off of my head and cool air flows through the filter of my mask. I'm able to draw in full breaths. My mask is working perfectly. In my panic, I was clogging my own filter with the sleeping bag. With my breathing back under control, I calm down and look around to see if anyone is watching me fumble around in the dark like a panicked jackass. Everyone is masked up and hunkered down like me, just trying to stay alive.

Half an hour later we get the "all clear" sign, and I take off my mask. There wasn't any gas to begin with.

WEAPONS OF MASS DESTRUCTION 1: IT BEGINS

During Desert Storm, Saddam Hussein lost much of his army, most of his access to international trade, and a large portion of Iraq's industrial infrastructure, but he didn't lose belief in himself, and he didn't lose his cunning or brutality. Before the US invaded and wiped-out Iraqi forces in Kuwait, Saddam pulled his most loyal troops back to Baghdad to protect the regime. As the US pushed into Southern Iraq, nearly every province openly revolted against Saddam, but the sectarian groups couldn't get organized, and the US didn't want to get entangled in an Iraqi civil war. Once Saddam realized the US wouldn't intervene, he deployed helicopters and his remaining forces to crush the revolts one by one until he was firmly in control of an Iraq that was even more oppressive than before.

With his people subdued, Saddam turned his attention to dealing with the West. As part of the Desert Storm ceasefire, Saddam agreed to disband Iraq's WMD programs, but that was something he never intended to do.

Chemical weapons had saved Saddam from annihilation during the Iran-Iraq War and had proven useful in quelling resistance from Shiites and Kurds. Biological weapons had been useful for assassinations and were easy to produce with limited space and equipment with the technical expertise that Iraqi scientists had. And nuclear weapons were like the Holy Grail. To Saddam, a nuclear weapon was a symbol of relevance that would immediately change regional politics by equaling Iraq with Israel and elevating Iraq above Iran. A nuke would also make it more difficult for Western countries to treat Saddam like he was beneath them.

Soon after signing the ceasefire, Saddam met with his inner circle to discuss how to proceed. They decided the best option was to appear to be cooperating with the UN while moving forward with weapons programs in secret. Saddam's son in law, Husayn Kamel, met with Iraqi scientists and security forces to give them their marching orders. Iraqi Intelligence would sanitize all sites prior to UN inspections. Key materials would be moved and hidden. Key documents would be placed in scientists' homes. Interviews with research personnel would be forbidden. Interviews with government officials would be so full of lies they were meaningless. Anything accidentally discovered by UN inspectors would be punished by a minimum of 5-10 years in prison. Anything intentionally given to inspectors would be punished by death.

Everyone knew the price of assisting the UN, and no one was willing to get themselves or their families butchered for crossing Saddam Hussein. Even as UN inspectors roamed the countryside decommissioning what they could, Iraq was figuring out ways to move forward. They established secret labs, expanded biological agent capacity, started new long-range missile programs, began new research on chemical pathways, manipulated UN surveillance equipment, bribed UN officials, and infiltrated UN inspection teams. But it wasn't until August of 1995 that inspectors became aware of how completely they'd been duped.

In that month, Husayn Kamel got in a fight with Uday Hussein, Saddam's oldest son. Fearing for his life, he took his family and fled to Jordan. Kamel was a dipshit thug, but there couldn't have been a worse person for the regime to lose. He knew every dirty secret Iraq was hiding from inspectors, and he was the kind of man who'd trade his children for asylum in the West. After crossing into Jordan, Kamel sought immediately to contact Western Intelligence, and Saddam's regime scrambled to figure out what to do, but there was no way of getting ahead of this. Kamel knew too much. As a last resort, Iraqi security forces loaded boxes and boxes of incriminating evidence into trucks and dropped them at Kamel's chicken farm. The regime decided to play dumb and pretend Kamel had continued WMD programs without their knowledge.

What was revealed by the documents in the boxes was much worse than inspectors imagined. Iraq had massively underreported its chemical weapons program. Their research was highly advanced and their production of VX gas alone was ten times what they'd declared to the UN. Similarly, Iraq's nuclear program was further along than previously thought. The documents showed Iraq likely would have had a nuclear weapon by the end of 1991 if their infrastructure hadn't been crippled by bombing campaigns during Desert Storm.

Perhaps the most alarming revelation was about Iraq's biological program. Iraq had claimed it never existed, but it was highly developed, ongoing, and expanding. Iraq had produced large quantities of botulin and anthrax and had worked feverishly to develop an aerosol delivery system that could be equipped on aircraft. This was seen being tested on beagles and donkeys in grisly videos found among the files at Kamel's chicken farm. Just a few inhaled spores of Anthrax is lethal. Iraq had produced thousands of liters to be distributed through this type of delivery system.

After the chicken farm incident, inspections became much more aggressive, but many gaps in accounting were never resolved. Scuds went missing. Anthrax was never found. Evidence of destroyed munitions didn't match claims. This is just how Iraq was. Nothing was ever how it seemed, and America's default position became, "When in doubt, Iraq must be hiding something." This is an important piece of how things played out in 2003.

As for Husayn Kamel, after the documents were discovered at his chicken farm, Western Intelligence had no more need of him, and he was stranded with his family in Jordan. Saddam eventually reached out to his son-in-law and offered amnesty. Kamel accepted, returned to Iraq, and was gunned down at his home.

MOASS

In Southern Iraq, the ground is like baked clay, so hard you need a pickaxe to get past the top crust. On top of that hardened crust is fine layer of dust, like powdered sugar, constantly being whipped up into the air by the slightest disturbance, a light breeze, a scuffling boot, it doesn't matter, anything will send the dust flying, and it gets into everything, eyes, ears, noses, throats, Humvees, packs, tents, gas masks, ammo crates, chow boxes, water pallets. The battle against the powder never ends.

During the invasion in '03, the largest Iraqi sandstorm in fifty years totally shuts down the American advance. Avoiding blown up bridges and highways in Southern Iraq, our endless convoy of military vehicles drives over dried up marshland. Thousands of tons of rolling metal grinds loose the hard-packed surface, turning the thin layer of powder into a thick layer. When the wind whips up and the sandstorm comes, it picks up all this loose powder and kicks it in our faces. We call it the MOASS—Mother of All Sandstorms.

At the height of the storm, winds gusting 50-60 miles per hour, the dust in the air is like thick brown soup. No one can see anything. Even driving at idle speed, we lose the Humvee in front of us, twice. Other teams get lost as well, so finally, we just hunker down to wait for the storm to pass.

One of the teams that gets lost is Sergeant Watson's. I'd only ever talked to Watson once, when we were still in Kuwait. It was a strange conversation about geography.

"It's pretty cool, ain't it? In a few days, when we enter Iraq, we get to cross the equator."

"Equator?" I said, "What are you talking about?"

"When we go into Iraq, we'll cross the equator."

"We aren't anywhere near the equator. That's way south of here."

We're in the desert, so I can't just pull up a map and show him we're roughly at the same latitude as Florida.

"I've seen the maps," he said, "We're definitely crossing it."

"Whatever you say, Sergeant."

"Fucking eeequator. Can't wait to check that one off my list."

The area the sandstorm hits was once part of the biggest marshland in Western Asia, an ecological marvel filled with fish, wild pigs, and dozens of types of migratory birds. It was also home to the Marsh Arabs, a complex culture of people who for thousands of years lived with their water buffalo on floating islands of vegetation, fishing and hunting from their canoes by day, harvesting giant marsh reeds to make their homes and meeting houses. In the 1980s and 90s, Saddam drained the marshes, in part to root out Shi'ite resistance fighters who would attack his forces then disappear in the labyrinth of reeds, and in part to get rid of the Marsh Arabs who he regarded as backward and beneath the dignity of the new modern Iraq. By 2003, only ten percent of the marshland remained, and the Marsh Arab civilization was mostly wiped out. Now, in place of that once vibrant ecosystem was lifeless desert, pock-marked with silty pits six to ten feet deep.

When Watson got lost, the storm was so bad he couldn't see his own feet let alone what was in front of his Humvee, but he wanted to push through and try to link up with the rest of our unit, so he popped a green chem light, stepped outside in the storm, and led his vehicle on foot. Peters, his driver, idled through the wall of brown, following the bouncing green light in the haze, when suddenly the green light disappeared.

"What the fuck?" Peters said, hitting the brakes.

"Where'd he go?" Jackson said from the back seat.

The two waited, not knowing what to do. Then a muffled voice called out from somewhere in the brown haze.

"That Watson?" Jackson said.

"Must be," Peters said, getting out of the truck.

"Sergeant Watson! Sergeant Watson!" Peters yelled out.

"Get me out of here!"

"Where the hell are you?"

"Look down!"

Peters spotted the green glowing light well beneath his feet.

The sand was so thick, Watson couldn't see the giant gaping pit right in front of him. He stepped off the edge like a cartoon character and tumbled face-first ten feet down to the bottom. Peters and Jackson dangled a cargo strap down the hole and pulled Watson out. They cracked up telling us the story later. It just seemed like such a Watson thing to have happen.

The powder isn't all bad. It makes for interesting skies. Sometimes after a storm, wind totally calm, the dust hangs in the air for hours, thick enough to block out the corona around the sun. You can look directly at it without hurting your eyes. As the sun sets, the sky turns a murky pinkish brown. This is the only place I've ever seen the sky turn that color.

Mostly the powder is obnoxious though. It lodges in your mucous membranes, turning your snot into grainy brown slurry thick enough to chew. You constantly hack and blow, trying not to gag on the chunks.

After our second time getting lost, my team eventually finds our unit and we merge into their perimeter. I can barely see the outline of the next truck over, five or ten feet away. I just have to trust the rest of our unit is out there somewhere, forming a perimeter. For the rest of the day, I stare out into the brown cloud, sand pelting and ripping at my face. I wear a surgical mask to help some with breathing and a set of green dust goggles over my glasses. The goggles are what save me. This storm would be impossible to endure without them, but the powder is so fine even with goggles on, my eyes water and cake with muck. They stick shut whenever I blink, so I periodically pull the goggles off my face to wipe the inside lens and scrub the dirt crust out of my eyelashes, but there's so much dust on my hands and sleeves, I'm not sure if this helps or hurts.

I do my best to stay in the turret. I figure I'm already screwed, so why not let my guys stay out of the storm as much as they can. After about fourteen hours in the storm, my head starts pounding and my breathing turns to wheezing. I start wondering if this is going to kill me, so I crouch inside the Humvee and ask for a replacement. Baker pops up, and I wheeze in the back seat instead.

After I drop inside the truck, we get a report on the radio of guys with AKs driving near our position in white pickups. My rifle is caked with dirt. The M240G up top is plastered with mud from dust and rain sprinkles. There is no chance either of these weapons is functional. I'm sure no one else's rifle is functional either, but the enemy AKs will still probably fire in this shit. The only functional weapons we have in the truck are hand grenades, which are probably not the best to use when you have no idea where other members of your unit are. If men with AKs come and decide to take a chance and engage us in the storm, we might be fucked.

My second to last thought before my body shuts down is *I might have to fight with my e-tool* (military issued folding shovel). My last thought is *Fuck it. If they come, let 'em kill me.*

On the outside, I look like a powdered donut. On the inside, my lungs feel like they're coated with mud. I need to throw up, but I'd have to step outside to do it, and my body can't take breathing in more sand, so I choke the vomit down, curl up, and pass out, hoping my body will repair itself while I sleep and any attacks will wait until morning.

The morning after the MOASS, my machine gun is fused shut. I scrub the joints for half an hour with my little green toothbrush just so I can pry it open. When I finally do, the innards are a hardened-plaster nightmare. I don't know where to begin. It'll be hours before this weapon is close to functional.

"Mount up! We've got to roll," Chilcot says. "How's that 240?"

"Totally fucked, Staff Sergeant."

"We'll get to it later. We need to move."

I throw the pieces together. Chances are low we'll get hit. There aren't many people out here besides half-starved farmers and herders, and they don't have much love for Saddam. But if we do get hit, I'd be better off grabbing my MRE spoon and trying to stab our enemy than shooting this machine gun.

"GOOD, GOOD, USA!"

A couple weeks before the invasion, two Iraqi men wearing Iraqi Freedom Fighter patches came to our camp and spoke to our unit.

"Our people are ready for this," the older one said, tall, thick around the middle, thin grey hair ringing his bald head. "They were ready thirteen years ago for their nightmare to end, for the Americans to come and end the bloody reign of Saddam Hussein, but Bush stopped at the border, and life became a new level of hell."

This was a perspective I'd never heard. I was a boy during Desert Storm. I remembered how quick the war went, how invincible our army seemed. Iraq was our enemy and Iraqis were bad. They picked on a smaller country and got what they deserved. No one ever said that maybe some of the Iraqis fighting in Kuwait didn't want to be there either, but they didn't have a choice.

"Thirteen years ago, my people prayed the Americans would come," the younger man said, "To end Saddam Hussein, to end the terror. I remember the prayers of my sister, how she believed we might finally have lives without constant fear and blood, how she wept when the Americans left us. But now you are here to finish the job."

The younger man, Akish, would become our translator. A decade earlier, knowing his death or imprisonment were imminent, he fled to Europe seeking political asylum. His family stayed behind under constant surveillance. He's coming back for the first time with us as a volunteer, throwing himself into a war without a weapon to help us communicate with his people.

"You have no idea what this means to us, what this means to me," Akish continued. "No one in the world cares about Iraqi people, about what we've endured, but now you are here to fight a battle that is not your own. I can't explain my gratitude that you would spend your lives this way. I wonder at your courage."

I'm looking for a reason to fight. I'm not sure what I'm doing here besides keeping my oath. I'm not from a military family. I don't have a personal legacy to uphold. I don't care about weapons of mass destruction. What I do care about is not losing my life for nothing. I need something worth fighting for. Akish gives me something.

"You will see for yourselves. There will be celebrations in the streets. The people of Iraq will forever be grateful for young men like you."

When the war starts, Akish's words are validated. After just a few days, Iraqis line the streets. The braver men shout, "Good, Good, USA!" as we roll past. The less brave men smile and give a thumbs up before looking anxiously around to see who might be watching them. These first few weeks, I never have to open a pack of cigarettes. Any time mine burns even halfway down, a stranger walking by on the side the road opens a pack and says, "Cigaretten, mister?" with a broad smile on his face.

Often, someone just hands me a pack of Sumers, the local brand. They're shitty cigarettes. Half the tobacco falls out the end before you can light up, but the gesture is nice.

These are special days. The suffocating black cloud of Saddam's regime is lifting, and the people are euphoric. Akish spends most of his time laughing, talking with crowds on the side of the road. But when American forces take Baghdad, Iraq becomes a free-for-all, and these crowds of people start robbing whatever they can. We just watch it happen. In the morning, thousands of empty-handed people stream past us toward town centers and residential areas. In the afternoon, thousands stream back the other direction with armloads, cartloads, truckloads of assorted goods. Women carry food—bundles of grain or sacks of potatoes. Children roll tires alongside their families, or carry whatever small items they can—clothing, trinkets, smaller sacks of grain. Men carry furniture—shelves, tables, desks—or drag heavier items—air conditioners, automotive engines, random machines—pausing every few steps to catch their breath and encourage their wilting children. Four teenaged boys push a 1930s Studebaker convertible past my Humvee. Either they couldn't find the keys when looting the house, or the car has no gas. The boys grin from ear to ear, but avoid my eyes, like if they look at me, I might confiscate their treasure.

Part of me understands what's happening. All wealth used to flow through Saddam Hussein, and he doled it out as he saw fit. Many profited greatly under Saddam's reign. They were given lavish lifestyles and almost total freedom to commit whatever crimes they wished against the less connected. These Iraqis flowing past us now were the people living on the crumbs of the old regime. But families taking food and clothing is one thing. This is something else. Just after the boys with the car pass, eight young men hanging out of the cab of a front-end loader roll past me. On the front forks of their vehicle is a brand-new Cadillac. The men smile and laugh. As they pass, one of them shouts at me, "Good USA!" and gives a thumbs up.

I sneer at the young man, and he looks away. Is this why I'm in this shithole? So you can steal cars? Is this why me and my friends are getting shot at and blown up? So you can act like assholes and loot your country blind? The looting continues for several days, sunrise to sunset.

My unit gets called farther north to block one end of a half-exploded bridge crossing the Euphrates. The river beneath the bridge is wide and deep and murky brown from churning silt. A fall from the bridge would probably mean death. I don't know why we post here, maybe to stop further attacks from collapsing the bridge completely. The road portion of the bridge is impassable, an explosion having left a fifteen-foot hole across both lanes of traffic, but the footpath on the side of the road is still intact. Hundreds of Iraqis gather at our position, begging to cross the bridge, and the crowd is swelling.

Frantic men and women jostle for position, all with stories of babies and sick loved ones they swear are in the nice residential area on the other side of the bridge. They know that even though we're Marines, we're still sentimental Americans moved by stories.

One young man sticks out in the crowd. He's beardless, clean, and where most of the people around him look half-starved, he's muscled like a high-level athlete. He also wears western clothing, jeans and the kind of T-shirt guys wear when they want to show off their arms. I wonder if he's Republican Guard. He's too well taken care of for normal military. This young man pushes his way to the front of the mob, yelling at Akish. Akish won't even look at him.

It's a hot day and several elderly men and women are in the crowd. We need to get them out of the sun and out of the fray. Respect for elders doesn't exist in a mob, and their frail bodies get tossed around in the throng until some look on the verge of collapse. Akish pushes through the crowd, ushering the elderly men and women out toward the bridge so we can send them on their way. Shouting voices come from every direction and people climb all over each other trying to get ahead. I can't say I'd be any different in their position, but watching this mob snarling for resources and grinding their elders into the dirt weighs on me. I'm not the only one. I see it in Akish's face too.

Eventually, we let the mob trickle across the bridge and as soon as people reach the other side, they start coming back with armloads of goods taken from houses. I feel sick inside.

After about a week, we get ordered to stop the looting, but the damage is done. We patrol through neighborhoods picked clean, shooing away the last desperate stragglers grabbing shit no one wants—rags, rusty machine parts, broken furniture. The looting has done something to Akish, turned him fierce. Sometimes he can't even look at us anymore. He told us over and over about how ready his people were, how all they needed was a chance, how we would see for ourselves. Now he stalks from straggler to straggler, yelling at them to drop what they carry, tearing it out of their hands if they hesitate. My Commanding Officer decides to make a point. He gathers looters around, has them dump their stolen trash in a pile on the street. My team leader and a couple other Marines kick through the pile to see if there are any trophies they want. I can't even look at them. After Marines are done picking through the trash, the captain douses the pile with diesel fuel and lights it on fire.

Iraqis stand around the circle watching their stolen goods burn, contempt glowing in their eyes. What the fuck are we doing? The damage is already done, just let them keep their garbage. We drive away, leaving them with the flames.

WEAPONS OF MASS DESTRUCTION 2: SANCTIONS

1991 to 1996 were brutal years for common Iraqis. Many people believe sanctions are a more tolerable alternative to war. You get fewer images of exploded corpses lying on the highways. But for countries like Iraq that rely heavily on exports for income and imports for essential goods, sanctions do enormous damage. After Desert Storm, 150 countries joined the sanctions on Iraq. This eliminated 90 percent of Iraq's imports and essentially all of its ability to sell oil which is what kept Iraq's centrally planned economy running. Per capita income in Iraq went from $3510 to $450 in five years. GDP went from $66.2 billion to $10.8 billion, and total lost income and productivity were estimated at over $260 billion. In addition to this, inflation was astronomical. In 1991, the exchange rate of Iraqi dinar to dollars was 10 to 1. By 1995, the exchange rate was 1674 to 1.

Over 200,000 bombs were dropped on Iraq during the first Iraq War, damaging much of the country's infrastructure. Because of sanctions, much of the damage to Iraq's electric, water, and sewer systems couldn't be repaired. Widespread outbreaks of previously eliminated diseases like cholera and typhoid ravaged the country. This was not felt by the Iraqi elite, of course. While his people starved, Saddam built monuments to himself. He had over eighty palaces, and in his eight main compounds, the floor space of the buildings alone was over twelve square miles. It's hard to calculate how much money was spent on gold, marble, and other fine materials, how much was paid for carvings, gildings, giant chandeliers, and paintings across his miles and miles of homes, how much was spent on gardeners, chefs, security, drivers, and servants at locations he wasn't even at. Maybe the most miserable fact of all this was he never even slept at these palaces. He was so afraid of being killed by his own people or blown up by American missiles that he usually slept in non-descript safe houses only he and his security knew about. All the billions spent were just a demonstration of power, a reminder to the people of Iraq that no matter where they went, Saddam was always near.

Despite all this, Iraq's economy was so bad in 1995, Saddam started to worry his regime might not survive. By that point, the government food ration system could only provide 1100 calories per day. 31 percent of children under five years old were malnourished. Excess mortality of children under five years old during the sanction years in Iraq was around 500,000, and Saddam used these dead kids to his advantage. He forbade parents from burying their children. The bodies were collected and stacked at mortuaries for use as props in parades through Baghdad where Saddam hired professional mourners to sob and wail in front of Western media. The sight of these dead kids created international outrage and forced the UN to distance itself from accusations that it was causing the widespread death of Iraqi children. As a response, the UN created the Oil for Food program, a program designed to alleviate the suffering of common Iraqis, but like most things the UN does, it soon became totally corrupt. It was the open-door Saddam needed.

REMNANTS

The first time I saw a bunch of dead bodies, I couldn't look away. I grew up in a peaceful Midwestern town with two ethical parents. I never worried about violence, never even thought about it. So now, when I see four dead men lying shoulder to shoulder on the highway, it doesn't seem real.

I can't tell if the men are Iraqi or American. They look Iraqi, but they're wearing American camouflage, and the soldiers watching over them are treating the bodies with respect, which makes me think they're probably ours, maybe a few translators or some sort of Civil Affairs Group. Either way, my first time seeing dead bodies seems surreal. By the end of a couple weeks, I hardly notice anymore.

★★★

On the second day of the invasion, the entire sky is blanketed with thick black smoke from burning oil fields. Midday looks like late evening, like the sun has already set and the darkness is coming. The smoke cloud is oppressive. I feel like I'm in a cavern underground instead of open desert. My unit stops next to a burning pipeline, one of dozens in an area the size of a few football fields.

The fire burns hot and high, thirty-foot flames belching greasy fumes into the sky. When the wind shifts, I feel the heat on my skin.

A couple hours into the day, an Iraqi man with a thick moustache approaches our position and begs us to put a sandbag over his head while he talks to us. Our CO doesn't want to do this. For weeks, US forces have been dropping leaflets in Southern Iraq telling the people we're here to help. A sandbagged Iraqi man on the side of the road sends the wrong message. But the man continues to press.

"Please, sir. Please cover my head," he says to our translator. "If anyone sees me here, my whole family will be murdered."

The man is the commander of the local army, and he has come to surrender. Some of his men surrendered to us the day before, and he told the rest to stack their weapons and uniforms and go home. But he knows Saddam's spies are still everywhere, and if they see him talking to US forces, those loyal to the regime will make an example of him.

"Jesus Christ," Romero says, coming back to the Humvee. "You believe that shit? Murder a dude's whole family just for talking to us?"

★★★

Sometimes it's hard to tell the war is still going. It's obvious there used to be an army here, but for days all I see are remnants, smoldering Iraqi tanks, troop transport trucks in flames, wide fields of charred artillery hit by aircraft at night. That's what's left of units that stayed to fight. The other eighty percent simply abandoned their gear and melted into the populace. Anti-Aircraft guns point up at the sky from empty sandbag dugouts. Surface-to-air missiles lie dormant on abandoned truck launchers. Piles of rifles, uniforms, gas masks, and bayonets litter the Iraqi countryside.

There are caches of explosives everywhere, some concealed, many out in the open piled on street corners and highway off-ramps. Young boys clamber over stacks of mortars and landmines as we talk to their parents. They stumble over Rocket Propelled Grenades asking us for candy or if they can wear our hats. We brush them off the explosives, but they're like little boys everywhere—they can't help being stupid.

★★★

We set up camp in a palm grove off the street. When guys aren't working checkpoints, they go back deep into the trees where the sounds of the city dissipate to nothing.

When it's my team's turn for a day in the palm grove, I feel like I'm in paradise. I didn't know palm trees could grow so thick and lush. Bright green canopies totally block out the sun, leaving us cool and relaxed in the rich brown underbelly of the grove. For a couple hours, I forget where I am and lay totally content on the roof of my Humvee, soaking up the refreshing air and reading a book about ancient Arab warriors. Then I notice something sticking out of a tree a few feet from my head.

I sit up and look closer. It's the tail of an RPG. The grenade didn't explode on impact, and it buried itself in the center of the tree trunk. I look around the palm grove more closely now. Unexploded rockets are lodged in tree trunks all around us. There must have been a huge attack here. Suddenly, I'm not so relaxed. I can't stop thinking about the grenades in the trees, wondering if one of them is going to randomly blow up in my face or if the guys that shot them are going to come back for more.

★★★

We stay one night at a businessman's mansion. Our CO has been talking with him for a few days about local issues, and the man invites him to stay.

The mansion has a huge loop driveway out front, with a jungle of palm trees and bushes in the middle. My platoon posts on one side of the loop. Second platoon posts on the other. We can't see or hear each other from our positions.

Inside the mansion are all sorts of pictures of this businessman with Saddam and members of his family. This guy was clearly well-connected in the old regime.

"The captain says we're sleeping here tonight," Staff Sergeant Chilcot says, addressing the platoon. "He says there's plenty of room inside for anyone who wants sleep there. I'm telling you right now, there ain't a single Marine from our platoon sleeping in that fucking house."

"This is so stupid," Baker says, "Why are we taking the risk?"

"Everyone sleeps with their boots on tonight," Chilcot says, "Be ready to move."

The platoon meeting breaks, and we start watching the long night. There are elevated chain-link fences all around our position so we can't patrol, and we can't get a good vantage point to see what's happening around us. We're all clustered together at the bottom of a bowl with nowhere to run. It's like we're begging to be shot.

When the sun rises the next day, none of our guys look like they've slept. A few Marines from Headquarters Platoon come out of the mansion clean and rested.

"Did you guys check out those heated tiles in the showers?"

"Hell yeah. Did you see all those pictures of this guy with Saddam and his family? Dude knew all of them."

Great, fellas. Glad you slept easy with the old regime.

★★★

A Civil Affairs Group and a few of our guys take four prisoners at a granary—Fedayeen loyalists who have been threatening to mutilate and murder the family who operates the granary as soon as American forces leave the area. My team drives up as two Marines heckle the prisoners.

"This was your boy, right?" one Marine says, holding up a painted portrait of Saddam Hussein.

The Iraqis look confused, so the Marine uses hand signals.

"You." he points at the prisoners then rubs his index fingers together side by side, which means something like "friend", then points at Saddam.

The prisoners spit at the painting and shout curses. One fat young man, obviously moneyed, with milky soft skin like no Iraqi man I've seen, kicks his sandals at it, saying,

"No Saddam! Bad Saddam!"

"Yeah, right, motherfucker," the Marine says, dropping the painting on the ground and leaving to search more of the granary.

As soon as the two Marines leave, the fat milk-skinned boy blows kisses at the painting and fervently mutters while bowing his head like he's repenting of a sin. I guess he doesn't notice me watching.

When the CAG doesn't need my team anymore, we head back down the road to link up with our platoon. I feel good that we were here. I'm glad for the family at the granary. These guys had nasty intentions. I'm sure of that. Hopefully now the family can find some peace.

On our way out of the compound, we drive past a forklift on the side of the road. A dead Iraqi man is stuck on the end of the forks, flopping in the air while the operator tries to shake him free. The body jiggles up and down, legs and arms flailing for several seconds. A soldier steps out of the forklift with a long metal rod. He wedges the rod between the body and the metal frame of the lift. He pries at it, throws all his weight behind it. The body pops free and drops into an unmarked pit in front of the lift. The soldier gets back in the cab to look for more bodies.

IF YOU'RE _____, LEAVE THE CITY

Last week Parker shot a looter in the face. After many days of sitting by, watching Iraqis steal everything from Cadillacs to potatoes to industrial air conditioning units dragged behind those Cadillacs, we get ordered to stop the looting. When Parker and Rhodes see a man stealing a flatbed truck, Rhodes steps in front of the truck and yells at the man to stop. The man doesn't slow down; he speeds up, so Parker levels his M-16 and shoots him several times through the windshield.

Back at camp after the shooting, a group of Marines gathers around Parker to congratulate him.

"Look at this killer!" one Marine says, shaking his hand.

"Nice tight grouping on the windshield," another Marine adds, patting him on the shoulder.

Parker looks uncomfortable, but the Marines in the circle want him to be excited, so he pulls back his shoulders, puts on an icy killer face, and says, "Just doing my job." But his eyes look like question marks, like he's not sure how he should feel about what he just did.

The next day, a white bed sheet with hand-painted red Arabic appears draped over a wall where the shooting took place. More sheets appear the day after that. I'm curious about the sheets. It seems strange that they started to appear right after Parker killed that man. One day when I'm walking by, I ask Akish.

"Hey, Akish! Can you tell me what those sheets on the walls say? It's been bothering me not knowing."

"Niggers go home."

"What? Really?"

"Some say, 'Niggers go home.' Some say, 'If you're black, leave the city.' But they all say similar things."

"Huh."

Parker is black. He and Stanley are the only two black Marines in our unit. I don't know Parker well. He's in a different platoon, but I've gotten to know Stanley a bit. He's a religious guy, lends me his bible now and again when I get interested. He's kind to Marines and Iraqis alike, and I've never seen him angry, even when shot. There are a lot of shitheads in the Marine Corps; Stanley isn't one of them.

There are a hundred-fifty-thousand US Soldiers and Marines in Iraq daily pointing their guns at people and barking orders. I've been one of those guys, machine gun trained on a man's face while he begged me in the only English he knew, "Please mister, no." I've watched wives and children collapse, sobbing on the ground, convinced that my team and I would do unspeakable things to them. I've watched the chaos, seen the bodies in the streets. Violence and death are everywhere. When you're living in a world where exploded remains of corpses are stacked on the highways, does the skin color of the invading soldier really matter?

Nonetheless, the signs say, "Niggers go home."

A week after Parker shot the looter, Stanley sat in his Humvee eating breakfast near the shooting site. That's when the Iraqi man walked up to his truck, pulled a pistol, and shot him in the face. That's when Stanley's white teammates turned on that man and wrecked his body with bullets. That's when a white corporal walked up behind the man as he swayed on his knees and blew his brains all over the street.

EXIT SOUL

Our three-vehicle convoy pauses on the highway while Lieutenant Huff radios for directions. Our unit, somewhere across the city through a maze of houses and alleys, waits for us to link up. Huff wants to make sure we know where we're going before we dive in. As Huff talks on the radio, my vehicle idles beside a pile of Iraqi corpses behind a sandbag wall. It's a hot day, probably in the 90s, but the bodies look fresh, like the men died a few hours before we arrived.

The corpse closest to me sits on the asphalt, back leaned against the body stack. His face angles up toward the sky, glassy eyes looking right past me, mouth a sneer of pain, violent death frozen on the rigor mortised muscles of his face. When he was alive, he was probably a decent looking guy, lean, well built, with a trimmed black beard. I can't tell what killed him. There are bloodstains on his chest where bullets passed through but also slashes across his belly through which rubbery grey intestines spilled into a pile on his lap. Both of his hands cup his guts making me think he tried to hold them in as he died. At some point, a tank or AAV ran over his legs, turning his calves into a meat smear on the asphalt, clear tread pattern ground into the human mush. His upper thighs are split open from pelvis to kneecap, like burst tomatoes, skin peeled back, fissures in orange muscle all the way down to femur.

The bodies behind the sitting man are a jumble of heads, torsos, and limbs. I can't distinguish much of the pile, except one smooth-faced teenager who had his foot blown off. The foot sits a few yards away in a dried pool of blood, ragged bits of skin and sinew at the edges where the body ripped apart.

As I stare down at these men from behind my machine gun, Huff transmitting behind me, I don't think about the violence that killed them a few hours before. I don't think about their hearts ceasing to pump blood, or their cells, deprived of oxygen, beginning systematic self-digestion. I don't think about their bodies cooling to air temperature or their final degradations, last meals seeping out anuses, cocks gorging with blood. I don't think about rigor mortis setting in, that final muscular clinch, like a body's last vain attempt to keep its inner workings in place.

I don't think about the nightmare time bomb of the human body, tens of trillions of cells outnumbered by tens of trillions more bacteria, bacteria kept under control by a functioning immune system, now set free, the greenish hue on the abdomen indicating they've eaten through the intestinal wall and are infiltrating of the rest of the body.

I don't think about maggots, how split open orange muscle will soon wriggle with white, like a perverse nursery rhyme: There once was a maggot who lived in a thigh with thousands of others from foot up to eye, or how those thousands, tens of thousands, hundreds of thousands will crawl into every putrefying crevice, underneath skin, inside muscle, through heart, nasal cavity, throat tissue, eye sockets, inner ear mechanisms.

I don't think about putrefaction, organs liquefying, brain turning to seething mush, liver, spleen, and kidneys, cloudy bags of goo ready to rupture. I don't think about blisters on skin swelling with liquid as bacteria gorge, or body cavities and blood vessels bulging with gas, turning humans into bloat-sack abominations until they pop, painting the ground with red-brown slurry, and exposing layers of decomposing yellow fat.

I don't think about the smell of putrefying bodies, like diarrhea, mushrooms, skunk, and rose petals; or eggs, vomit, cooking ground beef, and water drained from a can of tuna; or garlic, mothballs, leaves in a rain gutter, and shit sitting unflushed for weeks in a public toilet; or maybe a combination of all these; or maybe worse than all these.

I don't think about death spasms, feet and legs twitching, like spirits fighting for control of their lost bodies, or corpses collapsing in on themselves, skin loosening, sliding off in thick sheets, hand skin pulling off like gloves, foot skin like socks—nails, hair, everything sliding, pulling away, finally turning black-green like rotting fruit.

I don't think about family members not finding these bodies, not bathing and shrouding them for burial because an American crew already scraped them into a pit on the side of the road, where they'll molder until nothing remains but anonymous skeletons.

As I look down at these corpses of men, I don't think any of these things. All I can think about is how fake they look. When I see living men and women suffer it bothers me.

When they carry away their dead in boxes and cry out their lamentations, I feel it. But as I look down at these corpses, I don't feel sorrow, regret, or shame. All I feel is confused. Why don't these bodies look real? This whole scene looks like a macabre sculpture, like the curator of a museum put together a "Realities of War" exhibit: ashy yellow skin made with locally farmed organic bees wax, plastic grey-purple intestines imported from a novelty factory in China, rubber legs complete with orange thigh fissure bought on special at the city joke shop. The face of the sitting man doesn't look like it's ever been alive. His eyes are two glass beads, doll eyes staring at the ceiling of a child's bedroom. His arms hang limp at his sides, hands folded over his intestines like a marionette cut from strings. These aren't men. These are clay puppets. Why would I grieve for these?

I look at my hands, one on the ridged pistol grip of my machine gun, the other on the warm plastic buttstock. I feel my flak vest rise and fall as my lungs inflate and deflate. Huff ends his transmission and shouts "Mount up!" My team squeezes their combat loaded bodies—flak vests, ammo, grenades, knives, med kits, canteens—into tiny Humvee seats. As they fight the inconvenience of living out of a Humvee, they look real to me.

We turn off the highway into a nice neighborhood—driveways, windows, tiled sidewalks—then down a narrow alley between houses. I should be scanning windows and rooftops for threats, but I can't get those bodies out of my head. Why did they look like that? I know they were men. I know they moved and breathed and had passion enough to stand and fight an unwinnable fight. They should've looked real.

Our convoy exits the alley near the Euphrates. A hundred yards away, our unit is camped on a mud bank by a pontoon bridge. Marines lounge on hoods of Humvees, shit or shave by the river, wipe their balls and armpits with baby wipes. These men wiping their asses and scrubbing their crotches are all the same parts as the dead men on the road, but they look real.

"Look at these shit birds," Peters caws, pulling his hand and a dirty baby wipe out of his trousers.

"Finally found their way," Jackson says.

Peters throws his dirty baby wipe in Jackson's face.

"Mother Fucker!" Jackson tackles Peters against the side of their Humvee. "You're gonna eat that nasty cheese-crotch rag."

They grunt and roll across the hood of the Humvee, skin flushing red as they claw for each other's throats.

Huff looks unimpressed. Chilcot intervenes.

"Knock it off, you stupid fucks. Show some goddamn discipline." They stop wrestling, suck wind, grin the dipshit grins of brothers who will wait until no one is watching to beat the hell out of each other.

Why do they look real? Their faces are boy's faces, eyes active, barely able to hold down wild mirth, eager to test their limits. They're nothing like the faces of the dead men on the street, the sneering masks, vacant eyes staring off into nowhere, no mirth, no rage, no fear—the spark that made them men gone.

Why? Why were they so empty? This question hounds my brain.

A thought comes, something I haven't considered and don't know if I want to consider. I stare down at the mud, away from the eyes of other Marines. I smile, almost laugh out loud—it seems so ridiculous.

Souls? Is that the difference? Do people have souls? Is that what left those bodies looking empty? Exited souls?

WEAPONS OF MASS DESTRUCTION 3: THE INTERNATIONAL CASH PIPELINE

Oil for Food was a great example of what the UN is, a place for well-connected people from regimes all around the world to come together and make sleazy deals behind the scenes. That's exactly how Oil for Food played out.

The international community always underestimated Saddam. They treated him like a two-bit thug, but he was a tough and cunning man who raised himself up from beneath the gutter. He was a tireless worker with absolutely no scruples who had destroyed every Iraqi aristocrat that ever got in his way. Along his path to power, he learned many things beyond the brutality he is known for. He was a gifted manipulator and propagandist with an innate understanding of how to leverage people and situations. He also understood how to mix gifts with fear. Militarily, Saddam was a liability, but in the arena of power politics, he was well suited to succeed.

The Oil for Food program was supposed to alleviate the suffering of common Iraqis. According to the program, Saddam could sell a limited amount of cheap oil to buyers around the world, and payment would be deposited in a UN monitored escrow account for distribution toward humanitarian goods. It didn't take long for Saddam to turn it to his advantage.

When Oil for Food began, it gave Saddam something he hadn't had since the end of Desert Storm, leverage. France and Russia had been involved with Iraq for decades. France sold it its fighter jets and nuclear reactors. Russia sold it its tanks, guns, and technical expertise. After the Iran-Iraq War, Iraq owed these countries over a hundred billion dollars, a debt Iraq would never be able to repay under sanctions made after Desert Storm. Saddam needed French and Russian officials to exert pressure at the UN to end sanctions. French and Russian officials needed sanctions to ease on Iraq so they could get the money they were owed. Oil bribes using Oil for Food greased the wheels.

A few prominent people known to have accepted Iraqi oil bribes were two counselors of President Jacques Chirac, two well-known French businessmen, officials in Chirac's election office, the head of Russian parliament, the head of the Communist Party in Russia, and members of the Russian Presidential Office. The top three countries receiving oil vouchers from Iraq through Oil for Food were Russia (30%), France (15%), and China (10%), three of the five permanent members of the UN Security Council. This was not a coincidence. Saddam needed all three to begin to break the stranglehold of sanctions on his country, but weakening the UN wasn't all he needed. Maintaining control of millions of people through force, fear, and surveillance takes resources. His regime was on the verge of collapse. Fortunately for Saddam, there is no shortage of corruption among the world's power players. Everyone and their brother was willing to make a secret deal with Iraq.

Oil for Food was supposed to save common Iraqis from starvation and disease, but it became just another means to exploit them for profit. The chief of the program at the UN accepted bribes from Saddam Hussein and looked the other way for all sorts of corruption. Saddam funneled over ten billion dollars a year of humanitarian aid from designated civilian purposes toward military applications. Trucks shipped to Iraq for civilian transport became Military trucks once in Iraq. Construction equipment meant to rebuild Iraq's public services became equipment used for rebuilding Iraq's WMD infrastructure. And then there were oil surcharges. Oil buyers would purchase Iraqi oil according to UN rules then purchase the privilege of buying Iraqi oil in secret by paying ten to thirty-five cents extra per barrel in cash dropped at embassies around the world or deposited in bank accounts in Syria, Egypt, Lebanon, Jordan, UAE, and Belarus. Some very well-known international companies were involved in this scheme, and Saddam pocketed billions of dollars.

The most disgusting abuse of Oil for Food came with food and medicine imports. The UN would pay member nations like Egypt to supply Iraq with top quality food, medicine, and other necessities for Iraqi citizens. Egypt would take the money, buy spoiled, cut rate, or impure goods and ship those to Iraq, then take a cut of the profits and convert the rest to dollars or gold bullion to deposit in Saddam's international bank accounts. If Iraq ever did get quality humanitarian goods, Saddam's inner circle would sell them to other nations or leave them to spoil in the sun. Saddam made over ten billion dollars from importing cut rate humanitarian goods.

By the end of 1996, with the help of Oil for Food, Saddam was no longer in danger of losing power from economic pressure, and he was able to turn his attention more fully toward reestablishing military strength. He sent agents all over the world to recruit businessmen and government officials who could help him.

WOMEN

Back in Kuwait before entering Iraq, we used to get all sorts of intelligence briefings for things we might encounter. The brief about Iraqi women went something like this:

"Don't stare, don't gawk, don't initiate verbal communication, don't smile, don't wave, don't wink. If they need to be searched, wait for a female Marine to do the search. If there aren't any female Marines around, which will likely be the case, use the backs of your hands, not your palms. We want to avoid confrontation with the male population. Messing with women is the quickest way to make things escalate. You might see interactions between men and women that you don't agree with. Don't interfere. Things are different here. It's not your mission to change the culture."

Okay. Avoid the women. Got it. Easier said than done.

★★★

My Humvee parks next to a wood plank fence in a dirt alley between tight-packed houses. I'm behind the gun, scanning rooftops and windows for threats. Chatter starts behind the wooden fence, low whispers. I focus on the whispers, readying myself for anything that might pop over the edge. A set of eyes peeks over, then drops out of sight. The whispers become giggles, and I relax. I turn back to what I was doing. But now that one girl was brave enough to look over the fence, others follow.

At first, I ignore the girls. I've got more pressing things to worry about. Maybe they'll get bored. But they don't get bored, and as much as I want to resist, to play my part as a gruff, professional Marine, I'm nineteen, and their giggles are fun. Soon, I can't focus on anything else. I've been so focused on the war, I haven't thought about girls in months. It feels great being looked at this way.

Corporal V shouts up from inside the truck that we're leaving. Romero fires up the Humvee.

The next time a girl peaks over the fence, I look her in the eye and smile. She shrieks and ducks, talking a mile a minute to her friends on the other side of the fence. We drive off, and I grin like I haven't grinned in months.

★★★

The greatest feat of strength I've ever seen was performed by a four-and-half-foot tall, late-middle-aged Iraqi woman stealing a desk.

It was at the tail end of the major looting. Most stuff people wanted was already gone. I'd been watching stragglers walk past for hours with armloads of garbage—dirty rags, hunks of scrap metal, balled up wads of paper. Then there she was, sturdy like a tree stump, like the years had squashed her into a hardened ball of fat and sinew, plodding step by step, exhaling in quick bursts like she was giving birth. On top of her head, she balanced an extra-long steel tanker desk, the kind from the 1950s that could double as a bomb shelter in a pinch. I remember moving one of these desks across a storeroom one day. I had two other guys helping me, and we still had to put it down every few steps. I can't imagine the strain on her head and neck, all that awkward weight focused on a single point of her skull. The desk, almost as tall as the women, hovered a few inches off the ground, like it had fallen from the sky and crushed her, but her steps never faltered. The desk didn't even sway as she plodded on, red-faced, neck and forehead veins bulging.

I stared open-jawed as this woman passed. I was so impressed, I wanted to cheer, but then a man approached who I hadn't noticed before. The man waved his hand angrily in front of the woman's face and scolded her for how slow she moved, clicking his tongue and shaking his head. If he had a switch in his hands, I'm sure he would have whipped her right there to push her along. Going any faster probably would have killed the woman or caused serious damage to her neck and spine, but the man continued berating her, clicking his tongue like she was an animal. The more I watched, the more I wanted to jump out of my turret and smash my rifle into the man's teeth.

If it was me a few years later, I might've said "Fuck it," grabbed the man by his throat and slammed his old ass on the ground, but then what? What would happen to her? What do men like that do after they've been humiliated? Who would he take it out on? I'd have to shoot him in the face, or he'd probably just beat her to death when I was gone.

"Things in the culture will make you uncomfortable. Don't intervene." That's what the Lieutenant said during our briefing, so I don't intervene. I just wasn't expecting it to sting like this. I quit looking at the woman and glare at the man. I can't help it. His eyes flicker up toward mine and then back down. He watches me out of the corner of his eye. He knows I'm watching him, hands on my 240. Eventually the discomfort gets to him. He leaves the woman and resumes walking several paces in front of her, not looking back.

★★★

I'm alone with my rifle turning back civilian vehicles on a road outside a busy market. A suicide bomber blew up a different market a few days before. We're trying to stop that from happening here.

During cultural briefings before we invaded, we were taught a few Arabic words, mainly commands, like kif (stop), aitaff hawlah (turn around), imshee (move), and arfae ydyk (put your hands up). I shout commands now while motioning with my hands for cars to stop and turn around. Most of the drivers get my meaning, but one man pushes forward, trying to inch past me. I run to his open window and shout "Kif! Kif!" He motions with his hands for me to get out of his way and keeps rolling forward.

"Kif, motherfucker!" I raise my rifle to my shoulder. Point it at the man's face. He stops.

Seeing the situation escalating, a young Iraqi man who speaks English approaches me.

"Can I help you, sir? Tell me what you need him to do?"

"No cars are allowed past this point. He needs to turn around, now."

The young man translates my message. The middle-aged driver argues with him, insistent on moving forward, but the young man keeps talking until the driver relents.

When the man turns his vehicle around, the tension releases, and a crowd of middle-aged Iraqi men and women gather around me. They seem eager to talk to me but didn't dare approach without a translator. The people are in good humor, not angry or scared, but curious, like they want to connect in some way. Several of them show me pictures of family members and smile, others make jokes that I don't understand. An insistent woman, probably in her forties, works her way to the middle of the group and speaks. The young Iraqi translator looks embarrassed. She speaks again, and the young Iraqi man ignores her. When she speaks a third time, I don't let the translator demur. Maybe she's in trouble.

"What's she saying?" I ask. The translator looks at his feet.

"It's not important, sir."

"I need to know what she's saying."

The translator raises his eyes from the ground, though not quite meeting mine.

"She says you're pretty like a flower."

The crowd of men and women bursts out laughing. My face flushes hot. I suddenly feel every bit a nineteen-year-old kid.

★★★

We're sitting on a highway somewhere in the middle of Iraq surrounded by desert on all sides. A couple miles south of us, a Syrian suicide bomber blows up an American checkpoint, killing a large group of soldiers. We get ordered to stop and search every Iraqi car driving up the highway from the direction of the attack. Two fireteams of Marines handle this order. Four guys stop and search cars. Four guys provide security. A few minutes after setting up our checkpoint, a black Sedan with tinted windows coming from the direction of the attack slows down and stops on the highway about fifty yards from our position. For several seconds they just sit there watching us. And we watch them, waiting to see what's going to happen. When the sedan turns off the highway into the desert and speeds off to avoid us, Chilcot tells us to go get them.

My team jumps in our Humvee and tears off into the desert after them. The Sedan takes a narrow path between a canal and a dirt berm, and as Romero floors it in pursuit, the width of our Humvee becomes an issue. The sedan makes it through the choke with little problem, but our Humvee wheels are right on the edge of the canal. It's a ten-foot drop, and who knows how deep the water is. As I look over the side of the Humvee, I expect at any second our front wheel is going to catch the edge of the canal and fling us over the cliff into the water. I get ready to jump.

If I can launch myself out of the turret as the Humvee goes over, I figure I'll have a better chance than if I roll with the Humvee, half my body inside, half outside. If the water is deep, I'll still probably die. I'm wearing a full combat load, so I'll sink pretty quickly.

At fifty miles per hour on loose sand and grit, Romero somehow manages to keep us straight and the tire never catches the edge. When the road widens out, Romero catches the car, and pulls up alongside it. I'm pissed off and juiced up from almost rolling into that canal. I point my 240 at the driver's face and scream, "Kif! Kif, motherfucker!"

The middle-aged Iraqi man driving the car looks up at me. His eyes don't look so much angry or panicked as pathetic, like he's saying to himself, "Please, God, don't let this happen to me. Please make them go away." I'm in no mood for mercy. The adrenaline is pumping, and I know this asshole is hiding explosives. Why else would he be avoiding our checkpoint?

"Kif!" I shout again, louder and angrier, staring through the man. He slows, then stops.

Romero slams on the breaks, and Valdez jumps out of the Humvee, rifle at the ready, shouting "Get the fuck out of the car!"

I shift my aim to the tinted rear window. Valdez works his way around the front of the car and shouts to Romero, "One more in the passenger seat."

"Got him," Romero says, standing in front of the car leveling his SAW. With Romero at the front of the vehicle and me in the turret, we could put a hundred rounds in this car in a few seconds.

Valdez barks again at the driver, "Get the fuck out, now!" this time using hand signals to indicate what he wants.

The driver complies and steps out of the car with his hands up.

"You too, motherfucker!" Valdez snaps, pointing at the man in the passenger seat. "Baker! Get that fucker out!"

Baker walks around the front of the car to the passenger side and points his rifle at the man, waving him out. The man complies.

"Hey, V?" Baker says, "We've got women in the back seat."

"Get them out of the car." Valdez says.

Baker opens the door to the backseat.

"No, mister," the driver says, but his English is only as good as our Arabic.

"Did you say no!" Valdez says, getting in the man's face.

V is keyed up. We're all keyed up. These people are enemy. They're probably hiding explosives, and they almost killed us on that stupid high-speed chase across the desert. The Iraqi man can tell that this is not the time to protest, out here alone with us in the desert. He bows his head and frowns, telling the women to get out of the car. The response from inside is muffled but shrill. The women are panicked and don't want to comply.

"Imshee! Move!" Valdez yells, pointing his rifle. The Iraqi man speaks more urgently to the women. They step out of the car whimpering, pulling a young boy and girl with them, each maybe three or four years old.

"Romero, cover me. Kub, Baker, lock down those passengers."

Baker herds the passengers away from the car while Valdez has the driver open all the car's compartments. When I point my 240 at the group with Baker, the women cry, one of them collapsing to her knees. Both children pick up the panic of their mothers and sob.

Valdez has the driver pop the hood and trunk, but the distress of the women and children softens him. He stops barking at the man and instructs him quietly by pointing. When the man has opened every door and compartment, Valdez returns him to his family and searches the car from engine to trunk. When he finds no explosives or weapons, he returns to the driver and his family and quietly signals that they are free to go. We load up in our Humvee and drive back down the dirt road to our unit. There's usually chatter inside the truck, Romero and Baker giving each other shit, V chiming in now and again to call Baker an old man. Now there's silence. I imagine everyone's wondering the same thing as me, "What the fuck did we just do?"

WILD DOGS (2)

Fifty yards in front of my Humvee, an elderly Iraqi man slogs through a field of calf-high mud, barely keeping upright as the mud sucks down his feet. A scabby pack of tan wild dogs runs out of a palm grove at the edge of the field. The dogs sprint past the old man, seemingly intent on business across the field, then the leader stops as if something just occurred to him. He turns and stares at the old man. When the other dogs catch up, they turn and stare as well.

The old man knows what's coming. He pulls a thick stick out of the mud and faces the dogs, wispy-thin arms barely lifting the stick off the ground.

When the dogs charge, I look around our perimeter to see if anyone else is watching. Most guys are sprawled out, relaxing inside the protective circle of Humvees. Romero, Baker, and Valdez are across the circle, thirty yards away, bullshitting and drinking coffee around a camp stove. I wave in their direction trying to catch someone's eye, but they aren't paying attention. I think about calling them on the radio, but our CO has been pissed recently about Marines filling the channel with chatter. I want to help the old man, but I can't go sprinting across an unidentified field. Too many Marines have gotten their legs blown off that way already.

Two of the dogs grab hold of the man's robes trying to pull him off balance while a third dog circles behind to attack his legs. The stick is too heavy for the old man to swing, so instead he uses it to jab each dog in the snout. Each time a dog releases its hold to get away from the jabs, it wheels around the old man, looks for a new angle, then lunges back in. All I do is watch this unfold, a small pack of starving dogs looking for meat and a wobbly legged old man desperate to keep it. I feel like this a lot in Iraq, like I'm watching something obscene but can't do anything about it. This time, the old man is superior to the dogs. They eventually get tired of the fight and move on to easier prey. Other Iraqis have not always been so fortunate.

★★★

Saddam Hussein took a special interest in training his sons. He wanted to turn them into beasts that could do whatever vile thing he needed done. He'd beat them with iron bars if they did something wrong, and if either one of his boys ever acted timid or turned away from violence, Saddam would make him watch videos of executions and tortures. In time, the boys watched torture videos like most kids watched cartoons—jaws pried open until shattering, fingernails ripped off, spikes through skulls, heavy hammers shattering noses, and of course, lots of rape.

Uday Hussein, Saddam's oldest son, once said, "Just wait until I become president. I'll be crueler than my father ever was. You mark my words. You'll yearn for the time of Saddam Hussein." From the time Uday was a boy, he was intrigued by blood and pain. When he was eight years old, he'd have playmates hold down live sheep so he could practice slicing off their testicles and pulling out their intestines. In time, he could keep the screaming creatures alive for hours while he cut them apart.

★★★

Peters finds a puppy abandoned by one of the roving packs of dogs. He takes it in, cares for it, feeds it, and tries to teach it tricks. For a few days, this puppy becomes a mascot for our unit, guys stopping by to pet it and watch it play. The puppy responds to the love and attention the way that puppies do, with happy yelps and a lot of tail wagging.

I don't know why Peters bothers. In a few days we'll have to move again, and he'll have to leave the puppy behind. He'll feel terrible about it because he's a warm-hearted guy. And now the puppy will be under the misapprehension that humans are friends. When we leave the puppy, he'll likely be shot or run over by a convoy, or he'll be hunted down and eaten by other dogs. If he somehow manages to fight his way to adulthood, he'll become just like the other dogs in Iraq, a scabby mutt with nothing on his mind but hunger, roaming the countryside subsisting on garbage and corpse flesh.

★★★

Nahle Sabet was a pretty, Christian architecture student Uday Hussein noticed walking one day on his daily

"Grand Tour" of universities and coffee shops looking for young girls to rape. He pulled up in his car behind her on the sidewalk, honked his horn and revved his engine, but Sabet pretended not to notice and kept walking. Not one to be denied his desires, Uday found out who she was and where she lived. Later, as Sabet walked home, Uday's men snatched her off the street outside her house and brought her to a remote farm near Baghdad.

When the men brought Sabet to the room where Uday waited, he greeted her, saying, "It's your lucky day. You get to be my new girlfriend."

"You're crazy!" Sabet said, "I want to go home."

Uday motioned to his guards, who ripped off Sabet's clothes and threw her to the ground. "First I'm going to beat you," Uday said, standing over her naked body, "Then, if you're lucky, I'll allow you to please me and my men."

Uday and his men raped and tortured Sabet for months, beat her unrecognizable. When there was nothing left of her and Uday decided he was bored, he slathered her naked body in honey and threw her alive into a kennel with his starving dogs.

MARINE CORPS

When I was in ninth grade, I used to get in trouble in health class for goofing off with my best friend. One day, the coach decided to bring us to the front of the room and teach us a lesson.

"Since you two bozos can't seem to be quiet in class, we're going to have a little push-up contest to see what you big mouths are made of. Get down on the floor."

I knew I wasn't made of much. Greg was stronger and more athletic than me. I was taller and weighed more. I knew that if we started this competition, I'd look like a noodle-armed fat kid, which was probably what the coach was aiming at, a good public shaming to shut me up. I did the only thing I knew to defend myself—acted like a smart ass. When Coach said go, I flopped flat on my belly then stood up and brushed myself off.

"Well, I guess that's all I got."

Not knowing how to deal with my non-compliance, the coach tried another tactic.

"I know one thing's for sure," he said, "I would never want a guy like you on my wrestling team."

"I know one thing's for sure," I shot back, "I would never want to be a part of any sport where high crotch lift is a maneuver."

The class erupted with laughter, and the coach looked like I backhanded him across the face. He told me to sit down and shut up, and for the rest of the semester would fit words like jerk and punk into his lecture and make a point of looking at me.

I had nothing against wrestling and probably wished I could be more like the guys on the team, but I fought back with what I had. Part of the reason I joined the Marine Corps was I didn't want to be that way anymore. I didn't like that I couldn't deal with confrontation directly. I either ran from it or hid behind a smart remark.

★★★

The summer after high school I started my first full-time job packing windshields into crates at the factory where my dad worked. The physical labor did my body good, but I was an awkward kid, an easy target for the guys I worked with. I made the mistake early on of blushing and looking away when they made crude jokes. Once they saw that, it was open season. I was ashamed at how easily they got to me every day.

As summer wore on, anyone and everyone ran me over at will. I couldn't stand up for myself. Every day I went to work, I came home feeling smaller and weaker, but I saw no way out. I wasn't a good enough student to get scholarships to college, and I wasn't skilled enough in any way to get a different job.

I spent hours each day pacing back and forth in the humid upstairs hallway of my parents' house trying to think my way out, but nothing was coming. Then one day, the phone rang.

"Michael!" my mom shouted up the stairs. "A recruiter is on the phone. Do you want me to hang up?"

I'm not sure what happened then. I had talked to this recruiter before, and just like with the coach, I spent most of the conversation making smartass remarks about his job. I never wanted to be a Marine, and my family certainly didn't want me to be a Marine, but that afternoon, something clicked down deep inside. I knew I needed to change my life. I knew I needed to change myself. And I knew this was the way to do that. I ran down the stairs and grabbed the phone.

That weekend, just after my eighteenth birthday, when my parents were out of town visiting my sisters, I joined the Marine Corps. I was nervous about the commitment and didn't know any Marines I could ask about it, so I signed up as a reserve.

Two months later, the Twin Towers were destroyed, and everything changed. I had never even held a gun until I joined the Marines, and now I was heading straight into a war.

FUCKING RESERVISTS

It's 25 January 2003, and we're at the Fort Snelling drill center in Minnesota for our scheduled weekend training. Our three platoons—First, Second, and Headquarters—are formed up in a small basketball gym for morning muster. At 0630, the First Sergeant walks through the double doors of the gym, wide grin on his face.

"Alright gentlemen," he says, standing in front of formation. "Pack your bags. We're going to the sandbox."

It's Saturday. We're dismissed until Wednesday to get our affairs in order. I just started a semester of college, so when the Housing Office, Registrar's Office, and bookstore open on Monday, I'll cancel my room lease, drop my classes, and sell my books. Tuesday afternoon, I'll drink with my friends, pack up my shit, and say my goodbyes. Tuesday night, I'll stay at my parents' house. They'll make a nice meal, maybe steak and shrimp, but it'll taste like sawdust. Not because it's not delicious, but because the dread in our house is so thick I can hardly stand to be there.

I report for active duty on Wednesday morning, and for a week we prep weapons and gear, take "smoke" breaks to get away from prepping weapons and gear, and stand guard out front of the drill center in negative twenty degrees. The morning of 5 February, before we fly out, I have breakfast near base with my parents. My folks are mostly quiet. When they do talk, it's about anything but the deployment. I don't blame them. This isn't something they wanted me to be. Now I'm going half-way around the world to start a war. As we're about to leave, a grey-haired gentlemen thanks me for my service. This is the first time someone approaches me like this, and I don't know how to respond. I haven't served anyone yet and feel like a fraud for accepting his gratitude. But he expects a response, so I say, "Uh, yeah, for sure."

My parents drop me off with my pack and sea bag at the drill center parking lot. I hug them both, not knowing if I'll ever see them again, then grab my gear and walk away. In a way, it's a relief. I need to be around Jarheads who grunt and bark and meet shit head-on.

Late that evening, our plane lands at Cherry Point, North Carolina, and we catch a bus to French Creek, Camp Lejeune. It's after midnight when we get to our barracks, and no one expects us. We wait in the grass yard out front with our packs and seabags while Command figures out where we're going to sleep. A few Marines on the third-floor meander out to the concrete catwalk and stare down at us. Their scowls say what they're thinking, "Fucking Reservists."

There's a clear order of prestige in the Marine Corps, starting with Infantry and Recon at the top, then going down to other combat and direct fire support units like Tanks, Light-Armored Reconnaissance, Tracks, and Artillery, then reserve combat units, then way at the bottom, somewhere above reserve cooks, is us, reserve MPs.

Around 0230, our company breaks up to sleep in random occupied rooms. I'm with two hazy-eyed Navy med-techs who just got pulled out of bed and don't know why some strange-fuck Jarhead is dropping his gear on their floor. As they roll over and go back to sleep, I pull my sleeping bag out of the stuff-sack in my Mollie and lay it on the cool concrete floor. Reveille is at 0530.

When I can't sleep, I get up to piss and splash some water on my face. I stumble into the dark bathroom and flip on the light. The whole room flutters with motion, hundreds of cockroaches streaming toward cracks in the walls. I can't piss anymore; I'm too grossed out. I flip off the light, pop back in my sleeping bag on the floor, and pull it tight over my head. At around 0430, fatigue takes over, and I fall asleep for an hour before reveille.

The next few days are a rush. We need desert equipment and chemical gear—boots, utilities, head covers, MOPP suits, mask filters, second skins, canteens with functional NBC drinking caps. Some Marines get the stuff they need. Others have to make do without. That's what happens at the bottom of the pecking order. When 150,000 mobilizing troops need equipment, leftovers fall down the line.

We line up at a basketball gym converted into a vaccination center. Navy Corpsmen and medical personnel stand by tables full of needles and solutions. One by one, we walk through the assembly line, green t-shirt sleeves rolled up to our shoulders. Alcohol swab, needle-stab, step forward, repeat. Alcohol swab, needle-stab, step forward, repeat. Hepatitis A, Encephalitis, Meningococcal, Typhoid, Yellow Fever, Cholera, one after another. The multiple jabs of Smallpox. The deep-down tissue burn of Anthrax. What else? Plague? Ebola? It's not for us to know but step forward and take what we're given. Blue pills for Malaria and nerve agents? Okay. Uniforms soaked in DEET to prevent sand flea bites? Sure thing. Bodies inundated by microbes and chemicals, we march on.

In a white cinderblock room, my platoon practices gas drills, nine-line medivac reports, and calls for fire. A Captain from Lejeune walks in, introduces himself as our new Platoon Commander, then sits in front of the room.

"In a few days, gents, we'll be up to our elbows in blood." he says, "Not just the blood of our enemies, but the blood of our brothers. Look around you. Look to the guys on your left and right. These are faces of men you'll watch die. Make sure you're ready for that."

Every day in Lejeune, we keep training: flak-jacket runs, machine gun classes, hasty ambushes, whatever we can think of. When our rifles are locked in the armory, we patrol with sticks, looking like little boys playing war on the paved streets, giving hand and arm signals, halting, crouching, standing, moving, scanning for imaginary threats, squad rushing fake objectives. As we patrol, more and more Marines come out on balconies to watch.

"Fucking Reservists!" a chorus starts. "You dipshits going to war with sticks!"

We keep practicing, more shouts coming as we continue. When we patrol past the chow hall, a fat cook, wearing a white jumpsuit covered in sauce-stains, bursts out of the back door. He's breathing hard, must've seen us from inside and ran out to catch us before we got away.

This is probably the one time in his Marine Corps career he'll get an opportunity to give shit instead of take it for being a cook, and he's not going to pass it up. He catches his breath for one glorious moment before we're too far away and shouts, "Fucking Reservists! You dipshits going to war with sticks!"

On 10 February, our Master Sergeant finds us on the road near our barracks. "Pack your shit. We got our flight order."

We scurry for the last couple hours, packing up, calling loved ones, mailing crap home we don't need. The last thing I do before we leave Lejeune is shave my head and put on my military issue glasses. With a bald head and thick-rimmed marbled-brown glasses, I'm ugly. And when I'm ugly, I feel more ready to do what needs to be done.

At 0230 on 11 February, we board a plane to Kuwait. When we land, we walk down the stairs onto the tarmac and get herded onto buses that smell like body odor and sweat. Marine MPs with 50cals escort our buses to our desert camp. About two weeks ago, I was in college, probably skipping class to have a beer with my buddies. Now I'm part of the first wave of an invasion. Fucking Reservist.

CHOKE

(A couple days before I leave for Kuwait in 2003)

I'm lying on my back, staring at the ceiling, somewhere in that state between asleep and awake. I don't know when I cross over or if I do at all, but on the edge of my vision a cloud begins to grow, a thick fog creeping toward me. I'm afraid of the fog; I want to get away from it, but as the fog swells toward my body, I'm frozen in place. It drifts up my legs, across my chest, settles on my face like a plastic garbage bag. I gasp and choke in the black.

A pinprick of light pulses through the fog like a lone star. As I near unconsciousness, I focus on that speck of light and beg for my life. The light swells, then explodes, blowing the fog off my face. Cool fresh air rushes into my lungs. Above me, where the ceiling was, is an open sky, stars extending into forever.

The fog recedes into the periphery but doesn't disappear. It stays on the edge of my vision, waiting.

We set up camp along a highway north of An Nasiriyah. A Marine Civil Affairs Group is trying to build relations with leaders in the area, but the Ba'ath party is too strong here. Its members go from house to house, threatening death to anyone and their families if they aid US troops in any way. No one is willing to talk. My company leaders, like many of us, are eager to be a part of this war, to make a difference, to be Marines. So, when the CAG asks for help, we help. We accompany them on a raid of a Ba'ath party headquarters up the road from our camp.

As guys prep their gear for the assault, there's a palpable energy in the group. Romero is usually a level-headed guy, now he bounces up and down and chatters with everyone around him like he can't stop his mouth. Baker is quiet. He's older than most of us, 28, and just had his second kid. He wants nothing more than to get back to his family. The look in his eye says today might jeopardize that wish.

I'm a little like Baker and little like Romero. I'm as anxious as I've ever been, but I also feel like this is a chance to do my job, a chance to see what I'm made of. Some guys in my unit have waited their entire careers for a gun fight. I'm getting one less than a year after basic training. In that way, it's kind of a privilege.

Before we leave, I step away from the chatter of my platoon, walk to the edge of the road, and look up toward the sky. I don't know if I believe in God, and I've never prayed outside the rote prayers I learned in church as a kid, but I pray now.

"If you are up there," I say, "Please forgive me for what I'm about to do. I don't want to kill people, but I want to do my job. I'm going to do my part in the fighting, and I'm willing to bear whatever consequences result on my soul. I just want you to know that I don't have any malice in my heart. I'm just doing the best I can with what I understand to be honorable."

Mike Kubista

(During my deployment to Ramadi in 2004)

The dream starts in an empty room without windows, its walls and floors made of polished wood planks. An open doorway leads out to corn fields and blue sky. That's where I want to be, but I can't move my arms and legs.

Something invisible slides me across the floor like I'm gliding on ice. When I stop gliding, the invisible thing lifts me off the ground, pulls my arms above my head like they're hanging from strings. My legs dangle in the air. The invisible strings dance me from one end of the room to the other, and I laugh. It's kind of fun floating through the air without any control. But the longer it goes on, the less fun it becomes. I look at the open door with longing. I want to walk outside with my own strength and breathe deeply the fresh air.

I talk to the invisible thing, tell it I'd like to leave. Suddenly, the movements become violent. I'm hurtled against the walls, shaken in place like a defenseless infant, slammed against the ceiling. The invisible thing pins me there, then lets me drop to the floor with a thud. The crash knocks the wind out of me, but I can move again, so I crawl for the door. Just as I reach the door frame and feel the outside air against my cheeks, something grabs my legs and yanks me back to the center of the room. The door slams shut.

We drive up the highway in a column of Humvees. I'm rear security with my 240 pointed straight down the road behind us. Our objective turns out to be much closer than I think. When we started driving, I expected to have a few minutes to prepare myself mentally, but we go less than a mile and then exit, and the headquarters is right there, a hundred meters from the exit ramp. As rear security, my back is turned to the convoy and our objective. Just as my truck completes the turn onto the road to the headquarters, gunfire erupts at the front. A lot of gunfire. They were ready for us.

With the amount of gunfire going on behind my back, I expect to see Humvee wreckage and Marines' bodies lying all over the street, but when I swing my turret around to join the fight, I see neither. My guys are fine. Some of them are more than fine, hopping around like idiots, whooping into the air. Romero is so out of control, when he finally gets close enough to the building to engage, he hops out of the truck and accidentally shoots three rounds into the dirt in front of his feet, almost blowing off his own toes.

The complex is a two-story stucco building about the length of a short city block. The gunfire started when an Iraqi man jumped into the open doorway at the front of the complex and leveled his AK-47. Peters, at the front of the convoy spotted him and dropped him. After that, there were scattered muzzle flashes inside the dark windows, and our side erupted.

By the time my truck roars up to the edge of the compound, I don't see anything, no targets, no flashes, but the firing from our side is beyond reigning in. This is everyone's first contact. Fear and adrenaline run thick. The Iraqi in the door and the shot that dropped him are a trigger that releases everybody, and once the avalanche begins, there is no stopping it. Our guys unleash everything they have: 50cals, Mark 19s, M240Gs, M203s, SAWs, and M16s. Thousands of rounds of various calibers and capabilities fly at this building in a matter of seconds;

stucco debris cascades down the walls in waves. Rhodes takes a step toward the complex and lobs an M203 round at the building's external fuel reserves. He grins when the explosion starts a fire and thick streams of black smoke billow into the sky.

I forget my job as rear security and aim my 240 at the windows like everyone else. When I pull the trigger, my gun pops out a single shot and then goes dead. I rack the bolt to the rear and fire again. Again, my 240 shoots a single round then stops. I don't know what's happening.

(On leave in Minnesota before I leave for Ramadi)

A bright moon crests over the tree line next to the river. I'm in a speedboat with a Marine buddy, and as we accelerate, we holler into the night. He looks at me, grins, and banks sharply. I lose my balance and tumble over the edge into the black water. I bob in my life jacket as he circles around, laughing.

"Fucking asshole," I say, as he idles up, and I reach for the boat.

Then my head is under water. I gurgle and spit, not knowing what's happening. I thrash, fight to break the water's surface again, but the harder I struggle, the quicker I sink. I panic, scream, and then watch the precious bubbles of air escape out of my mouth and ascend to the surface.

An unseen hand grasps me firmly by the collar and yanks me deeper. Towers of seaweed grow around me like ladders to the surface just out of reach. I fight the pull, but nothing I do changes my direction. My lungs spasm in my chest trying to draw in air. When I start to black out, my mind shouts, "You are about to die, Wake up!" I wake up, chest heaving in my bedroom in Minnesota. I'll be heading back to Iraq shortly.

A few weeks before the invasion, I was in a tent in Kuwait waiting for the order with the rest my unit from Minnesota. An active-duty MP unit from Pendleton was a couple tents down. The ships hadn't arrived with our gear yet, and the guys from Pendleton were undermanned, so my CO made a deal with their CO, equipment for Marines. Eight of our guys went to them. A few shotguns and a soft-back Humvee came back in return. I was the youngest and most inexperienced Marine in my platoon, so I got shipped.

This was devastating. Not only would I be crossing into Iraq with a group of total strangers, the shame of knowing I was worth about half a pump-action shotgun to my Minnesota unit almost broke me before the war even started, but there was nothing for it; it was what it was. So, I held my head up, did my best, and took up smoking.

When I met my new fire team leader, the first thing he said was, "You're the gunner. My guys don't want to do it because that's the first guy to get shot." I had never handled an M240G before. I didn't even know how to take one apart. When I brought this up, Valdez said, "You'd better learn quick," and walked away. That was that. No time for self-pity, I swallowed it and learned as much as I could before we crossed the border.

Now I'm in front of a Baath Party Headquarters with a malfunctioning weapon. I try over and over to do the things I know how to do. I clear the ammunition, check for bent rounds, slap the belt back in the feed-tray, rack the bolt, and attempt to fire. I clear the ammunition, swap out ammo cans, feed in new rounds, rack the bolt, and attempt to fire.

Nothing I do helps. I just don't know the things I need to know, yet.

Without a functioning weapon in an unarmored turret, I feel a bit like I'm naked with my ankles behind my head facing a swinging baseball bat. Then things get worse.

The CAG Commanding Officer orders a hasty retreat, and instead of everyone doing an about face, the lead Humvee U-turns at the far end of the complex and each following Humvee drives forward and U-turns at the same place. Our unit doubles up on itself, some trucks going one direction, some going the other. Most Marines stop firing to avoid shooting each other. My truck, the last in the convoy, idles across the entire length of the complex, twice, no one covering me and me unable to cover myself.

The complex is only about fifty feet off the road, and as my wide-open head and torso glide past every dark window, I expect to see the muzzle flash that will end my life, the one that'll send a bullet through my face. About halfway through my crawl across the kill zone, my body starts to take control of itself. With my hands, I still claw away, loading and unloading ammunition, but my head starts jerking backward violently every few seconds, like it's anticipating the death blow.

When the convoy completes its U-turn, Chilcot yells at me, "Lay down some cover fire! What the fuck are you doing?" His directness and urgency snap me out of my head, and I find my voice enough to yell back that I can't fix the gun. Romero jumps up top, and I slide into the back seat and take a deep breath. When Romero can't get the 240 working either, he grabs his SAW and covers us the rest of the way back to camp.

When we get to the clearing where the rest of our company is parked, black smoke rises over the palm trees in the distance. It's unsettling realizing that that smoke came from us, but adrenaline is still pumping and the mood in camp is celebratory. Marines smile, shake hands, and congratulate each other on their escape. Romero jumps down from the turret and slaps me on the back, and even though my experience was a disaster, it still feels like an initiation of sorts.

Our XO gathers us for a mission debrief and congratulates us on how we handled ourselves. A chorus of grunts and approving barks meets his words. He goes on to say, "If anyone comes around asking questions, don't tell them what happened. We don't need anyone poking around in our business. You tell them that we were sitting in camp when we heard the Civil Affairs Group get ambushed. They called for assistance, and we went in to rescue them." The grunts and barks of approval die out.

I'm confused by the order. The silence of the group suggests I'm not the only one.

Why would he ask us to lie?

I'm a new Marine, fighting alongside Marines I barely know. I found out today that I'm a liability on the battlefield, maybe worth less than the half pump-action shotgun I was traded for. I'm unqualified for the responsibility I've been given as a turret gunner. And today, when I couldn't get my weapon working, I was so scared that I lost physical control of parts of my body for which I'm enormously ashamed. The war is just getting started, and no one is coming to save me. I'm going to have to deal with these issues one by one, and I will, but now our XO is asking me to have no honor. Honor is about all I have left that tells me I have some value. I decide if anyone asks, I'll tell them exactly what happened.

No one ever asks.

(During my first deployment)

In my dream, the shuttle hovers ten feet off the surface. I leap out the open hatch and thud on the ground. The ship accelerates back into the sky. I'm totally alone.

There was a village in the forest we flew over on our way here. Smoke from its cookfires drifts over the trees. I walk toward the smoke until I reach the outskirts of the village, where a fat bald man stops me.

"No one is allowed in the village until they prove themselves in the militia," he says.

He pushes me back toward the forest. I don't like this man. He's someone I feel I shouldn't trust, but I have nowhere else to go, so I let him lead me into the woods. When we reach the trees, we meet a platoon of soldiers and a handful of recruits like me. The soldiers all carry guns, the recruits carry nothing.

"When do I get a gun?" I ask the fat bald man.

"When I know I can trust you," he says.

The platoon pushes deep into the forest. Brush snags my clothes and slaps my face. When we emerge in a clearing, the platoon sets up in a semicircle with the recruits in the middle.

I don't see the creature approach, don't hear any footfalls or snapping twigs, but when I turn, he's there: pink flesh, nearly translucent in the sunlight, like an unborn fetus; blue-black veins full of thick pulsing liquid, spider webbing just beneath the skin's surface; eyes, a clear reflective black without expression. He stands in front of me, close enough that I see myself in his eyes, like I'm watching a recording. I watch my body tremble, my eyes widen with confusion and panic. The arteries in my neck throb so hard against my skin, it's like my blood is trying to escape. I reach my hand reflexively to my throat to keep the blood back. The creature's lips curl in a smile of uneven reptilian teeth.

I shift my eyes to the others in our group and realize this creature is not alone. A dozen more like him stand near the recruits in the center of the formation. The fat bald man steps forward.

"Please accept these tributes in the name of our village," he says.

The fat-faced recruit next to me whimpers and collapses to his knees.

Fuck this. I bolt for the forest.

"Halt!" a soldier barks as I fly past him.

The creature next to me doesn't move. He just smiles and says, "The offering flees. The treaty is broken."

I don't turn around to see what happens next, but I hear the fat man beg, "No, please! We will bring you more offerings!"

The clearing erupts in shrieks as I reach the tree line.

With smoke rising in the distance like a witness and the captain's comment about us keeping this quiet, I wonder how much damage we did, but I don't think I'll ever find out. Our skirmish was more of a massive drive-by than a raid. No one seemed to care or want to talk about it.

A few nights later, on radio watch with a lance corporal I don't know very well, I bring up the raid, saying I really want to know the consequences of what we did. He tells me he was on radio watch the night of the skirmish and higher command sent out a small team to scout the aftermath. They reported 44 people dead, a few of them women and children. I never heard anyone else say anything to confirm or deny this. I never heard anyone talk about it again.

UNKNOWN IRAQI MAN

I saw you there, crouched on the ground, cradling your knees in your arms. You in your long white robes, dirty at the hem from walking the sandy streets. You with your skinny long body, gaunt face, and wispy black beard. You with your hands covering your eyes, like if you couldn't see, it wouldn't be true, like somehow you would no longer be there in front of a line of machine guns just as they opened up without restraint on the two-story sand-colored complex behind you. You shook. You peered through your hands, eyes hysteric wide, whites bulging. Your lips worked frantically back and forth as I imagine you prayed for your life, prayed for another day, prayed to see your children's faces one more time, as the bullets impacted feet above your head, showering you with shattered pieces of mud-brick walls. I saw you over the barrel of my M240G midsized machine gun as it made an empty click-click sound, as it malfunctioned in my hands and left me in a stupid panic. Me nineteen years old, me in my first gunfight, me with my trembling feet on the Humvee's metal grated floor. My fingers fumbling with belts of ammunition as I cleared and loaded over and over again, my face jerking involuntarily toward the back of my head, like shrinking away could stop the bullet I knew was coming out of the dark window above your head to smack me game over senseless.

It was that look in your eyes that briefly made me forget myself. It was the way you clasped at your face, like your hands would protect you from armor piercing 50 cal rounds, like they could stop you from being vaporized into pink mist. It was that wide-eyed animal fear that saved you. You looked like a man in the wrong place at the wrong time, and so magically, thirty-five Marines, all of them unhinged, pointed their guns in your direction and pretended like you didn't exist, spraying thousands of rounds but letting you cower unharmed—just beneath the hail of bullets devastating the people in the building behind you.

UNKNOWN IRAQI GIRL

We're on our way to a meeting with local elders about reopening a hospital. The neighborhood is friendly. You can always tell by the kids. If the kids are excited to see you and run along following your convoy, you're probably okay. If the kids kick the air, make obscene gestures, and throw shit, you might be in trouble. In this neighborhood, dozens of kids run alongside our convoy, waving and laughing, and more spill out of houses to join them.

One little girl, about six or seven, wearing western clothing, follows closely alongside my Humvee. When we speed up, she runs to keep pace. When we slow down, she slows down, always about five feet away just under the scan of my eyes.

This little girl is lovely, thick black hair down to her shoulders, bright blue eyes, deep tan skin. Iraqi kids are beautiful. Many Marines get charmed and softened by interactions with kids in those early days. What amuses me about this little girl is she won't look at me. I want to smile and wave at her, but she keeps her eyes on the ground and keeps speeding up and slowing down to stay about five feet away. A couple of times, her eyes drift up, and I try to wave quick, but then she snaps them back to the ground.

When we turn down the road to meet the elders, we're swarmed by so many kids we come to a dead stop. I forget about the girl. The street is bracketed on both sides by buildings with crowds of adults standing in front. For the most part, they look happy too, but now I'm nervous. We're at a dead stop in the middle of a massive crowd, and the guys we're fighting aren't above using crowds to hurt us. They've pulled that shit all over the country. This is an ideal scenario for them. We're stuck in this crowd, and if we take fire, we'll have to choose to either protect ourselves and destroy dozens of innocent lives or let ourselves get killed because we can't fire back into a crowd of kids.

I wish I could enjoy being here. I wish I could be like the captain out in the crowd shaking hands or the first sergeant tossing handfuls of candy like it's a parade, but I'm with the machine gun, scanning the crowd for the start of the fucking nightmare that's going to make me choose. Thankfully, after an hour of watching and waiting, the elders cut a path for us through the crowd, and we start to move again.

As we leave the neighborhood, boys and girls run after us for several blocks with bare feet through the muddy streets. I smile and wave now that I know I'm not going to have to shoot them. I think about the little girl again, wish that I could see her one more time, maybe get her to smile at me just once.

That little girl sticks in my mind for weeks after. Sometimes when I'm on a building top with my 240 looking down on crowds of Iraqis, I daydream about her being my little girl, me getting out of the Marine Corps, finding an honest shitty factory job. She'll go to an elementary school with oak trees in front and corn fields in back, no gunfire, no explosions, no streets piled with garbage or human waste. She'll go to high school and break all the boys' hearts, and I'll scrimp and save to send her to college where she'll study whatever she wants, probably something stupid like creative writing (like her dad). Maybe she'll find a boy she likes who will cherish her, and they'll get married and start a life together. And when she's out of my house and into her own life, I'll feel like I lived a life worth living.

That's how the story plays out in my head, but I'll never see that little girl again. When I'm out of Iraq and out of the Marine Corps, I'll still think of her sometimes. When insurgents blow up schools or marketplaces, I'll wonder where she is. When roving gangs kidnap children for ransom or sex, I'll wonder if her family has been able to protect her. When nothing's left of cities but charred bodies and rubble from years of civil war, I'll wonder if she's still alive and how her life turned out. Then I'll go to the grocery store, pick up some chips and a twelve pack of Coke and spend the afternoon watching college football, trying not to think about the little girl with the blue eyes or how much I wish I could've done more.

BUSH'S WAR (1)

Before the war, President George W. Bush said that the United States' only interest in Iraq was removing Saddam Hussein and his top officials. This was a statement many Iraqis did not oppose. Even many Sunnis hated Saddam Hussein and only submitted to him because in Iraq, you either submitted or you disappeared. Unfortunately, this statement wasn't true. In May 2003, the American government showed it had a much broader agenda in mind than just removing top leadership. Against recommendations of military advisors and intelligence analysts, US officials made two sweeping decrees that entirely reshaped Iraq. The first was purging the Iraqi government of Baath Party members, and the second was disbanding Iraqi Security Forces.

What these US officials didn't fully appreciate was the role of the Baath Party in Iraq. It wasn't just a political party. It was the state. It may have been a corrupt and brutal state, but every aspect of life ran through the central government and through the party. This meant that anyone looking for a decent job had to be a party member. Any professional with the technical skill necessary to run the nation's systems had to be a party member. Under the new

US decree, Baath Party members were dismissed from the top three layers of every government ministry and barred from ever holding high office again. Over 85,000 people suddenly had no jobs and no path forward because they were denounced as Baathists. Many of these were not thugs or leaders from the old regime but professionals with essential technical skills—the people necessary to keep Iraq running. Iraq's ability to run basic infrastructure disappeared overnight. Things like electricity, water, communications, transportation, and hospitals quickly crumbled, and the 85,000 people that could have stopped it were left idle and angry.

The decision to disband Iraq's security forces was perhaps even more devastating. With the swipe of a pen, 385,000 soldiers, 285,000 police officers, and 50,000 presidential security officers no longer had jobs. This went directly against promises made on leaflets dropped by American planes at the beginning of the war which said if soldiers didn't fight, they'd be welcomed back into the army when Saddam was gone. But the damage went well beyond broken promises. The US needed these soldiers. We invaded Iraq with 150,000 troops. This was not a large force. A decade earlier, when kicking the Iraqi army out of Kuwait, we invaded with 400,000 troops. Kuwait was 1/25 the size of Iraq, had 1/10 the population, didn't have the same complex history of sectarian violence, and wasn't a candidate for regime change. To deal with the size and complexities of Iraq, American military leaders were counting on using much of the Iraqi military and police force to stabilize the country after the invasion. Instead, policy makers unleashed 700,000 trained and angry men who now had no way to feed their families into a country quickly falling into chaos where piles of weapons and explosives were on every street corner.

With the weakened security situation, foreign fighters flooded into Iraq. The head of al-Qaeda in Iraq, Abu Musab al-Zarqawi, took full advantage. He began indiscriminate terror attacks at mosques, shopping malls, and markets to sow general fear and make sure Iraq couldn't stabilize. He then launched targeted terror attacks against Shiite holy sites and leaders to provoke Shiites to violence. He knew that if the Shia got violent, it would stoke Sunni fears, and he could use that fear to gain Sunni support for his continued operations in Iraq.

Zarqawi wasn't alone in causing chaos and bloodletting. Iranian elements supported Shiite militias in the south. Saddam loyalists ran insurgencies in old regime strongholds. Rapists and murderers released from prisons by Saddam during the invasion, roved the city streets. Iraq became a nightmare of warlords, militias, and thugs. Looting and theft were rampant. Kidnappings for ransom became common. And when people tried to defend themselves by carrying weapons, they'd often be misidentified as threats by US forces who didn't know any better.

The more Iraqis saw their country falling apart, the more they couldn't get basic necessities, the more they had their children kidnapped, their property stolen, and their families and friends killed by roving gangs and militias, the less inclined they were to accept America's "vision" of the future.

From 2004-2007, roughly 85,000 Iraqi civilians died from violence in Iraq. About 6,000 were caused by coalition forces. The other 79,000 were killed in terror attacks, lawlessness, and sectarian violence, problems largely influenced by those two decisions made by US officials. 79,000 people died because we destroyed the institutions of Iraq, alienated the people that could've helped us, and failed to make safeguarding the Iraqi people our number one priority.

IRAQI PASTORAL

How does anyone survive out here under the merciless sun? How do shepherds feed their flocks? How do families feed their children? There's no pasture in the south and even scrub brush is scarce. All we've seen for hours is one room mud huts with fenced in "yards" where a few green shoots brave the desert sun.

I wonder about the fences. Every little mud hut has a fence, and all of them are made of strung together pieces of sun-bleached driftwood. This plaster dust desert seems to extend on forever. Where would people find driftwood? The old wetlands must have been massive.

There's a sort of beauty in the emptiness, in this land of Bible stories—Jonah preaching to the people of Nineveh; Daniel reading Nebuchadnezzar's dreams; Shadrach, Meshach, and Abed-nego refusing to worship the golden image and being thrown into the furnace. Maybe it's because I wasn't born here that I'm charmed by it. I don't understand this harsh land seemingly orchestrated for human suffering, but in the emptiness of the desert, a strange yearning sinks into my heart. Maybe I should find something simpler, find what really matters to me and spend my life doing that. The stuff I used to think was important has no meaning out here. Maybe if I'm alive in a year, I should get rid of that old life and build something new.

★★★

One of my favorite photos of Iraq is of some shepherds on a bus. Not wanting to walk their flock home, the shepherds herded their sheep into a bus's luggage compartment, then boarded the bus to catch a ride. I love the broad goofy grins on the shepherds' faces when my buddy asked if he could take their picture. They knew they got caught doing something ridiculous. The funny thing was how calm and patiently the sheep waited in the bus's undercarriage to be closed in. This was obviously not their first time riding a bus.

One of my favorite photos not taken but stuck in my mind, is of a little boy, half-running half-walking on the side of the road, trying to keep pace with his father. The father carries two fistfuls of dead chickens. The little boy carries one chicken in each hand, heads almost dragging on the ground as he struggles to emulate his father. I watch these two for some time—little boy struggling, father measuring his pace so the boy can keep up, patiently continuing onward, allowing his son to learn.

★★★

A soft sandstorm rolls over the highway. It's more of a brown fog than a storm, but as it crosses my field of vision, everything disappears, the small house up the road, the palm trees a few hundred yards away. The sand completely envelopes me, makes me feel totally alone. Then suddenly, I'm in the middle of a camel herd. Dozens of thousand-pound animals appear out of the fog, and more stream out every second. A lone, scruffy man in robes and a head dress emerges from the haze. The man seems as surprised to see me as I am to see him. I nod in acknowledgment. He nods back, and for a few seconds it feels like we're the only two people in the world. He looks back toward his herd, takes a few steps forward, and is absorbed again in the brown haze.

★★★

We pull off the highway after dark, set up camp next to a muddy pond near the Euphrates. The night is total calm, no city lights, no clouds, no breeze, no animal sounds. The pond surface is perfect glass. I stare out past reedy grass at reflections of starlight, thinking how peaceful this must be.

A line of rumbling steel on the highway breaks the silence with screeching tank tracks and diesel engines. Four Cobra attack helicopters cut across my vision. Their huge rotors slap at the air, breaking the surface of the pond.

How peaceful the water was under the stars.

★★★

I like watching the old men walk, hands clasped behind their backs, nowhere to go in particular, eyes watchful but full of peace. They seem to see something I don't, something their years have taught them. I feel the strain of the war in every beat of my young heart. I don't see that same strain in their wrinkled eyes. I watch them stop by ditches and rinse their hands and faces. I think of the grime and powder on my own face from hours up in diesel exhaust and dust. I want to wash my face in the ditchwater too, take off my helmet and mill about with the old men. Maybe they can teach me what all of it means. Maybe they can teach me how to have peace.

A farmer drives by—donkey and cart heading to market. There's so much I don't understand.

★★★

A white pickup truck pulls up at our bridge a couple blocks from the local market. Jackson and Peters jump out with a live goat they bought. No one knows what to do with a live goat, but we're all tired of vacuum-sealed food. While guys argue about how to kill and butcher the goat, I take my post on the roof. In a few minutes, I peek over the edge and see their solution: three Iraqi kids, two boys maybe twelve and eight, and a little girl. After puncturing the goat's throat and hanging it for bleeding, the kids are flurry of motion, knives slashing and trimming. In short time, the goat no longer looks like a goat, but like a giant turkey ready for the oven laying in the courtyard.

A couple hours later, Peters calls me down from the roof and tells me to bring my canteen cup. I rinse out the sand and whisker residue from my morning shave and step over to the goat pot. Peters scoops a steaming heap of goat stew into my cup, and I head back to the roof. The sun sets over the expanse of palm trees behind

Mike Kubista

our building. The call to prayer starts, Arabic chants blaring across deserted streets. I scoop goat stew into my mouth with my plastic MRE spoon. It's fantastic—goat, potatoes, onions, salt, thick broth. The air takes on the chill of night. Soon I won't be sweating anymore, and I'll catch a chill. I take another bite of hot goat stew. The sun slips below the tree line.

MORNING PISS

I'm walking through the scattered bodies of Marines asleep in the dirt. It's just before sunrise, and I step from bag to bag, shaking guys until they give some sign of life.

"Uggh,,."

"Go away."

"It ain't morning yet."

"Fuck off."

When a few guys are up yawning and tying their boots, I walk outside our circle of Humvees and piss in a little ditch by the road. It's a calm morning, and I pee in relaxed circles, amused by the dry powder, how it sucks up every bit of moisture and turns it into slick brown paste. When I'm done, I button my fly, lean back and stretch my hands over my head, enjoying the last bits of cool night air while the sky softens from purple to pink overhead. It's a perfect morning.

As I walk back inside the perimeter, the captain brushes by me with his canteen cup and razor.

"Good morning, sir," I say, not because I want to, but because it's what's required.

"Good morning," he says, not looking at me.

When I get back to my truck, Valdez, Baker, and Romero are up and in good spirits.

"I'm just saying you're an old-ass man," says Romero.

"I'm only twenty-eight," says Baker.

"Twenty-eight is like forty here," says Romero.

"Back me up, V," says Baker, "Twenty-eight isn't that old."

"Twenty-eight isn't that old," says Valdez, "but you move like you're forty."

"Fuck you guys," says Baker.

I settle in beside my team. Romero heats me a cup of coffee on his camp stove.

When the coffee is hot, I add a pouch of powdered MRE French Vanilla, and presto, I'm sipping gas station quality cappuccino. "Thanks man. This is pretty fucking good for the desert."

The captain finishes his shave outside the circle of Humvees and climbs down the little ditch slope stepping directly in the slick wet muck of urine and powder where I just pissed. His foot slips out from under him, and he thuds down flat on his back. I snort and almost spill my coffee.

The captain scrambles to his feet, looking around to see if anyone saw. When he realizes someone's piss is soaking through his uniform, he sneers in disgust and glares around the circle. I snort again and hide my face behind the hood of our Humvee.

"What the hell's up with you," Romero says.

"Nothing," I say, bent over, unable to hold back my laugh.

"What is it?" he says.

"The captain still over there?"

"Yeah. He looks pissed."

"I'll tell you later, man."

★★★

I've been with 1st MPs awhile now, and I finally feel in rhythm. I didn't know what to expect back in early March. When I walked into their tent in Kuwait with my pack and seabag it was like walking into a pit of retarded monkeys. Guys next to the doorway were cawing at each other, flapping their arms shouting "Shit bird! Shit bird!" Two other Marines were taking turns stabbing each other in the chest to see if their flak vests would stop knives. A few guys at a makeshift table introduced themselves and invited me to play a game of spades, but then a knife flew across the tent and stuck in the ammo crate just below one of their asses.

That was my first impression, but after a couple days, I realized every guy in my new unit was a better Marine than me. Most were about my age, nineteen or twenty, but they were so much more proficient at their jobs it wasn't even close. Every day, Valdez would find another Marine to teach me something to try to get me up to speed, communications, tactics, weapons, vehicle maintenance, etc. None of these Marines ever treated me like I was stupid. They were unexpectedly kind and patient, running me through basic shit I should've already known. One of these guys was Corporal Brady, who in a couple weeks, would chop off the head of a corpse with a machete and lose command of his fire team, but right now he was teaching me how to load a 240.

"Cover closed, you push the rounds into the feed tray like this," Brady grabs a belt of ammo and feeds it into the slot on the side of the weapon. "Keep pushing until you feel it click. Then all you have to do is rack the bolt, and you're ready to go."

He unloads the 240, moves over, and hands me a belt of rounds.

"Give it a try."

I push the rounds into the slot like he says. The rounds are awkward and won't go in the slot. The link twists and slips out of my hand.

"You'll get it, man. It just takes repetition."

I pick up the rounds and try again.

"Just push a little harder. You're not going to break anything."

The rounds click into place.

"Good. You feel that click? Now rack the bolt and you're ready to go. Pretty easy, huh? That's how I'm supposed to teach you to do it, now let me show you what you'll really do."

Brady opens the feed tray, pulls off the belt of rounds.

"During a gun fight, you don't want to be fumbling around trying to fit those rounds in the slot." He opens the feed tray cover. "Just slap them right down on the feed tray over the bolt, close the lid like you mean it. Rack the bolt, and you're ready to go. Simple shit."

I misjudged these guys when I first walked into their tent. They do stupid shit without thinking sometimes, but most of them are decent guys who want to do the right thing. I've been through basic training, combat training,

MP school, and a few months with my Minnesota unit, but it's with 1st MPs I start to grow up.

★★★

I never cared much for officers during my time in the Marine Corps. I served under fifteen and respected two—Solaris, who got shot beside me on a highway overpass outside Fallujah in 2004, and Huff, my Platoon Commander during the invasion.

Huff was professional. Other officers walked around with their chests puffed out trying to show who was in charge. Huff treated us like men, expected us to act like men and do our job. And most of the time, we did.

I was only with Huff a couple months and then the invasion was over, and my Minnesota unit wanted me back. When we got to the exchange point at Ad Diwaniyah, I said my goodbyes to Romero, Baker, and Valdez, and a few other guys I'd gotten close to, then grabbed my pack and walked across a dirt lot toward my unit. Huff caught me on the other side of the lot.

"Kubista! Kubista!"

I was surprised to see him. "Sir?"

"I just want to say thanks for the work you did with us. I've only got good things to say about how you handled yourself."

"Thank you, sir."

"I know it wasn't easy getting shuffled around like that. The other guys from your unit didn't do so well. Thanks for sucking it up and making yourself an asset."

"Yes, sir," I mumbled, a little embarrassed.

"Take care of yourself."

I never would have thought of myself as an asset. In my head, I was living day by day, just trying to do the best I could, and at the beginning of the war, I was a disaster. Now, a man I respected told me he valued my contributions in an extremely complex and challenging environment. That had an impact on me going forward.

SWEATY BALLS AND DYSENTERY

I'm perched on a two-story building next to the Euphrates with a rifle and my 240. The only access to the roof is a metal ladder I can raise and lower at will, so I'm not worried about anyone sneaking up on me. I can see a lot from where I'm at—nice houses along the riverbank, people milling around the street market, minarets calling to prayer. Behind me is a lush grove of palm trees that seems to go on forever next to the river. When the sun sets over the trees and over the river, it's one of the most perfect sights I've ever seen in my life. But I'm not thinking about any of that. Right now, all I can think about is how much I have to take a shit.

I don't want to tell Valdez I need a replacement, but I've been crapping my brains out for the last two days. A section of the roof is covered with several inches of gravel, and every twenty minutes or so, I've been scratching holes in the roof gravel and using it like a litter box. After I've put a dozen or so diarrhea pockets in the roof gravel, I wonder about the people who used to live in this building. They probably spent some time on this roof enjoying the river on hot days. It'll be less appealing up here once I'm gone.

Doc finally sees me looking pale one day and asks me what's up. When I tell him I've had the shits for two days and continued standing post in the sun, he's not happy.

"You've got to tell me this shit, man. Are you trying to hurt yourself?" He gives me some pills and tells Valdez to keep me off the roof.

★★★

Several years after I got home from Iraq, I read an article in an American magazine interviewing Iraqi citizens. One Iraqi man, when asked what he thought about American Marines, said, "I lost a lot of respect for them when I saw how dirty they were. Their faces, their clothes, everything was filthy." That made me chuckle. I knew exactly what he was talking about. I was filthy all the time during that first tour in Iraq, nothing but swamp-crotch, caked on dust, and diarrhea. Most guys looked haggard and dirty. Most caught the shits at some point. It was so common we called it Saddam's Revenge.

It's not surprising we all got sick. There were human and animal corpses all over the place, festering, breeding clouds of flies; the air was filled with noxious fumes from burning vehicles, bodies, and oil fields; and who knows what sorts of chemicals were getting released from the massive weapons caches periodically blown up by EOD.

In addition, we were an army of a hundred-fifty thousand, sweating all day every day in heavy chemical suits, living in the same nasty skivvies for weeks on end, sleeping in the dirt, eating nothing but processed vacuum sealed food, and shitting and pissing wherever we went. At any given time during the push to Baghdad, there'd be Marines and Soldiers lining the highway with their pants down, squatting a few paces off the road over little crap pits they dug with their E-tools, not wanting to go too far off the road for fear of landmines.

It's probably been about the same for every invading army across millennia. Alexander the Great's army probably crapped up and down the Indus River valley before he died of Malaria. Hannibal's army probably left a slick trail of human sickness and waste behind them as they crossed the Alps with their elephants. The Mongolians who sacked Baghdad in 1258 and stacked piles of skulls from the thousands they slaughtered, probably also stacked piles of human shit and disease. Now it was our turn.

★★★

Toilets played a more important role in my experiences in Iraq and Kuwait than I would have thought, taught me stuff I wouldn't have learned otherwise. The first time I used an Iraqi toilet was in the police headquarters in Ramadi. I was on the second floor asking a Marine if he knew where a bathroom was. The Police Chief overheard my question and motioned me to follow him. He led me through his fancy office with its floor to ceiling wooden bookshelves into an immaculate room with marble floors and shiny brass rails.

"Use this one," he said.

I thanked him, and he put his hand over his heart. I was surprised at the deferential way he treated me. I was just some random trigger puller, not a person accustomed to nice things.

When I closed the door behind me, I realized there was no toilet in the room, no urinal, nothing I was used to besides a sink. At the other end of the room, where I'd expect the toilet to be, was a porcelain bowl laid in the floor, about the width of a basketball. What the hell am I supposed do with that?

I needed to get out on the roof. There was a Black Opel-sedan car bomb supposedly coming our way. Me and my 240 were the main lookout. I didn't have time to think about how to use this porcelain indent in the ground in front of me, so I unbuttoned my fly, pulled out my junk and aimed down. Piss splashed all over, spraying my boots and several feet of the marble floor next to the toilet hole.

Son of a bitch.

I looked around the room for toilet paper or paper towels so I could clean up the mess. I didn't want to leave urine sprinkles on the man's floor after he'd been so kind to me. But there weren't any paper products anywhere in the room.

I had to get out on the roof and eventually decided there was nothing I could do. I was just going to have to be a pig.

Later, when I had to piss again, an Iraqi Policemen showed me the lower ranks' bathroom. It smelled like a clogged-up stadium piss trough, and I immediately felt more at home. But again, there weren't any toilets, just porcelain holes in the ground to squat over. It never occurred to me before then that people in other countries had different kinds of toilets.

★★★

The propensity for young Marines being stupid is astounding. Just before the war kicked off, one dude at our staging camp ate a handful of shower gunk from the drain on a five-dollar bet. This wasn't normal shower gunk with pubic hair and general filth. This was desert filth from thousands of sweaty, dirt caked bodies, mixed with scabs and Smallpox-infested band aids from the inoculations we'd all gotten. I don't know what happened to that kid, but if he didn't die from that, he probably died from something else stupid. But at least he was five dollars richer.

I had my own bout of stupid in 2004 at the police headquarters in Ramadi. One day, to thank us for our help, the police chief threw a banquet. I was on watch in the courtyard with my 240, but while I sat alone on my Humvee, an Iraqi Policeman approached carrying a plate of food.

"Your commanders thought you might like something to eat," he said. It was roasted lamb and slices of ripe tomatoes and looked fantastic compared to the cheese spread in a metal tube I was eating.

"Thank you," I said, "That looks terrific."

"You're welcome, sir," he said, putting his right hand on his heart. "Where would you like it?"

"If you could set it in the back seat, that'd be great."

After the Iraqi Policeman left, I debated if I should eat the food or throw it away. We'd been warned about microbes in the local food affecting our bodies in ways we weren't used to. I was also hesitant to accept anything from an IP. I wanted to believe this was a decent man just trying to do me a favor, but I also knew there were plenty of Iraqi Police working for the other side. Probably several in this complex wouldn't mind killing me themselves. It wasn't a good idea to trust this man with my food when no one was watching.

I let the plate sit in the back seat and continued eating my partially separated vitamin fortified cheese spread. The roasted lamb smell wafted up through the hole in the turret, and I glanced down at the plate. The tomatoes were red and juicy, perfectly ripe.

Maybe just a taste.

I set the cheese down, leaned into the back seat of my Humvee, and picked up the plate. I bit into the lamb. It was juicy and well-seasoned. The tomatoes burst with flavor in my mouth.

What the hell.

I gulped down every scrap on that plate.

Later that night, back on base, I had midnight watch. Fifteen minutes into my shift, my head started pounding, and the strength sapped out of my arms and legs. I collapsed on a stack of sandbags behind our trucks and radioed my Sergeant for relief. When no one answered, I panicked. Something gnarly was brewing inside me, but I couldn't leave my post. We had weapons and ammo out here staged for the next day's mission. I was responsible for this stuff. I thought briefly about running to the tent to get a replacement, then my intestines shifted, and I almost shit down my legs.

I ran instead to the porta john across the gravel road from my position, holding my butt like I was five years old. I whipped open on the door and tore down my pants, diarrhea bubbling out my ass on the way down to the seat.

As soon as my butt hit seat, I exploded. Then the vomit came. I didn't know what to do. I couldn't stand and lean over the toilet, or I'd spray shit all over the door, but I also didn't want to puke on my lap. Maybe I could puke in the space between my dick and the rim of the toilet. I looked down between my legs, scooted my butt back as far as it would go.

Nope, that seemed like a really bad idea.

I turned my head to the plastic urinal by my left arm and fire-hose vomited straight into it. Maybe it was my last nagging bit of civility but puking in the urinal felt wrong. Something about making the next guy piss on my vomit crust felt like a violation of some unwritten code.

I spent the next hour and a half in this porta-john shooting lamb and tomatoes out both ends. When the lamb and tomatoes were gone, I puked up a seemingly endless pile of rice I didn't remember eating, wondering if this was how I was going die, alone in my filth in this dirty porta-john in Ramadi.

In between volleys, I wondered if other Marines were looking for me yet. I worried about the penalty for abandoning my post in a combat zone. I worried about other units fucking with our gear. Then I started puking again, and those thoughts gave way to the more immediate situation.

When my body was out of material to spew and my internal convulsions stopped. I used a whole roll of toilet paper cleaning myself up, pulled up my pants, and staggered back to post. I had spent most of my two-hour shift in that porta john. About a minute later, my replacement showed up.

"Anything going on out here?" he said.

"Nope, pretty boring," I said, "Have a good one."

I walked to my tent, woke up Doc, and told him I was dying, then staggered to the med tent and collapsed on the ground. Doc gave me an IV and pills and ordered me to bed rest for a few days. After that, I was good to go. No one ever asked me about that night, so I figure nothing went missing.

★★★

Whenever I think of gallons of human waste, I think of Ad Diwaniyah, Iraq. That's where Saddam's Revenge hit my unit full force, unleashing a literal shit storm like nothing I've ever seen. At Camp Ad Diwaniyah, a group of engineers had made makeshift toilets out of plywood and fifty-gallon oil drums. The first time I used one of these toilets, I couldn't believe the luxury. The plywood stalls had doors that opened and closed, and the cutout plywood holes had real toilet seats. The feeling of crapping in privacy on actual toilet seats and not in some self-dug hole on the side of the highway was incredible. Things were looking up. We even had promise of a roof over our heads. It'd been well over a month since I'd crapped in a toilet and slept under a roof. I was thrilled, until I saw the building we'd be staying in, an old tanker bay, covered in dust, grease, and a half-inch of pigeon shit. A couple of Marines grabbed palm branches from outside and swept most of the pigeon shit off the floors, but we didn't have any way of disinfecting the area. We just bedded down on top of the filth, and I remember thinking, "If guys weren't sick before, this'll get 'em."

What I remember most from that old tanker bay was the sound of Marines' scurrying feet at night and the pitter patter of vomit splashing on the floor when they didn't quite make it to the door. Also, the "Sugar Shack," a little room jutting off the main bay some Marines designated as a jerk-off room. Or maybe they called it "Protein Palace," I can't remember. I never went in the Protein Palace. Something about a community masturbation room disturbed me, but it definitely added to the feeling that we were living dirtier than farm animals.

★★★

Problems understanding foreign toilet designs didn't only happen to me. In Ramadi, Iraqi contractors worked on our base each day, building structures, collecting garbage, sucking out porta-johns etc. Now and again, when you'd open a porta-john door, you'd see two footprints up on the plastic ledge next to the toilet seat from someone trying to squat over the opening. Usually, those footprints were accompanied by a fat turd in the middle of the toilet seat from a miss-fire. As those Iraqi men squatted on porta-john ledges, struggling to get their anus angles right in such a cramped space, I wonder if they thought to themselves,

"What a stupid design. How am I supposed to get my shit in that hole?" Or maybe they just thought crapping on our toilet seats was funny. I guess I'll never know.

Iraqi worker turds were far from the grossest thing happening in our porta-johns. Our porta-johns in Iraq and Kuwait were often so full that guys had to shit standing up, hovering over the massive piles, careful not to crouch too low and touch their butts on the multicolored hills of sick-looking feces. In Kuwait this happened because there were just so many damn people using the toilets. In Ramadi this happened because we couldn't always get someone to come on base and clean them. Supply and service trucks were constantly getting blown up, and Al Qaeda operatives in the area had no qualms about going to the homes of people aiding the US and murdering them or kidnapping their kids, even if those people were just sucking crap out of our toilets to earn money to feed their families.

★★★

The most putrid part of living at Ad Diwaniyah wasn't the tanker bay. It was the plywood toilets I was initially so excited about. When Saddam's Revenge got going full force through the division, Marines were using the makeshift toilets twenty to thirty times a day. And as Marines kept shitting, the fifty-gallon drums kept filling. Even though I didn't love walking in the distance, digging a hole, squatting in plain sight, and praying to God no one shot me with my pants down, it wasn't long at Ad Diwaniyah before I wished for those days again. Those makeshift toilet stalls were like diarrhea saunas. As the gallons of liquid filth broiled in the sun, the air in the enclosed wooden boxes got hot and moist. The stink was thick enough to taste.

The barrels filled at an alarming rate. Almost every day, a Marine would need to pull them out of the stalls, pour in gallons of diesel fuel, light the mixture on fire, and stir it for hours until the shit burned away. It was usually Orlovsky's job. He was a smart ass, so usually got tabbed to work the barrels, but the smell of diesel-diarrhea smoke permeated everything. Like rotten corpse, it's a smell that sticks in your brain.

The worst thing about the toilets though wasn't the smell or moist heat. It was the biblical plague of flies. The juicy gallons of diarrhea were a fly buffet and every stall was a buzzing hive. Every time a Marine sat down, hundreds of diseased little shit-eaters enveloped his body from face to asshole. Flies, whose feet had just been bathing in the sludge below, walked on his neck, in his ears, over his closed eyelids. They touched his lips, crawled on his thighs, landed on his penis and testicles. They even crawled in his ass-crack as he added more sludge to the barrel.

We only stayed in Ad Diwaniyah for about a week before getting sent to Kuwait to start customs work for units shipping back to the States, but it sticks out in my mind as the only place I've ever lived that made we wish I could sleep outside in the dirt and dig holes in the ground to crap in.

★★★

The prize for most disgusting thing I saw in Iraq would have to go to PFC Freemont for a very special night in Ar Ramadi. On that night, Freemont went to the porta-john with a porno mag and flashlight in hand, hoping to beat a nasty windstorm heading our direction. But the windstorm, strong enough to tear a tin roof off a neighboring building and send it flying through the canvas-top of our barracks, hit hard and quick. As Freemont squatted in his plastic cube, gazing over naked women under his red lens flashlight, the wind lifted his porta-john and the entire row of porta-johns it was attached to and flipped them all over, door down. Trapped inside with gallons of raw sewage sloshing up his legs, butt, and back, Freemont, in true Marine Corps fashion, pulled out his trusty Leatherman multitool from the pouch at his hip, unfolded the short blade and got to work.

I don't know how long Freemont laid there cutting his man-sized hole to freedom with his tiny knife in the top of that porta-john, but he walked into the tent later that night dripping filth and scowling like he'd been dipped in a vat of liquid dog shit, turning his nose up in the air like he was trying to escape his own body. He grabbed soap and a towel and made a bee line to the shower trailer.

The next morning, after the storm had died, I went outside with a couple Marines to check out Freemont's handiwork. Sure enough, there was the porta-john tipped over, door down, with a shoulder width square hole cut in the top. I peeked inside at the pool of sewage where Freemont had lain and half-gagged half-laughed.

In truth, I was kind of impressed. I never carried a knife with me to the porta-john. If it had been me in there, I probably would have puked myself to death while clawing at the plastic wall with my fingernails. My unit would have found my body the next morning steaming in my raw-sewage casket. Good on Freemont for not dying that way.

I was also impressed that he didn't catch some nasty disease, something that rotted off his testicles or grew mushrooms in his butt. Though maybe he did and never said anything.

WILD DOGS (3)

Cruelty was a common means of control in Saddam Hussein's regime, but it wasn't the only means. Saddam was a student of power, a cunning, unscrupulous man with tremendous capacity for reading and manipulating people. He plastered his image everywhere. Cities were covered in grandiose murals. Thirty-foot painted figures of him towered over city entrances. And he built massive memorials to himself immortalizing his glory. On a typical radio broadcast, his name was mentioned thirty to fifty times an hour along with reams of titles like Leader-President, Leader-Struggler, Standard Bearer, Knight of the Arab Nation, Hero of National Liberation, Father Leader, and Daring and Aggressive Knight. His goal was to be everywhere, in homes, on city streets, in conversations, in news broadcasts, in books, in speeches, and in schools.

The object of education became mass-producing boys and girls with the correct ideology. Saddam once said, "Some fathers have slipped away from us for various reasons, but the small boy is still in our hands, and we must transform him into an interactive radiating center inside the family." Independent thinkers were simply executed.

Teachers became a new form of moral agent, taking children from their parents and replacing historically strong bonds of family and clan with submission to party politics and thereby submission to Saddam Hussein.

The Baath Party consumed the Iraqi state, and Saddam's grip tightened until he reached into every aspect of Iraqi life, student organizations, sports groups, literary and science clubs, artistic societies, hobby and craft groups, trade unions, peasants' associations, and any other organization or gathering anywhere for any reason. Even literacy was a weapon. Ignorant farmers were sometimes hard to control. Their loyalties leaned toward tribal leaders and local customs, so Saddam's party created literacy mandates, fining or imprisoning Iraqis who couldn't read and making it illegal to employ them. This forced uneducated Iraqis into Baath Party literacy centers where they were coerced to learn to read through party propaganda materials.

Propaganda also helped Saddam control the flow of resources in Iraq. Any time someone had something he wanted, he could just take it and have the person killed or imprisoned, then lie about them in the state-run media and denounce them as traitors working with the Jews. This was common operating procedure. He then used that stolen wealth to give money, opportunity, and gifts to people who served him.

MATILDA

After Ad Diwaniyah, my Minnesota unit heads back to Kuwait. The war seems to be winding down, and a massive troop rotation home is just beginning. The US needs more customs agents to check everyone's gear on their way home, so they pull us back to Kuwait to do that. When we get to Camp Matilda, it looks like the start of a horror movie, rows of deserted eighty-man tents, no one around for miles, a small group of filthy Marines drives up, haggard from months in the dirt. On screen, some doofus PFC looks into the camera and says something stupid like, "Gee Sarge, this don't feel right." One of the tent flaps slowly opens, and out of the dark, a mutant cannibal peaks its head out to get a better look at its victims as tumbleweed rolls in front of the row of tents.

We unload our Humvees, and I go take a shit. When I step inside an empty porta-john, I'm relieved to see it's clean. Sand has collected on the toilet seat, and most of the chemical water has evaporated, leaving a shallow dark-blue pond on the plastic floor, but it's the cleanest toilet I've seen in months. I pull down my trousers and sit in peace.

It's been a couple months since my last shower, a couple filthy, filthy months, so after the porta john, I go the shower trailer. Inside, in the mirror, I see how grungy I look—short greasy hair matted from my helmet, dark face, partially from sun, mostly from road grime. I haven't shaved in a couple days, so I pull out my razor and step in a shower stall. At first, the wetness shocks me. It's been so long, the water hitting my body is uncomfortable. But eventually, I relax into the warmth and watch the grime circle the drain. After I get out of the shower and dry off, I put on a fresh pair of skivvies and a new undershirt. It's amazing how being clean affects my mood. I feel instantly lighter, more optimistic.

When I get back to the tent, a couple guys already lay on the ground, set up for the night, heads resting on packs. As I head to my gear, something the size of a small rat crawls in the door and charges toward a Marine on the floor.

"Holy Fuck!" Polenka shouts as the thing zooms by his feet. He stomps it under his right boot before it reaches the sleeping Marine's head, but the thing doesn't die from one stomp, and Polenka stomps it again and again until it goes limp, then he picks up the carcass and brings it over.

"Look at this fucking thing!" he says.

This is the first camel spider I've seen. It kind of looks like a spider and a scorpion had a baby in a vat of nuclear waste. Its body is the size of Polenka's palm but its legs make it longer, and unlike a normal spider, it has ten legs, two extra up front which act like antennae arms for feeling and fighting. Its huge jaws make up a quarter of the length of its body. When I'm back in the States after this deployment, I have the same dream several times. In my dream, I'll be face down on my pillow when something strange starts tickling my face. When I pull my head off my pillow it's a camel spider, legs wiggling in the air. I usually wake up mid-flight, my body violently propelling me off my mattress to my feet.

Polenka lays the camel spider carcass on his cheek.

"Take a picture of this!" he says.

When US Customs Officials come to Matilda to train us, the training is mainly about microbes in the sand that could devastate American agriculture. Not even trace amounts of sand are allowed home, which is not easy. The guys coming through our inspection lines have been rolling through powder for months. It's embedded in every stitch of gear.

Besides sand, our list of contraband includes weapons, gas mask canisters, and porn. Most Marines coming through inspection do what they're told and give shit up without a fuss. They just want to go home. And after a month-long flurry of inspections, hour after hour of Marines laying out gear on plywood floors or on sweltering rock lots where temperatures get 140+ degrees, the rush is over, and camp is empty again except for us.

Guys start talking about when our turn will be.

"End of June. It's got to be end of June."

"I heard July 10th."

"Where'd you hear that?"

"I overheard the Major talking earlier today. The bird home is already scheduled."

"Bullshit!"

"Mark my words, boys. July 10th."

"I heard Gunny say this morning sometime in August.

"Fuck no! Mid-July at the latest, but definitely July."

June passes. July comes and goes. August comes and goes, and we're still in Matilda, nothing but the sound of generators dying in the heat, and no one around for miles but a few camel herders in the distance. We man metal guard towers day and night around the camp perimeter. Flat brown nothing in every direction, day after day, night after night, no end in sight.

Shit gets stupid. We gamble all the time, poker at night, Nintendo golf during the days. A few guys start a competition to see who can masturbate the most times during a single guard shift. One day, Orlovsky decided to set a new record, so to keep himself in the zone and reduce time buttoning and unbuttoning his fly, he stripped down completely naked in his tower. Unfortunately, fate had other plans. Another unit had just come into camp to be processed out of country, and their crusty old First Sergeant who hadn't been on a run in a while, decided to run the camp perimeter. His "WHAT IN THE FUCK?!!!!" must have echoed out to the camel herders when he found Orlovsky naked in his guard tower.

Our company Gunny stormed into our tent red-faced and mortified. "I want every swinging dick at the front of this tent, NOW!!!"

As he told us about Orlovsky and the First Sergeant, Marines snorted and chuckled.

"Is this funny?" Gunny growled. "Other commands telling me this shit about my Marines? Why don't we just build a tower in the middle of camp so you can jerk-off in front of everyone?! I swear to God if I hear any more of this kind of shit..."

When Gunny left the tent, laughter exploded, and everyone turned to Orlovsky.

"You were totally naked?!" one Marine asked.

"Shut up," Orlovsky said.

"How many did you get?"

"I don't want to talk about it."

The jack-assery at Matilda wasn't all harmless. LCpl Lester had psychological problems. He was one of the guys traded with me to 1st MPs at the beginning of the deployment. When our CO announced eight of us were going, I knew I'd be one of them. I was simply too young and inexperienced to be of much value. But the other guys had different issues. Hill was full of shit, always telling weird stories about how many languages he spoke and how many women he'd screwed in his church group. Luthor was a pussy. He could bench press twice his body weight, but the first time he heard gunfire in Iraq, he collapsed from the turret into the belly of his Humvee and refused to get back up. Schoener was belligerent. I liked Schoener, had a lot of good conversations with him, but he always thought he was smarter than everyone. And then there was Lester, always a little twitchy and always trying to one-up other people. I wasn't sure what to make of Lester, but I knew I didn't like him. I avoided talking to him as much as possible.

At some point during the deployment, Lester started sending stories to his family about "The Great Eight." According to him, the eight of us had been transferred because we were elite Marines needed for special missions. The stories got wilder and wilder over time until he sent one home about a particularly difficult mission in which half of our unit got killed. Lester's family, filled with fear for their son's life and pride at his courage, sent the story to a newspaper back home. It was published, and other Marines' family members started asking what the hell was going on with their sons and husbands. The staff in Minnesota did some fact finding and Lester was exposed. When he got transferred back to our Minnesota unit, things were bad for Lester. The Marines in his platoon were relentless. One day, one of them came into our tent with the firing pin from Lester's rifle. They'd been giving him so much shit they started worrying he might try to shoot them, so they disabled his weapon. I felt sick. None of our leaders intervened, and there was nowhere for Lester to go. He was stranded in the desert with a group of bored Marines who loathed him. When command finally shipped him home for a psych eval, I was relieved.

I never saw Lester again or thought about him until a decade later when a buddy sent me his obituary and told me he committed suicide. I may have never been close with Lester, but he was a part of my history, and it stung hearing things went so badly for him. His obituary haunted me, not the message, that was the usual "loving brother, son, and father" crap, but the accompanying photo. The picture wasn't of Donald with his family at a barbeque or Donald with his golden retriever. It was of Lance Corporal Lester in his desert camouflage utilities, exactly the way I remembered him, and his gravestone read:

Donald Lester
Marine Corps Lance Corporal
Served in the Iraq War

Apparently, even in disgrace, his service in Iraq was still one of the most important parts of his life. I started thinking about what the last ten years must have been like for him, all the "Thank you for your services," well-meaning strangers, relatives, and friends who didn't know the whole story, bragging about their Marine cousin, buddy, or uncle, or the guy they used to work with at the video store. How does a guy like Lester respond to that? How does he not feel like a fraud every minute of his life, knowing he got discharged for being mentally unstable, knowing the Marines he worked with thought so little of him, they traded him for shitty old equipment before the war, then bullied him so badly after the war they worried he'd lock, load, and spray rounds in their chests? Lester was spastic and weird. He told tremendous lies. But should he be cursed for the rest of his life?

LCpl Lester served with me in Iraq. He was treated by his own like he didn't matter but did the job he was asked to do for another unit anyway. Desperate to be highly thought of, he acted stupid and paid a heavy price, both in an empty desert camp in Kuwait, and probably in interactions regarding the war for the rest of his life. Even in disgrace, he sacrificed more for our country than most people ever will. I hope he rests in peace.

As months pass by in Matilda, days blend together. I'm asleep one afternoon because I'm on night shift and someone shakes me awake.

"Kubista. Kubista."

I barely open my eyes and see Staff-Sergeant Chilcot standing over me.

I'm surprised and must look pretty dazed, because he asks if I remember who he is. Chilcot was one of the best Marines I ever served with, no nonsense, totally professional, the kind of guy you hope for as your platoon Sergeant because he'll look out for you. He tells me he'll wait outside, and I shake myself awake, put my boots on and step out in the sun. Romero is also outside waiting for me. I grin.

"How's it going, devil," Romero says.

"Shit, not bad, how the hell are you guys?" I say shaking their hands.

"Still kicking."

"You on your way out?"

"Yep. Got a bird home in a couple days," Chilcot says.

"Everyone make it out okay?"

"Rawls got hit by a rocket, lost an eye. Hearns got shot in an ambush. Fought em off bleeding out in the dirt."

"No shit? He still alive?"

"Yep."

We shoot the shit for a few minutes, then, when the three of us run out of things to say, Chilcot says, "Anyway, we just wanted to stop in and see you before we head off. You good?"

"Yeah, I'm good, Staff Sergeant. Shit's quiet here."

"Good. You take care of yourself."

"You too. Have a good flight."

We shake hands, and they walk away. I'll never see these guys again. I was a dipshit kid when I first met them. They took me in, expected me to learn and hold my own. Eventually, I did.

As time goes by at Matilda, motivation noticeably slips. Guys slime around the tent in PT shorts going from rack to TV to porn box, to porta john, back to porn box, then back to rack. Gunny gets tired of watching us mope around like whipped dogs and calls us to the front of the tent.

"I don't know why I see all these long faces," he says, "This is the easiest summer of your lives. All you do is sit on your asses eating popcorn and watching movies."

The response from the Marines in the tent is something like a forty-year-old man whose wife just left him, sitting on a bean bag chair in his underwear, scratching his crotch with Cheeto-stained fingers. It isn't so much a response as a groan barely acknowledging life. I've never seen a group of Marines look like that before. Guys I'd serve with in Ramadi the next year who thrived through ambushes, IEDs, rockets, and mortars, slimed through life here, no sense of purpose as our purgatory slipped by month after month, no end in sight.

In response to our apathy, our CO makes us practice drill movements in a tent in our free time.

"Are we really going to practice marching?"

"How many times did we march in Iraq?"

"It's like a blow-dryer's asshole in this tent."

"It's like a blow-dryer farted in an oven set on broil."

Bitch, bitch, bitch, bitch, bitch, bitch, bitch.

I want to go home like the rest of the guys, but Matilda hasn't been terrible for me. I don't mind so much being alone, staring out at nothing. The days and nights of stillness have given me time to think, to process things I did and saw in Iraq, process changes in myself. I've always been weak. But I see progress in myself. I can say what I mean, now. I made it through ugly things. I never quit working, never quit moving forward. I'm more resilient than I thought. And now, I'm kind of optimistic about my future. I've never been optimistic.

Matilda makes me appreciate shit. It's the little surprises, like fancy ice cream bars showing up in our freezer or fresh fruit in our packaged lunches. On the Fourth of July, I walk in the chow tent expecting powdered eggs, rice, and shelf milk. Instead, there's a catering line with mounds of steak and lobster. Where did this come from? Maybe we weren't forgotten here.

My squad leader brews coffee when we're on night shift, drives his Gator from tower to tower dropping off steaming hot 1.5L bottles. He doesn't have to do this, but I look forward to it every night, barely being able to touch the plastic water bottle, pouring the steaming liquid into my canteen cup, sipping it down staring out at the dark desert, climbing down the ladder periodically to take a relaxed piss in the sand. Life ain't so bad.

I see weird things out here, like scorpions under the generator lights at night. As they crawl through the top layer of powder, their bodies are covered by dust and look invisible, and their tails look like they're floating in the air over the desert. Sitting there under the flood lights watching the floating tails, I can't help but be grateful. It's like some strange show only I get to watch.

I see something huge flying around a generator one night. The twitchy way it flies makes me think it's a large bat, but I can't imagine a bat living out here. There's nothing for it to eat. When the thing lands on the ground, it's the biggest beetle I've ever seen. I have no idea how a thing like that could even fly. I wonder what it would feel like to have something like that land on your head at night. I'd have a fucking stroke.

The moon is different here, both its angles and brightness. When the moon is waning, it looks like a toenail clipping falling to the ground. When the moon is full, it's brighter than any I've seen. When the moon is gone, the night sky is so full of stars it still glows. It makes me wonder if a thousand years ago people couldn't help but believe in God, every night reminded how magnificent and vast the universe is without the constant glow of electric lights holding their attention to the ground. On one of these nights, Sergeant Adler teaches me how to find the North Star.

"You see the two stars that make the far edge of the Big Dipper?" he says, pointing up. "Draw a line between those two stars and follow it out the open side of the cup. You see Cassiopeia?"

"What the hell is Cassiopeia?"

"It's the one that looks like a 'W'."

"Yeah, I see a W."

"Draw a line out from the middle star of the 'W'. Where that line and the line from the Big Dipper meet, you'll find the North Star. It's the bright one with really nothing around it."

This is the stuff I learn from other Marines. Stuff I'll share with friends when camping. Stuff I'll show my nieces and nephew when they're still young enough to think I'm cool, when they leave the city and come to my hometown where they can see stars. They'll stand with me on the dark high school football field, and I'll explain to them how to draw the lines.

"Is it that one?" my nephew says.

"That's the one. Good job."

"I want to try!" my niece says, nuzzling up against my side.

"Okay, draw a line from the end two stars of the Big Dipper. Now draw a line from the middle of the 'W'."

"Is it that one?

"You got it."

"That's so cool!"

A simple piece of knowledge thrown out casually by an educated warrior in an empty desert camp.

GUARD SHIFT

The tower at the entrance of Matilda is twenty feet tall, placed on top of a ten-foot-high dirt berm. Its walls are tan, waist-high steel plates, front wall fortified with sandbags on which an M240G sits with four hundred rounds of ammunition pointing out toward a serpentine of concrete barriers on the dirt road below.

Orlovsky drops a brown pack of MRE garbage off the side of the tower and starts down the steel rebar ladder in full battle gear—desert camo Kevlar helmet with green dust goggles; flak jacket with six M16 magazines each holding thirty rounds of 5.56; two olive drab canteens; twelve-inch Ka-Bar knife; first aid kit with tourniquet, bandages, adhesive tape, airway nasopharyngeal, clotting agent, and combat gauze; 1.5 liter CamelBak hydration system; assault pack with beef jerky, cigarettes, tin of chew, M&Ms rat-fucked from a box of MRE's, two bottles of water, porno mag or *Maxim* for "reading"; M16A2 service rifle slung over his shoulder; and two pouches for M67 fragmentation grenades, empty because we're not in Iraq anymore, but guarding our abandoned desert camp in Kuwait and rarely see anyone but camel herders on the horizon.

"It's fucking gross up there, man," Orlovsky says, when he gets to the ground. "Good luck."

It's midday, summer, around 135 degrees. The metal guard tower in direct sun radiates heat, but the ladder rungs, shaded by the tower platform, are lukewarm in my closed fingers. When I reach the top of the ladder, the stink of MRE garbage wafts into my face. A pack of half-eaten spaghetti sits on the floor in a pool of sticky clear liquid leaking from a pouch of pears. The metallic sweet and rank smell tells me the food has been there awhile, maybe since the night shift. Before I even pull myself onto the tower landing, I'm peppered by the little feet of a metric shit ton of flies.

Mother Fucker! Which fucking pig left their trash?

I kick the garbage out of the tower then peel off my assault pack and flak jacket. Flies throng the sweat outline on my uniform from my combat gear.

I check the 240, make sure it's clean and ready to fire. I open the feed tray cover, lift the feed tray, check the bolt and rails for grit and lubrication, drop the feed tray, and slap on a belt of rounds. Flies blanket my face and the backs of my hands. I flick my hands through the air and whip my head from side to side, but there are so many, I can't keep them off me, so I try to ignore them, slam the 240 shut and sit on an unopened MRE box in the center of the tower floor.

It's two hours until I rotate out of this tower. Five minutes into my shift, I go ape shit. Flies crawl on my cheeks, lips, and earlobes, down my neck, around my throat, under my chin, up my nostrils. I snort, spit, slap, and swear. The more the flies touch me, the angrier I get.

I slap my body and face so hard my fingers bruise, but the flies are too fast.

A fly lodges itself in my ear canal. It squirms inside my head, garbage and shit covered feet rubbing against my ear canal walls, wings buzzing against my eardrum. I jump off my seat and claw at my ear. *It's laying fucking eggs in my head*! I claw at my ear because I don't know what to do. I can't jam my finger in my ear and smash the fly. Who knows what kind of problems insect guts smooshed deep in my ear hole would cause, but clawing is worthless, so I open-palm slap the hell out of my ear hoping if I hit hard enough the fly will get rattled and leave. After a few clubs, my brain goes fuzzy, and my ear rings like a TV end-of-broadcast signal, but the fly leaves.

The fly in the ear is too much. These flies need to die.

"Alright, you little mother fuckers. Let's go!" I snatch the floppy-brimmed desert boonie off my head and swing wildly. My boonie snaps against the wall, the sandbags, the sticky floor, my arms, thighs, calves, and boots, but no flies die, and now that my head is uncovered, dozens burrow in my hair.

"Fucking cock slut!" I shout, tearing at my hair, sure that the guys on the ground can hear me and are laughing their asses off.

I fold my boonie in half, doubling over the brim and creasing the top to decrease wind resistance, then swing some more.

Thwaap! Miss. "Donkey cunt!" Thwaap! Miss. "Sweaty fucktard!" Thwaap! Miss. "Cock waddle anal bead shit nugget!" The boonie cuts better through the air when it's folded up, but these flies aren't fat slow American flies hanging out on fast food windows, these fuckers are survival of the fittest flies fighting for limited resources in a god-forsaken shithole, and it's like they know they're better than me. The faster I swing, the faster they get. Little diseased fly legs crawl over every patch of open skin and hair on my body, and there's nothing I can do to stop them.

"FUUUCKK!" I yell, flailing like a monkey in a trap. Once I thrash away all my fight, I sit on the MRE box in the center of the floor, defeated, flies roaming my body like a corpse.

Slingshot. That's what I need.

A picture flashes in my brain, surgical tube stretched behind a U frame, pebble releasing with enough velocity to knock a crow out of the air.

I need to be like a slingshot.

I grab one edge of my folded boonie in my right hand, keeping tension in my arm. With my left hand, I pull back the other edge. The fabric doesn't stretch like surgical tubing, but as the elbow on my arm cocks, I feel increasing tension. On a section of the metal wall, four flies stand close together, idle. *They'll do.* I release my left hand while snapping forward my cocked arm. THWAAP!!! Four little carcasses fall to the tower floor, and four blood specks stain the camo of my boonie.

Game on, bitches.

For the next hour, I slingshot my boonie this way and bodies rain to the floor. I pause between swings only to wipe off clumps of yellow guts from particularly vicious hits. At around twenty minutes, I count blood specks on my boonie—157, and the air hasn't begun thinning out.

In another twenty minutes, enough bodies tumble across the tower floor that they flow like waves in the breeze.

After an hour, no flies remain alive. My boonie is covered with blood and guts, more specks and smears than I can count. For several minutes, I watch fly bodies swirl around the steel floor, eventually collecting in black mounds in the tower corners. This must be what victory feels like, sitting on your throne in your tower, staring down at the bodies of your enemies swirling at your feet. I look out at sand and clean blue horizon, hot breeze blowing in my face, king of nothing.

When my replacement calls up the ladder, I throw on my flak jacket and assault pack, slap my boonie against my thigh to clear it of clinging guts and put it back on my head.

When I get to the bottom of the ladder, my replacement says, "Orlovsky told me it's fucking gross up there."

"Nah," I say, "It ain't that bad."

WEAPONS OF MASS DESTRUCTION 4: SMUGGLING VICTORY

Saddam had smuggling partnerships with most of his neighboring countries that he used to get around international sanctions. Even Iran temporarily suspended their hatred long enough to help Iraq secure black-market commerce against common enemies.

To make the deals work, Saddam secretly sold oil to his neighbors at tremendous discounts. These countries then used Iraqi oil to meet domestic needs so they could export their own oil at higher market prices. In exchange for this premium, Iraqi elites got extra cash flow and Saddam secured willing partners for smuggling weapons, technology, and prohibited materials into Iraq. Syria was Iraq's most unscrupulous collaborator. They were willing to smuggle pretty much anything into Iraq.

Saddam's smuggling operation was vast. Iraqi agents were located at transport nodes all across the country and worked closely with agents from other countries to ensure smuggling went smooth. Iraq utilized over 500 official and unofficial crossing points between Iraq, Syria, Turkey,

Jordan, Saudi Arabia, Kuwait, and Iran, but most goods went through five major border crossings where traffic was so heavy it was impossible to inspect all vehicles.

Saddam also smuggled over water. Oil was smuggled out of Iraq using private dhows, barges, and tankers. Goods were smuggled in the same way. Qatar and Dubai were primary transshipment points, but Iraq also made deals with Oman, Algeria, Tunisia, Yemen, and Sudan. Occasionally, prohibited goods were discovered by the US fleet, but smugglers were usually able to reroute, change shipping dates, disguise cargo, or cover cargo with enough innocuous looking freight to avoid detection.

Two countries had direct air routes with Iraq. Russia smuggled high technology items on charter flights that flew from Moscow to Baghdad every Monday. Belarus had a joint airline with Iraq to transfer experts and government officials under the cover of humanitarian missions. For smaller, more sensitive items, Iraq used diplomatic couriers.

Iraq sent agents all around the world to find suppliers and bribe businessmen and government officials. These officials then worked behind the scenes through their own ministries and friend groups to procure banned goods for Iraq. Some countries were deeply involved at every stop. Russia, for example, had a regular sea smuggling route running through Yemen and Syria. They also regularly sent government ministers to Iraq to assist Russian companies in their work with Iraqi export ministers.

Out of fear of being discovered making illegal arrangements, many companies used sub-contractors to disguise the link between themselves and Iraq, for example, one British firm hired a Pakistani company to fill orders for Iraqi rocket fuel. Freight and shipping companies were often used as middlemen to disguise routing, destination, and purpose of acquired goods. Anti-aircraft systems were labeled as water pumps, tank engines as agricultural equipment, anti-tank missiles as illumination devices or plastic piping. This was especially prevalent in Syria where trading companies were headed by high members of government and relatives of President Assad.

Perhaps the most impressive part of Saddam's smuggling apparatus was the network of front companies created by Iraqi Intelligence. Front companies were used to smuggle weapons, search for foreign contacts, import sanctioned materials, and hide Oil for Food revenues. Upper management, middle management, and security of these companies were staffed almost completely by Iraqi Intelligence agents. The most commonly used fake company was the Orient Company, but Iraq set up at least 230 single use companies for more dangerous transactions like importing weapons and banned chemicals.

Iraqi smuggling was so lucrative, members of the UN Security Council began competing against each other to get on Iraq's payroll. The level of international corruption was astounding. Private companies from Jordan, India, France, Italy, Romania, and Turkey, engaged in probable WMD related trade with Iraq. Governments of Syria, Belarus, Yugoslavia, Yemen, and Russia directly supported private company efforts to provide Iraq with weapons and weapons technology, but nearly everyone was involved in some way—missile components from China, missile tech from North Korea, rocket fuel and expertise from India, missile engines from Poland, experts and UAV components from Ukraine, rocket fuel from Italy and Japan, aluminum powder from France, precursor chemicals from Croatia, high tech items from South Korea, HF comm systems and 16,000 channel receivers from South Africa, precision machining from Taiwan, gyroscopes, UAV motors, 30-mm cannon technology, carbon fiber filament winding, jet engines, helicopter engines, tank parts, missile parts, electro-chemical gun barrel machining, GPS equipment, technology transfers, technicians, scientists, experts on lasers and night vision, frequency hopping radios, electronic countermeasures, explosion resistant cables, compressors for nitric acid production, military computers, communication and radar equipment, patrol boats, infrared homing capability, test benches for missile engines, missile guidance and control systems, aerodynamic structures experts, vacuum furnaces, software experts, circuit boards, fiber optics, indigenous computer design and fabrication experts, hardened cpu notebooks, filters, oscillators, anti-tank guided missiles, shoulder fired SAMs, training engineers, tank engines, BMPs, CNC milling machines for aerospace and missile applications, inertial navigation systems, gyros, accelerometers, RPGs, heavy machine guns, munitions, nitric acid, nitric acid pumps, hydrofluoric acid, and several chemicals previously used in production of Iraq's highly developed chemical weapons program.

All of this was off the books. All of this was smuggled into Iraq by people who knew full well what Saddam was. Presidents of foreign countries were making 100-million-dollar deals. Foreign companies sent fleets of engineers and experts to Iraq and kept them hidden from UN inspectors for years. The US had little idea about most of this until intelligence was gathered inside Iraq after the invasion in 2003. Only then was the extent of what Saddam Hussein accomplished understood. Iraq's smuggling economy was roaring. Saddam had won the international politics game, and his most dangerous enemy didn't even know it.

CEREAL AISLE

It's my last night in Kuwait, and I stand outside our desert tent, looking up at the sky. We're the last unit in Matilda, so when the generators shut off, they won't come back on. There's no moon tonight, and the dark is so heavy I can't see below my knees. It's a darkness I haven't encountered before. I look up at the sky with tears in my eyes. How can there be so many stars? The Milky Way shoots through the black—pinkish star clusters and bright white clouds of light.

Gratitude courses through my body. I'm going home, and I'm okay. And now I have this perfect night sky.

★★★

After a couple days back in my hometown spending time with my family, I jump in my car and drive down a country road. I've never realized how beautiful Minnesota is, the thick air fragrant with grass and harvested fields, the blue sky full of puffy white clouds. I drive to the neighboring town where my buddies and cousins go to college. They take me to house parties, sneak me into bars, tell strangers wherever we go that I'm just back from Iraq. Those strangers shake my hand and buy me drinks while girls smile at me and work their way over from across the room.

★★★

A couple weeks after being home, my CO calls me into his office at Fort Snelling. I don't know what to expect, but I hate talking to officers. It's never good. My CO is a big guy, taller than me, looks somewhat like Mr. Bean, and when I enter his office, he motions to a chair and tells me to sit.

"There's no easy way to say this," he says, sitting behind his desk, "Our unit has been asked to provide volunteers for Iraq. We've got a few new guys, but not enough to cover the number. The simple reality is you don't have a wife or kids or anyone depending on you, so I volunteered you to go back. There's a group of former active-duty Marines getting called back from around the country. You'll be going with them. Do you understand?"

"Yes, sir."

★★★

After the news, I spend a lot of time just walking around my hometown. I walk to the gas station to buy cigarettes, walk around my parents' yard looking at the trees, the old oak stretching high overhead already almost bare of leaves, the chestnut nestled underneath, yellow leaves still fluttering in the breeze. I light a cigarette and walk past the crab apple tree next to the driveway. It's so pretty in spring covered in bright pink blossoms, but in fall it's like the straw arms of a scarecrow.

I walk down the block across the football field of my high school, past the stone walls of the Lutheran Church where I took communion. I walk to the edge of town, to my elementary school, past the oak trees out front that block the sun in summer. I walk along the yellow stripe painted on the sidewalk where kids wait for buses after school, where I used to wait. Now I'm just some weirdo roaming in front of an elementary school smoking cigarettes.

I walk to the store where I used to bag groceries. I don't need to buy anything, but familiar places are pulling me. When I step through the door, I feel like I'm in another world: carts stacked high with produce all around; tomatoes—cherry, grape, Roma, celebrity; onions—yellow, white, purple, green; green grapes, red grapes, purple grapes, cucumbers, carrots, celery, six varieties of potatoes. A few weeks ago, I was thrilled to have an apple, now there are carts of apples, eight varieties, engineered for taste and texture. There's fresh cilantro, basil, lettuce, cabbages, pre-chopped lettuce in plastic bags for salads, pre-shredded cabbage in plastic bags for coleslaw. There are a hundred varieties of chilled gourmet salad dressings because the half store aisle of non-chilled salad dressings isn't enough. This is a different world than the one where parents watched their children starve underneath portraits of Saddam Hussein.

Next to the produce section is a deli with every kind of food I could want, fried chicken, grilled chicken, rotisserie chicken, metal tubs of mashed potatoes, off-the-cob corn, baked beans, mac and cheese, macaroni salad, potato salad with mayo, potato salad with sour cream, various mixes of fruit with whipped cream and candy bits, dozens of varieties of turkey, ham, and roast beef, blocks of cheese for slicing—Colby Jack, Pepper Jack, three types of Cheddar, Swiss, Provolone, and cheeses with names I can't pronounce. There's a cooler full of ready-made pizzas for home baking, a heating unit full of already cooked pizzas, a made-to-order section so you can shop while someone bakes your pizza for you. As the store goes on, so does the food, Chinese food cooking in giant woks, bakery racks of breads, pastries, and doughnuts, meat counter with prime cuts of beef and pork. Food is piled everywhere I look.

I remember a skinny man in the desert near Safwan begging me for food for his equally skinny little girl. I remember wondering how they weren't already dead. We didn't have much. We were on short rations ourselves. I gave him a pouch of pears. Another Marine gave an energy bar. Whichever guys didn't have the stomach to just look away, gave what they could. There were people like this all-over southern Iraq that came to us, invading soldiers, for help. What kind of nightmare do you have to be living under that your best option is to take your young daughter to foreign soldiers?

I walk past shelves of cookies and cakes, past rows of chocolate bars and candy. When I get to the cereal aisle, I pause—green boxes, red boxes, yellow, blue, white, orange, brown—boxes of corn, oats, wheat, rice, crisped, flaked, puffed, rolled—skateboarding tigers, talking frogs, gold medalists, pudgy bears in t-shirts, friendly pirates, cartoon bees—rows of boxes, walls of boxes, boxes stocked eight deep. A paper-skinned old man pushes his cart behind me past Cocoa Puffs, Cocoa Pebbles, Cocoa

Crispies, Count Chocula, Oreo O's, and Reese's Puffs because sometimes chocolate alone isn't enough and you need a dash of peanut butter. As he shuffles along, nothing seems strange to him.

    I need to get out of here. I walk back past the Chinese food, deli meats, and vats of fried chicken, back past the shelves of chocolate and pallets of produce, back through the sliding doors and out into the cool air. I light up a cigarette and inhale deep, walking away from the store, away down the road, away toward the woods nearby. I suck up tar and nicotine walking along the mostly bare tree line, feet crunching on red and yellow leaves. The nicotine helps. The crunch of the leaves helps. The smell of autumn and the feel of cool air helps, but I can't shake the disquiet inside me. I don't feel right in this place anymore. Maybe it's better that I'm going back to Iraq.

WILD DOGS (4)

A buddy of mine found a video of Iraqi secret police before his first deployment to Fallujah. In the video, the police dragged a middle-aged Iraqi man to the top of a two-story building and threw him off. When the man didn't die from the fall, they dragged him up the stairs and threw him off again. It was like a game to them. They were enjoying watching the pain and fear of this man who had nowhere to run and no way to fight back.

Control of information and resources were pieces of Saddam's power, but by far the strongest and most devastating piece was his security apparatus. There's an old Tikriti saying, "Kill a man and end his news." This is an idea Saddam took to heart. People in Iraq disappeared all the time. Between several hundred-thousand and a million people were "disappeared" by Saddam's forces. Others, the government just murdered and didn't bother to hide, secret police taking people from work or home then showing up the next day with a box and a death certificate for the family to sign. Not only could they kill you whenever they wanted, they'd make you endorse it.

The security apparatus was everywhere, informants on informants on informants. You never knew who you could safely talk to, so people stopped talking. Any word of frustration about the government or its leaders was swiftly and brutally punished, often by cutting out a man's tongue in front of his family and the people in his neighborhood. Iraq was under constant surveillance. The security state kept detailed files on the Iraqi population, and escaping this nightmare was nearly impossible. Exit visas were extremely rare, and if people were allowed to leave the country, their families were required to stay behind as leverage, but none of this was the darkest part of the regime.

Saddam loved his state torturers, called them the "Sharp Sword of the Government." Many tortures were recorded and used later to train secret police, blackmail people who might not want them seen, or test the stomachs of men working for the regime. But sometimes Saddam watched the videos because he liked them. Cruelty wasn't a necessary evil to Saddam Hussein, but something positive. The crueler a man was, the better chance he had of finding place in Saddam's forces.

Iraqi state torturers used a broad array of methods: cutting off fingers and toes with bolt cutters; letting dogs rip into chained down victims and eat their flesh in front of them; drilling through hands, feet, and skulls; forcing naked victims to sit down on long neck wine bottles until their insides tore and blood streamed out their anuses; tying people to ceiling fans then beating them with clubs while they spin; suspending women in the air by their hair; attaching electrified alligator clips to nipples, eyelids, ears, and genitals; starving people then feeding them someone else's vomit; binding naked people to gas heaters and letting blue flames sear off their skin; severing arms and legs with axes or power saws; tying prisoners' hands behind their backs then lifting them off the ground until their shoulders dislocate; beating prisoners' genitals with heavy sticks or rock filled hoses; shoving needles under finger nails; drilling into teeth; nailing a standing victim's ears to a wall then leaving them standing, as their strength fades, their own sagging bodyweight rips off their ears; confining children in rooms with beehives, forcing parents to watch them get stung over and over; raping women while their husbands and children are forced to watch and applaud; leaving people in several feet of dirty water for days until their skin starts to decompose; holding a person's head under water with feces and urine until they gasp and are forced to drink; lighting men's beards on fire; slowly lowering people feet-first into shredding machines; keeping people in tiny sweatboxes without ventilation for months, throwing dead bodies into cells of live prisoners and letting them rot; plugging a prisoner's nose with wads of fabric, making them breathe out of their mouths for weeks; piercing tongues with needles; splitting tongues up the center with knives or scalpels; dipping feet and hands in boiling oil, spraying insect repellent in pinned open eyes; melting a prisoner's flesh to electric heater coils; making parents watch as men scoop the eyes out of their screaming infants.

Over the years, I've been surprised at how many people say things like, "Saddam wasn't that bad. He was just a guy who knew how to control Iraq." I can only assume people say this because they don't know better.

There are plenty of reasons to criticize how America handled the war. There are plenty reasons to criticize America's motives for invading Iraq in the first place. But Saddam Hussein was "that bad". He was probably worse.

NAPALM DITTY-BOP

But still the branches are wire
And thunder is the pounding mortar,
Still I close my eyes and see the girl
Running from her village, napalm
Stuck to her dress like jelly,
Her hands reaching for the no one
Who waits in waves of heat before her.

(From "Song of Napalm" by Bruce Weigl)

A half-hour before I entered bootcamp, me and three other guys from Minnesota stood inside the USO office at the San Diego airport waiting for the bus to the Recruit Depot. A kind old woman behind the desk kept us busy talking about our hometowns to keep the shakes out of our legs.

When the recruit bus pulled up long after sundown, a drill instructor stepped off, uniform immaculately clean and pressed, chest full of ribbons.

"Load up," he said, calm and almost kind. We loaded the bus while he lit a cigarette and cracked jokes with the USO staff.

On the empty bus, I sat alone in my seat, heart thudding. I stared out the window across a vacant parking lot at a grassy hill and palm trees in the distance. I wondered if I got off the bus now and ran if I could make it over that hill and disappear.

Too late.

The drill instructor stepped on his cigarette, said his goodbyes, and boarded the bus. As soon as he turned his back on the USO staff, the smile left his face, and a fire lit behind his eyes.

"Eyes down, bitches," he growled, climbing the stairs. "You're mine now."

The door closed behind him.

The first time I realized I could be physically dominant was in basic training. We'd been practicing bayonet drills, hundreds of young men in a dirt field stabbing dummies and slashing at each other with rubber knives, shouting "Kill, Kill, Kill, Kill." At the end of the instruction, my platoon lined up in a short tunnel made of sandbags and another platoon lined up in another tunnel thirty feet away. Both tunnels angled toward a small clearing covered in camo-netting. Two recruits at a time would charge down their tunnels, round the corner, and fight each other in the clearing with pugil sticks, using different slashes, stabs, and rifle smashes we'd learned. The fight would end when one recruit got a killing blow, and the judging drill instructors declared him the victor.

When it was my turn to fight, a drill instructor grabbed me by the collar and said, "When you see him come around the corner, just give him a straight jab. Don't waste your time slashing or swinging. Shove the knife edge of your pugil stick right though his face."

I did what I was told. I started down the tunnel, met the other recruit at a full run. He slashed at me, and I jabbed, then he was on the ground with a drill instructor crouched over him checking to see if he was conscious. Two other DIs cheered and laughed behind me. The way they roared when I drilled that kid in the face stuck with me. I had never felt like that before. Standing over this kid with dazed eyes in a heap on the ground in front of me, I loved it.

When I was in Military Police school after Basic Training, a classmate taught me a running cadence I would often use during future company runs. It was shocking and horrific, and that's why it appealed to me. It went like this:

> Bomb the village. Kill the People.
> Drop some napalm in the square.
> Do it on a Sunday morning.
> Kill the people while at prayer.
> Throw some candy in the school yard.
> Watch the children gather round.
> Swing my 50 cal around now.
> Mow them little fuckers down.

At this point the verse transitioned into chorus, and I'd switch my voice to a psychotic growl.

> Napalm sticks to kids.
> Burns their hair and their little eyelids.
> Napalm sticks to kids.
> Watch them fizzle and watch them fizz.

What was interesting about this song was how the other Marines in my platoon responded to it. Most of them were decent-hearted guys, many with kids of their own, but when I started that ditty, they'd turn savage with me, and like a pack of animals, we'd run in step, snarling, and thundering abominations about burning innocence to the ground.

The funny thing about savagery, though, is how much easier it is to stomach in theory than in reality. I have a hard time watching kids be mean to each other on a playground, let alone watching them get brutally killed. During my first tour in Iraq, there was a day when we handed out a couple dozen soccer balls to local kids. One little boy, maybe eight or nine, was so excited, and he immediately ran off toward his house to show his parents, but two older boys caught him on the way and cornered him against a building. When he wouldn't let go of the ball, one boy pinned his left arm over his head while the other boy punched him repeatedly in the ribs. After several punches, the eight-year-old dropped the ball and hunched over to protect himself. The bigger boys smiled, grabbed the ball, and walked off.

That little bit of cruelty from older boys against a younger one haunted me for days afterward. I couldn't get it out of my head. And that was several degrees of viciousness less than burning children with Napalm.

I lost my glorification of violence early on in Iraq. The dead bodies, wailing families, and my own fear when violence came my way took it out of me, but I didn't stop singing the Napalm song until an experience in the Minneapolis Airport on the way to my second deployment.

While we waited for a plane to California, I went to Burger King in the terminal to get a breakfast sandwich. A couple guys from my unit, Frank and maybe Cheeto went too. When we got close to the register, a voice behind me said, "Let me buy you fellas breakfast. It's the least I can do."

I turned to thank the man saying the words and almost lost my composure. I'd never seen anyone so horribly burned. He was a Vietnam Vet who got caught by some sort of explosion during the war. He didn't say whether it was Napalm or something else, but his face looked like it was melting wax dripping off his skull. I could barely look at him.

"I always want to let our troops know how much I appreciate them," he said, "I know what it's like making the sacrifice."

As the man talked, his eyes filled with tears. It was obvious he knew way more about sacrifice than I did. Standing next to him, my war experience seemed superficial. I felt unworthy of the appreciation he was showing, like I was lying by even accepting it. How would that feel, returning home with an injury so severe it would make people cringe at your approach for the rest of your life? What was that like, paying such a price then coming back to a country where privileged little assholes who didn't fight felt justified treating you like a criminal whose sacrifice was a disgrace? But this man didn't strike me as bitter. He was actually so damned sincere in his appreciation it was hard for me not to get tears in my eyes as well. We got our food and thanked the vet.

"God bless you guys," he said, and walked away.

As we walked back to our unit, Frank said, "I'm grateful and all for that guy buying us breakfast, but it kind of made me sick just looking at him."

I want to claim a moral high ground and call Frank a callous piece of shit. That dude paid one hell of a price and somehow still had the guts to be kind and gracious. But in cold reality, I was so repulsed by his melting skin, I didn't even want to eat my sandwich.

When we got back to the other Marines waiting in the terminal, I stepped away from the group and sat in an open chair staring at the ground. What kind of person am I? I couldn't even look at that guy without squirming, and I can't even be honest about it like Frank.

I never sang the Napalm song again. Every time I thought about it, it reminded me of that old vet, and a sting of shame filled my heart.

Several years after I got out of the Marine Corps, I came across a poem by Bruce Weigl called "Song of Napalm." In it, a Vietnam Vet tries to forget his time as a soldier and reintegrate into life with his wife, but he can't escape the memory of a little girl.

> And the girl runs only as far
> as the napalm allows
> until her burning tendons and crackling
> muscles draw her up
> into that final position
> burning bodies so perfectly assume. Nothing
> can change that; she is burned behind my eyes
> and not your good love and not the rain-swept air
> and not the jungle green

pasture unfolding before us can deny it.

By the time I read this poem, I was several years removed from my final deployment to Iraq. I'd gone far away from that life, about as far as I could, becoming religious, living as a missionary, consecrating myself to a different kind of life. But the Marine Corps didn't leave me. When I read that poem, it all flooded back, me, the tentative young man looking for guts, me, hardening, but naïve about the consequences of cruelty, me, seeing brutality everywhere, realizing that this world is diseased, people striving to dominate and consume each other, and in this diseased world, violence is often the only answer, but an answer that spreads like fire, an answer that consumed the vet with the melted face and the little Vietnamese girl covered in Napalm jelly, an answer that cost the lives of a hundred thousand Iraqis during the war and swallowed the lives of hundreds of thousands more after, an answer that leaves its mark in the hearts and minds of millions upon millions around the world who've been swept before it, an answer that runs as deep in human psyches as our history is long.

THE WALLS OF ABU GHRAIB

"What's the difference between a dead baby and a watermelon?" Frank asks. "One is fun to hit with a sledgehammer, the other one is a watermelon."

I snort.

"How do you know when a baby is a dead baby?"

I shrug.

"The dog plays with it more."

"What's the difference between 100 dead babies and a Ferrari? I don't keep a Ferrari in my garage."

Frank is a bit of a sociopath, but I'm glad he's here.

During the initial invasion of Iraq, the focus was on pushing to Baghdad. That meant other hotbed areas were mostly left alone, areas like Al Anbar province. In 2004, a large rotation of Marines was deployed to Al Anbar to start dealing with the problem. I'm one of those Marines. Now my company is gathered around our commanding officer at an Army base in Iraq just before the highway splits—North to Baghdad, West to Fallujah and Ramadi. The sun has set.

"Alright, gentlemen." the major begins, "Tomorrow we head into the viper's den. Convoys are getting ambushed all over Al Anbar. Chances are high we get hit tomorrow. Be prepared to watch the men around you die."

I've heard speeches like this before, officers telling me I'll spend my last moments writhing in the dirt, blood squirting out of whatever stumps are left of my body.

"Tomorrow is a day that changes us all," the major continues. "Best make your peace tonight." Fuck this guy. We might all die tomorrow, but if I am going to die, let me die snarling, teeth bared, bloodlust in my eyes that will haunt my enemy forever.

"Alright, you fucking pricks! All you worthless sacks of shit are going to die tomorrow! Suck it up and do your jobs. Dream about how dearly you're going to make those sandy cock-sluts pay for daring to attack United States Marines" This is the speech we need, but not the speech we get.

"Look at the Marines around you," the major continues, "Some of these have been your friends a long time. Prepare for their blood. This will be the last night for many of them."

After we're dismissed, our men return to their Humvees to contemplate their destruction in a few hours when the sun comes up. Some guys sit with tactical red flashlights, writing last letters to loved ones, others rustle in their bags in the dirt, trying to drift off and get a few hours sleep. I walk through our parked vehicles, cool air against my cheeks, looking up at the stars, pulling in the last few bits of flickering beauty.

We wake before the sun a couple hours later, no joking, no talking shit, men keeping to themselves. Everyone looks tired. My fierceness from the night before is gone, stolen by fatigue. Now I fight to keep the dread pushed down in my stomach. When we roll out the gate, starting toward Ramadi, I'm not the man I need to be.

The first hour of driving is uneventful, sand, palm trees, long grass, and the occasional farmer transporting goods by donkey cart. There are no cars on the highway, and only a few houses here and there. I struggle to stay awake behind my machine gun. *Wake up, motherfucker! What the hell is wrong with you? You want to die like this?* My senses are dull. My brain is slow. I'm having trouble focusing my eyes, scanning my surroundings for threats. *Pick yourself up, dumbass! You can't be slow today!*

Our convoy pulls to the side of the road in front of a massive complex with high tan walls, sentried guard towers, and machine gun nests covered with camo netting. Out front of the main entrance, Hesco barriers filled with dirt are stacked twenty feet high, reaching almost the top of the main wall. In front of the Hescos, concrete barriers funnel foot traffic toward the gate, and rows of concertina wire stacked three high run the length of the front wall. This place is a fortress.

"Dismount, stretch, take a piss," our Master Sergeant says, "This is our last stop before Ramadi. We won't be stopping again."

With the fortified walls of Abu Ghraib Prison on one side and an open field of sand and grass on the other, I relax some. There's nothing around us the towers won't see. Nothing that could attack us without fire support from machine guns on the walls. Right now is about the safest I've felt in Iraq.

I jump out of the turret, leave my machine gun, and walk to the edge of the road, stopping before it turns to dirt because you never know where there's a landmine. I unbutton my fly, flop out my junk, and piss in the dust. I button up, light a cigarette, grab a Coke from the cases we loaded up before we left Kuwait, pop it open, and lean over the hood of our Humvee. I guzzle the can down, feeling the burn of carbonation in my throat and chest, inhale deep on my cigarette, hold the smoke in, slowly let it out. The sun is warm on my face. The hood of the Humvee is warm on my arms. Nicotine, caffeine, a secure place to piss, a little time to feel the spring sunshine, and I feel like myself again. I'm not sure who that bitch was a few minutes ago, but I'm glad he's gone.

"Mount up," Master Sergeant yells. I jump on the hood of the Humvee, climb to my place behind the gun. It feels like my place again. Maybe we'll all die in the next hour. Maybe we won't even make it past Fallujah, but at least I'll be me.

In 2004, Abu Ghraib became synonymous with blood-stained concrete floors, naked prisoner pyramids, and Iraqi men on leashes being dragged down cell blocks by smiling female soldiers. It became an example of the degradation that unchecked power over people often leads to, an example of young soldiers in a wild world falling prey to the strange dark impulse that comes in those situations, the impulse to dehumanize others, to subjugate those caught in your sick little world and set yourself up as the absolute ruler in their lives.

But in this moment, outside these walls, I don't know about any of this. I don't know about torture by government interrogators in dungeon rooms. I don't know about soldiers herding naked Iraqi men like animals, pointing at their penises and giving a thumbs up to the camera. All I know are machine guns, concertina wire, and sandbag nests. All I know are concrete barriers, sentried towers, and high tan walls. All I know are ten minutes of peace to take a piss without fear of being shot, ten minutes to smoke a cigarette and guzzle a warm Coke in the morning sun, ten minutes to get my mind right, get back behind the gun, and face the day like a Marine.

LUCK

There's nothing like a war zone to show you the coldness of fate. One group of guys might accidentally drive a convoy of fuel trucks through a minefield and somehow take the exact right angle not to explode, while a gunnery sergeant up the road might take one step off the highway and blow off both his legs. That actually happened.

A group of seventeen Marines from my unit got ambushed one day because they wanted to shop at a better PX. They took an off-limits road between Ramadi and Baghdad and after they initially got hit, found a shack that insurgents were using for building IEDs. They called it in to Command who ordered them to hold position and wait for reinforcements, so they hunkered down and waited while dozens of insurgents surrounded their position. When they called Command again, they were informed no one was actually coming, so they should blow up the shack themselves and run, but the insurgents had other plans and hammered them with RPGs, RPKs, AKs, and mortars. Our Marines hastily retreated a hundred yards down the road then got slammed again by RPGs and small arms fire. Two Marines were shot, and a third was knocked unconscious by a blast that ruptured his eardrums.

All the Marines in that convoy could have easily died that day. I don't mean to take anything away from them. They fought like hell, and that's certainly a part of what saved them. But a million things could have gone differently. If just one of the dozens of RPGs fired at them had disabled a truck, suddenly, there wouldn't have been enough seats to get everyone out. Suddenly, their defensive capabilities would've been a fraction of what they were and panic might have become a bigger factor. Suddenly, an enemy smelling blood might have found the will to finish the job. But that's not what happened. Instead, this small convoy of Marines, tires shredded, windshields smashed to hell, Humvees looking like Swiss cheese, limped back to camp, and not a single Marine died, not even the gunner who got shot to hell.

A Navy Seabee Reserve unit who moved into camp a couple tents down from us was not so lucky. These guys weren't even in Ramadi to fight. They were there to build infrastructure on base and maybe help rebuild stuff in the city. During their first week on a familiarization run they got hit by a car bomb and lost four guys. A week later, on base, fixing vehicles in their motor pool, a mortar landed right smack in the middle of them. The explosion shook us in our tent fifty feet away, and after the blast, the bodies of Seabees were scattered all over the ground like bowling pins. They lost thirty guys that day. That's just how things went.

Sometimes, whether you live or die is just a matter of timing. We made a wrong turn one day on some back roads between Ramadi to Fallujah and ended up at a little farm. It was a beautiful place, a shaded cottage with palm trees and green gardens full of fruit and vegetable plants. It seemed more like a vineyard somewhere in California than a farm a few miles from Ramadi. The house windows were dark, and the place was quiet, but it was too well taken care of to be abandoned. We didn't spend long there, just long enough to figure out directions and get back on the road to Fallujah.

After dropping off a load of prisoners in Fallujah, we headed back down the way we came. The city was too dangerous for us to cut through to get to the highway, so we headed back past the little farm. It was a nice drive, away from civilian vehicles, away from people and commotion. I felt more relaxed than I'd ever felt around Ramadi. As we passed the little farmhouse, I felt like I was driving down country roads back home, enjoying the breeze and the sunshine and the look of the growing fields. Then suddenly, three explosions ripped through our convoy, a daisy-chain of IEDs. Through the smoke, all I could do was wonder how bad the damage was and get ready for follow-up attacks.

Before our deployment began, we watched some video clips of IEDs to familiarize ourselves. In one clip, a group of Chechen rebels holding a camcorder zoomed in on three 155mm artillery rounds in the back seat of a sky-blue hatchback. The video then cut to several rebels crouching in a field chanting "Allah Akbar," as a Russian troop transport approached. When the rebels detonated the artillery rounds, the blast threw the troop transport truck twenty feet in the air in a massive fireball. If a blast like that had hit my Humvee, they would've found bits and pieces of me a hundred yards away.

The explosions that hit our convoy were big, but not 155 big, and they hit the heaviest, best armored vehicles we had. The guys inside got tossed around and briefly knocked unconscious, but aside from a little brain damage, they were fine. Had the bombers hit our Humvees, there would have been a lot more blood.

Two days later, an army convoy rolled down the same road and got hit in the same place. They were driving a heavily armored medical vehicle with thick plate steel walls like a tank. They probably thought they were safe from almost anything. But this time the insurgents didn't use the explosives they used on us. This time, whatever they used left a crater in the road twelve feet wide and ten feet deep. The medical tank was shredded and everyone inside died. Had they driven down the road the day we did, they wouldn't have been scratched. But that's not what happened. Now they're all dead.

You want to believe you've got some say over your life, so you work and train and fight like hell and do everything in your power to make sure you're as prepared as you can be. But when it comes down to it, sometimes it's luck, and sometimes you just die.

TRANSITION

We're in Camp Habbaniyah, waiting for a group of Soldiers to escort to Fallujah. It's strange acting as security for other units, like shouldn't these guys be able to protect themselves? But part of me loves how it feels being responsible for other men's lives. While the Army guys get their trucks together, we sit in a dirt lot near camp entrance.

"I've been thinking," Adler says, "There's a section of road we'll be driving later that would be perfect for an ambush."

"How do you mean?" I say.

"Just past the big cemetery, the highway is bracketed by canals. There's good concealment in the fields from tall grass. Someone could hit us there, and we couldn't even see where it came from. And if we did, we wouldn't be able to pursue because of the canals."

"Fucking radio is broke," Gunny Patterson says.

"Vietnam era radios are always broke," says Captain Solaris.

The army trucks pull up to our position, ready to go.

"Should we hold up and see if we can fix the radio?" says Gunny P.

"We don't have time," says Solaris, "No guarantee we'll be able to fix it anyway."

"Murphy's Law," Adler says to me. "We got no radio, can't call for help. Today is when we get hit."

★★★

Burt was a kid in my neighborhood growing up. He was overweight, a little dirty, and spoke like his throat was full of phlegm. He got teased a lot by other kids, and I was embarrassed to be seen with him, except when we played in our neighborhood.

When we were in Junior High, Burt got a new Green Bay Packers jacket for Christmas. He was proud of that jacket, walked a little taller while he wore it. One day, riding the bus home from school, two girls, popular, pretty, and vicious, scooted up to the seat behind him, pulled out a tub of peanut butter, and scooped a massive glob on the back of his new coat. Burt screamed and tried to pull away, but there was nowhere for him to go. He just cried in frustration against the bus wall as the girls cackled and smeared.

I sat in the next seat over feeling sick to my stomach. We weren't great friends, but Burt was from my block. I'd been to his birthday parties. We'd played tag in the street together and micromachines on his front stairs. I felt like I should step in and stop these girls, but I was scared they'd turn on me. I didn't want to be their new target for the next few months, so I just looked at the floor and listened to Burt cry while the pretty little trolls laughed.

When we finally reached our street, Burt ran off the bus in humiliation. I stepped off wondering why I was such a coward, why I just let that happen.

★★★

At the back of the convoy, wind in my ears, I don't hear the explosion, but someone pops red smoke at the front, letting me know we got hit. My truck whips along the shoulder of the highway, past the rest of the convoy, and links up with my team leader Kowalchek and his gunner, who is shooting into a field of shoulder high grass adjacent the highway.

"Dismount! Let's go get him!" Kowalchek says.

"Get who?" I say.

"Let's go, Kub, get the gun off the truck!"

I release my 240 from the gun mount, jump off the roof of the Humvee, and run after Kowalchek toward the field. I still have no idea what's happening, but red smoke means we got hit by something. Before we get to the field, we come across a hidden canal that's too wide to jump behind tufts of long green grass. Kowalchek pokes down in the water with a long stick that doesn't hit bottom. Not knowing how deep the canal is, we can't just jump in with our battle gear and weapons. We'd go straight to the bottom and have a hard time getting back up. Just like Adler said, there's no way for us to pursue into this field.

The red smoke was popped after a rocket came out of this field and hit one of the large Army trucks. Kowalchek's gunner saw the man who shot it running away, but when he fired at him, the man dropped into the grass and disappeared. The army trucks are well armored, so no one got hurt, but the truck can't move, and soldiers scramble around trying to get it working again. Knowing that our enemy is still lying somewhere in that field, we punch out teams to secure the area as much as possible.

"Chewy, get on top of that overpass and watch the field," Gunny P says to me. "The rest of you, search them fucking houses up the road."

★★★

Before I joined the Marine Corps, when I worked at the windshield manufacturing plant, one guy in particular gave me lots of crap.

"Hey dumbass, you done nailing that crate?"

"You're about worthless, aren't you? Why are you using so much glue?"

"Jesus, you can't even cut a board right."

The guy was a real piece of shit, stringy blond hair matted down under his baseball cap, shirts always two sizes too small, acne-covered back-fat spilling out the bottom. The day for him was an ongoing battle between his ass-crack and his hands trying to keep his pants up between pallet loads. All he ever talked about when he wasn't ragging on me was how wasted he was going to get after work and how his life's ambition was to sleep with a stripper.

The summer I joined the Marine Corps, I hid my choice from the guys at work as long as I could, but when it was time for my swearing in, I had to tell my boss, and he told the rest of the crew.

When the blond man found out, he laughed in my face, "This pussy? The Marines? He'll wash out and be back here in two weeks."

★★★

I jump back up top of my Humvee and remount my 240. My driver, Ogg, takes me a hundred yards up the highway, then straight up a steep dirt embankment onto a paved overpass. From here, I have good vantage of the field, but our rocketeer isn't poking his head up.

Our main convoy radios aren't working, but our squad radios are still good. I listen to my guys on the ground as they work their way through the farmhouses next to the field finding no people and no weapons. I watch and wait, and as five minutes turns into ten minutes turns into twenty minutes, I get anxious. We've been stationary way too long. I look at my watch. We need to get the fuck out of here. What the hell is taking so long? I pull out a cigarette and light up.

Solaris comes running up the dirt embankment, huffing a little from the uphill sprint in full battle gear. "Put that thing out! We've got to maintain our aggressive posture."

"Yes, sir," I say, snuffing out my cigarette.

"You seeing anything up there?"

"Nothing yet, sir. But we've been here way too long."

"Yeah. They're taking their sweet time fixing that vehicle."

Frank calls in over the headset. "Hey, uh, we've got truckloads of men dressed in black offloading by our position."

I pick up my binos, look toward the tree line where Frank is, and see several pick-up trucks coming from the direction of Fallujah carrying men in black holding rifles.

A shot cracks out from the field somewhere below. The bullet pings off the highway guard rail and tumbles harmlessly up toward the rear tire of my Humvee.

★★★

When I joined the Marine Corps, I had never shot a gun. My first time on the rifle range in boot camp my commanding officer looked at my target, shots scattered all over hell and said, "Maybe you should be a machine gunner."

Pistol was different. With pistol, I had natural ability. From day one, I was high man in my MP class, even beating out a couple civilian cops. By the end of qualification week, my instructor told me I should practice and try out for Marine Corps Competition Pistol Team.

When qualification day came, I didn't shoot my best, but I was still solid and expected to win company high shooter. That would have been big for me, a little sign that I belonged. I was surprised when someone tied my score. Olander was almost thirty, our class leader, and I believe a cop before he joined the Marine Corps. He was also an asshole who most of our class despised. Our instructor decided we'd have a one-shot shoot-off from 25 yards to determine company high shooter, and guys streamed over to me before the shoot off.

"Come on, man, you've got to win this. Bring that fucker down a peg or two."

"Yeah, someone needs to knock that punk-bitch on his ass."

The more guys talked, the more nervous I got. I didn't want anyone counting on me for anything. When Olander and I lined up side-by-side twenty-five yards from our targets, my legs and hands went rubbery. The instructor gave us each one bullet, and we loaded. Olander brought his pistol up quickly and shot a nine, just off center. Nine was solid, but I'd shot mostly tens over the week. I brought my pistol up, aimed at the target, and squeezed the trigger, but nothing happened.

Did I forget the safety? No, the safety's off. What the hell is going on? Why isn't it firing?

My hands were weak from nerves. I should've dropped my arms, breathed, and started over. But my whole class was watching, and I couldn't do it, so I stood there like a jackass, arms swaying out front of me, pistol shaking in my hands. Finally, I yanked the trigger as hard as I could just to get it over with and was lucky my bullet hit paper.

"Seven?" My instructor said. "You kidding me? A fucking seven?"

I hadn't shot below nine all week.

★★★

"Where the hell did that come from!?" Solaris says.

"I don't know, sir!" I say, lowering my binos. "I didn't see it!" Judging from the angle of the round when it pinged off the guard rail, I'd guess it came from the same field as the rocket, but I don't have time to think about it.

"They're shooting over here too!" Ogg shouts from behind me. I swing my turret around just as another round hits in front of Ogg's feet.

What the hell do I do now? I just took fire from both sides of the highway and didn't see where either shot came from. Armed men are coming for my guys on the ground. I'm overwatch, the only guy with any sort of vantage on the battleground. The convoy below can't see shit because the road is bracketed on both sides by fields of shoulder high grass, and they can't move to engage any enemy because of the canals.

I've got no time to figure shit out, this all happened in a couple seconds. I have to make a decision. I have to respond somehow. Most of our guys are focused on the field south of the highway, so I focus on the north, quick scanning for anything out of the ordinary. A cargo van is parked a few hundred yards away next to a farmhouse. This whole area has been deserted by civilians for weeks. This van and the farmhouse are my best guess, so I rack my bolt to the rear, sight in, and squeeze the trigger.

As soon as I fire on the van, the world around me erupts in gunfire. The captain gets shot right beside me, and I don't even see or hear him fall. And it's not just gunfire, but explosives. Mortars drop from two mortar crews, one hitting our guys searching houses, and one hitting us on the highway, working its way up our lines.

My 240 is in perfect condition. The rounds come smooth. A year ago, not knowing my weapon, I fumbled with belts of ammunition and waited for a bullet to blow a hole in my skull. Now my 240 is like a piece of my body. My fingers know every rail, joint, and crevice. I take care of my weapon before I take care of myself, before I eat, before I sleep, before I shower, before I shit. I know the exact amount of lubrication it needs for our environment. I know how long that lubrication will last depending on what we're doing. So, when I need my 240 now, it doesn't let me down. The rounds come smooth. "Die, motherfucker, die. Die, motherfucker, die." This is the cadence for machine gunners to keep their timing, but I don't need a cadence. I feel the pattern.

★★★

When I first checked into my Minnesota unit, my hair was about a quarter inch too long on the sides. A sergeant sat me down in front of my platoon and shaved me bald and another sergeant pulled me aside and said I'd better fix myself real fucking quick. During my first deployment, I learned weakness had no place in a combat zone. I had to fix myself real fucking quick.

By my second deployment, I was different. I'd become sharp and capable. I knew my weapon inside and out, and the turret was my domain. I ran missions with the best fighters in my unit and held my own, and they treated me that way.

During one large operation in Ramadi, expecting heavy enemy contact as infantry flushed insurgents our direction, my Company Gunny wanted to replace me for the day. He had been a machine gunner as a young Marine, but never manned one in combat. It was something he felt he needed to do.

At the end of the mission briefing, our Master Sergeant asked Frank how he felt about the plan.

Frank said, "I'd feel a hell of a lot better if Kub was on the gun. We've seen him in these situations before. We know what he can do."

Mike Kubista

So, our Master Sergeant put me back on. Gunny was pissed at getting replaced by a Marine twenty years his junior. He walked around with an attitude the whole next day. I would have been more than happy to let him get shot at for a day, but it was still a nice compliment to me.

★★★

As the fight goes on, I still can't see the enemy. Everywhere I look is just shoulder high golden grass swaying in every direction. I crouch, make myself as small a target as I can behind my machine gun. I'm surprised I haven't been picked off yet. I'm on top of a Humvee on top of an overpass, basically wide open from the ass up.

My buddy, Mixon, rolls up next to me with his 50 cal and lays down rounds into the grass. The power of his shots rocks his Humvee back and forth. At a shooting range, a 50cal firing off next to your head without hearing protection would damn near make your eardrums explode. Right now, I barely hear it. With all the adrenaline, it sounds muffled, almost sweet. With Mixon next to me laying down massive firepower, I calm down, stop firing, start to think, start to watch.

I notice flashes coming out of the tall grass a hundred yards away, maybe muzzle flashes. I watch some more, sight in and wait. When the next flash comes, I hit it with a burst of rounds. My shots are good. The flashing stops. I scan the field for more targets. I scan, wait, shoot, scan, wait shoot, until the flashes on the north side of the highway stop.

As the fight continues, mortars close in. They hit along our guys on the highway, but their main target is the guns on the high ground, so they walk the mortars up the highway trying to get us zeroed. When a mortar round explodes just below the overpass, I know the next one will be on top of us, but the bridge is my responsibility. Our guys pinned down near the farmhouses need the bridge to link back up with our unit. Our guys fighting from the highway need us up here eliminating threats. I expect to die from the next explosion. I accept it. I'm not leaving this bridge.

The next mortar sounds like it explodes on top of me, but lands just behind. The explosion rattles our truck and shakes me all the way through, but no shrapnel hits me. A Humvee screams past me down the exit ramp. They've had enough. Mixon's truck follows the leader, and before I realize it, I'm moving too. Ogg has also had enough. As we flee down the exit ramp, I start to breathe again. We link up with the rest of our company, but we still have guys pinned down by the houses. We have to go get them. This means driving back across the overpass into God knows what on the other side.

Cowardice is poison. Now that we ran once, my body wants to run again, but Gunny P says, "Mount up, we're going to get them."

I'm like a feral animal, ready to chew off my own leg to get away, but I choke this feeling down, and we start rolling. I can't explain how much I don't want to drive back across the overpass into that field, but there's nothing for it. These are my guys. We have to go get them.

Suddenly, something happens I can't explain. A Humvee comes flying across the overpass in our direction, all seats full and four guys clinging to the hood for dear life. For some reason, after that last mortar hit, there was a lull in the action. Previously pinned down on their bellies by gunfire, our guys got up, sprinted for the Humvee, and piled on. I'm in shock seeing them zoom across the bridge. I have no idea how they made it out, but guys jump off the hood and hustle into open seats, and we take off down the highway, all Humvees, Army trucks, and personnel accounted for.

★★★

After being home a few weeks from my second deployment, we had an unexpected awards formation. The platoons lined up and the Gunny I replaced on the machine gun called me forward twice, once to give me a commendation for uncommon professionalism and once for valor. The citation went like this:

For heroic achievement while serving as a turret gunner, Military Police Company, 3D Battalion, 11th Marines, 1st Marine Division in support of Operation Iraqi Freedom II on 8 April 2004. During an enemy counterattack on a 14 vehicle, 37 personnel convoy, Lance Corporal Kubista engaged multiple enemy positions with superior and sustained M240G machine gun fire north of main supply route Mobile, near Al Fallujah, Iraq. From his unarmored and unprotected turret, he effectively suppressed enemy fire on an overpass, which proved instrumental in the evacuation of a Marine wounded in the engagement. His fire was also pivotal in maintaining the key terrain to further suppress the enemy attack that threatened all elements of the convoy. Under increasingly effective enemy mortar fire, Lance Corporal Kubista provided cover fire for another vehicle during its movement to link up with the main body of the convoy. Lance Corporal Kubista's initiative, perseverance, and total dedication to duty reflected credit upon him and were in keeping with the highest traditions of the Marine Corps and United States Naval Service.

The line about providing cover fire wasn't true. I was already off the bridge when the guys came flying over. And the award wasn't a Bronze Star or anything. It was a Navy Achievement Medal with a combat "V," the lowest ranked combat valor medal the Navy offers, but seven years ago, I was petrified of a couple teenaged girls on a school bus. Now I stood shoulder to shoulder with the toughest men I'd known in one of the worst places in Iraq and did my job. Something about those last words, "in keeping with the highest traditions of the Marine Corps," stuck with me. I joined the Marine Corps to find a little backbone. I got my ass handed to me more times than I could count and more than once felt like a liability, but somewhere along the way, I changed. Somewhere along the way, I became a United States Marine.

★★★

As our convoy starts toward Camp Fallujah, an Iraqi man pops up on a building-top thirty yards away. My eyes lock with his. He must have thought we were already gone, and now he looks like I'm his death sentence. In panic, he squishes back against his fortifications, but he can't make himself small enough to avoid my angle. I have a decision to make. Do I reengage or not? He's obviously an enemy combatant and will attack other Marines in the future, but I won't have an accurate shot because we're already rolling. In the end, I don't have it in me to restart the fight. Maybe this makes me a shitty Marine, but I'm happy we made it out as good as we did. I let him go, and we roll on to Camp Fallujah.

DESERT CHAPEL

It's night in Ramadi. There's scattered gunfire across the river, but it's far enough away to be background noise. A light breeze pushes away the stagnant heat of the day. I sit with Mixon just outside the wall of Hesco barriers around our barracks meant to stop shrapnel from explosions.

"It's good to get out of the tent," I say.

"Yeah. It gets a little hard to think in there," Mixon says.

Mixon is my best friend in Ramadi, an uber-Christian going to some bible college in Minnesota. For most of my life, I didn't like religious people. But there's an authenticity about Mixon I've never seen before. No matter what we go through, he's always kind and treats everyone with respect. And no matter what's happening around us, he's always hopeful. In a place like Ramadi, that's an impressive thing. Mixon is a better person than I am, and we spend a lot of time outside the Hesco barriers talking.

There's a little white chapel in Camp Ar Ramadi. It looks like a country chapel near my hometown, but instead of surrounded by cornfields, it's surrounded by hard-baked wasteland. Inside are rows of simple wooden benches and a plain pulpit. I was surprised that whoever built it put in the time to make it look like a real chapel. It looks out of place in Iraq.

Mixon starts going to church at the chapel, so I go with him a couple times. There's a group of southern soldiers who always sit in the front row. Something about these soldiers changes my heart. After running missions all day, when other Marines rack out for a few hours before our next run, I sometimes go to church to listen to these soldiers sing. They sing like no one else is in the building, like it's just them and God, a pure joy and faith in their voices I had never come close to. They sing like they're trying to lift the ceiling off the chapel, raise it up high to make space for God. They sing like they know he's present, like their voices are the realest sort of prayer, like he hears them, and the deepest parts of their souls actually matter to him. And while I'm in that little chapel feeling their joy and faith, I can almost believe that their god is real and would bless people like them. It doesn't seem to matter how many rockets hit or how many guys around us die. Those soldiers are always there, singing to God like he couldn't be any closer.

Jim was another one of my best friends in Ramadi, a big, tough dude who grew up in a bar in rural Wisconsin. Between our two tours in Iraq, Jim met his wife, moved to Utah, and turned Mormon.

Jim was a good dude. I trusted him completely. I would still trust him today with my life. Jim and I used to sit in the tent for hours talking. It was a strange kind of chapel, full of reeking feet and swearing, Marines all around playing poker, sneaking booze, watching porn, zapping each other with cattle prods, etc.

One night, after talking for a few hours, Jim asked if he could pray for me. I said of course he could, so he bowed his head and closed his eyes. I didn't expect anything. I'd sat through many prayers in church as a kid and nothing ever happened. It was just people mouthing words and following the crowd. But something changed when Jim began. My heart grew hot in my chest, and warmth pulsed down to my fingertips and the ends of my toes. I felt like some presence floated down through the ceiling of the tent and came toward me, like a hand reached into my chest and cupped my heart, and in that moment, all my fear and anguish were suddenly gone, and I was filled with a joy so powerful I couldn't speak or move. I could barely endure it. Tears gushed down my cheeks and snot ran over my lips onto my chin. I didn't know what was happening, but I was happy and fulfilled and exalted beyond anything I thought possible. Somehow, in the middle of all the darkness of Ramadi, something magnificent and pure touched my life, just for a moment.

Jim quit praying. I wiped my cheeks and eyes and blew my nose. The feeling stayed in my chest a few more seconds, but grew softer until it disappeared, and then I was back in a tent full of Marines just trying to stay alive.

BUSH'S WAR (2)

A buddy of mine got deployed back to Fallujah in 2008. He told me I wouldn't even recognize it. People had moved back, the city was being rebuilt, kids were back in school. He said there were cars everywhere. It made him nervous because he remembered the old days, but Fallujah wasn't the apocalyptic hell it used to be. In 2008, he never even got attacked.

For all his mistakes in Iraq and the horrible consequences, President Bush made one great decision that changed the trajectory of the war. "The Surge" in 2007 was wildly unpopular in the United States. Talking heads lambasted Bush. They all "knew" Iraq was an irredeemable disaster and that committing more troops was beyond irresponsible. The only correct move was to cut our losses, acknowledge our failure, and get out of Iraq. To Bush's credit, he ignored the pressure of the critics and sent 20,000 more troops to Iraq, mostly to hotbed areas around Baghdad.

What Americans didn't know was how the surge in troops would be received by Iraqis, especially Sunni leaders. America had often abandoned people in the past. After Desert Storm in 1991, George H.W. Bush encouraged all of Iraq to rebel and overthrow Saddam Hussein themselves. The population of Iraq did just that, but they couldn't get coordinated. There was too much mistrust between groups, and they'd all been living in a police state of propaganda and controlled information for years. That doesn't just change overnight. They needed outside help to give the movement stability, but President Bush didn't want to get involved in a political quagmire, and he didn't want to be seen as an occupying force, so he elected to stop at the border and let events unfold.

This gave Saddam Hussein the room he needed. Before the US stormed Kuwait and annihilated the Iraqi army, Saddam had brought his most loyal and best trained units back to Baghdad to protect the regime. When America stopped at the border, Saddam deployed those units around the country. The disorganized bands of resistance were no match for helicopters, chemical weapons, and heavy armor. Saddam crushed the rebellion. His men rampaged through those communities, burning and slaughtering, hanging young men from lamp posts, dragging their bodies through streets behind tanks, hanging Shia clerics from holy sites, bulldozing family tombs and graveyards, and putting up new portraits of Saddam over the ruins. American units just stood by, in some cases close enough to hear and watch, and Iraq entered a new era, even more despotic than before. From then on, Iraqis knew not to trust what Americans say.

This is what the surge in troops changed. It showed that America meant what it said this time. It wasn't just going to go away and leave Iraq with the chaos. Along with a surge of troops came a new military strategy:

safeguarding the Iraqi population. I don't know why it took so long for this to become the number one priority, but American troops started having more contact with local populations. They started living in communities among normal Iraqis. They started showing that they were going to be around when jihadists tried strong-arming these people and their families. And slowly, normal people started gaining confidence and started trying to rebuild their lives.

Sunni leaders, tired of all the fighting, and seeing this change of course, flipped on Al Qaeda. Instead of allowing these foreign jihadists to operate in their communities, they started handing them over to US forces. In short time, Al Qaeda was routed, about ¾ of their leadership was killed or captured, and the rest fled into the desert to regroup. With Sunni leadership reigning in the lunatics in their territory, the Shiites started reigning in their lunatic militias as well. Radical militant groups across the country started losing power. The Iraqi people wanted peace. And for the first time since the very start of the war, it seemed like peace might be possible. It may not have looked that way in the news back in the US, but Iraq had more than a little chance of success.

CRASH

Twenty of us stand in a circle outside the PX at Camp Fallujah. LCpl Bunt, long and lanky with an elastic band imprint on his forehead from his intra-squad radio, walks out loaded up with twelve packs of Coke and cartons of smokes, which he distributes to each Marine and Soldier in the group. I grab a couple cigarettes and a Coke, then walk to my Humvee. The hood is covered with metal links and spent cartridges from my 240. I sweep clean a little section, hop on the hood and sit.

We were lucky today. Only the Captain got shot. He's in the base hospital right now. Soon they'll fly him to Germany and try to fix him up, but the bullet tore up too many nerve clusters in his arm. He won't be back, which is too bad since he's the only officer I trust. I pop open the Coke and gulp half of it down, then lean back, admiring the pile of spent ammunition around me. I reach up and pat my 240 mounted on top of our Humvee. She ran good today.

I see a soldier I want to talk to, part of the group we were escorting. I hop off the hood and walk over to him.

"You are the luckiest motherfucker I've ever met," I say. He's got an ear to ear smile on his face, and I know why. "Did any of that shrapnel even hit you?"

"Just this one little piece," he says, pulling off his flak vest to show me where a marble-sized chunk lodged itself in the center of the trauma plate covering his upper spine.

"I can't believe that shit," I say, "That thing landed right on top of you. You should be dead." He shrugs his shoulders.

During the fight, this soldier was below the highway overpass I was perched on, crouched on one knee in the middle of the road, firing his pistol into the weeds. He looked so stupid, I briefly stopped firing to watch him. Where's your rifle, dumbass? Why don't you find some cover? All of a sudden, for no reason, this soldier stood up and turned to run. Just as he took his first step, a mortar fell from the sky and landed right behind his back heel, right where he had been crouched. The force of the blast blew him off his feet onto his belly, and I thought he was dead, but then he hopped onto his feet and ran off. I didn't see him again until now.

Our group is euphoric. It's the combination of being alive when we shouldn't be, and the adrenaline that's still in our systems. Everyone's telling their story, where they were in the fight, what happened around them, who was pinned down in what field, who had men unload from trucks at his position, who spotted a mortar crew in the distance and greased them with his 50cal. Even with all the details coming out of what everyone did and saw during the fight, I still can't figure out why we're here. One minute we were getting cut up by gunfire from three directions and mortars dropping from above, our guys scattered all over hell, and then it all went quiet enough for us to pull our guys together and bolt. I don't know why it went quiet, but I guess it doesn't matter. What matters is we're all here, and aside from the captain and an unlucky army truck, we're all good. I pop another Coke and light another cigarette.

After we wait around a couple hours for word on Captain Solaris, the sun gets low. To get back to Ramadi, we'd have to drive down the road where we just got ambushed. We decide not to attempt it in the fading light but park our trucks in an open dirt field inside Camp Fallujah to wait for morning and reinforcements.

The night is cold. I lie on top of my Humvee, shivering against the plate-steel. The skies are so clear here, I sometimes spend hours looking up at stars, but not tonight. Tonight, I'm trying to keep my shit together. The adrenaline rush that comes in a gunfight is unlike anything else I know. Your body buzzes with so much energy you feel like you can fly, your senses sharpen—small movements catch your eye and you respond rapidly, and as long as you have control of your fear, your mind focuses with such intensity everything gets muted but your purpose. When the fight is over and you're still alive, you feel like the master of the fucking universe, like nothing is too big for you to take on. But then the crash comes, body and brain drained from the exertion, adrenaline gone, left alone with the realization that tomorrow you have to go again, then the next day, then the day after that. Terror creeps in. You can't keep this up, but there's no way out. This is how you'll live every day for the rest of your short life.

This is what happens inside me as I shiver on the Humvee. Tomorrow we'll go back through the ambush site. Will they be waiting for us again? We were lucky today.

There's no way we'll be that lucky again. Is tomorrow my time? Is this how my life ends? On a stretch of highway outside of Fallujah?

Fuck, it's cold. We weren't supposed to be staying overnight. I didn't pack any warming gear. I'm not going to be able to sleep like this. I jump off the roof of the Humvee to piss. Adler told me your body wastes a lot of heat keeping piss warm, so if you're cold, you need to get rid of it. My piss steams in the night air, little drops of liquid splashing off the hard-packed dirt onto my boots. I'd jump in my Humvee to warm up, but it's crammed with gear and bodies. The ground would be warmer than the steel hardback roof, but I'm not anxious to sleep in the dirt with no bag with camel spiders and scorpions crawling around. I hop back up top. The top is my home anyway. In a couple hours, exhaustion will take over and the cold won't matter. I'll fall unconscious until sunrise.

The next morning is subdued, excitement and confidence deserting most of us overnight. Now we wait. We're a small unit, usually running with around twenty guys. Fighting has been escalating in the area, and we're supposed to link up with a bigger unit for the trip back to Ramadi, but they're on another run. We wait in the sun through the morning and the afternoon, but they don't come. Around dusk, an incoming rocket whizzes overhead and explodes in our field a hundred yards away. We decide it's time to go home. We pack up, ready our weapons, and hit the road.

Once we leave camp and start up the highway, the dread mounts. Something's going to happen today, I can feel it. I see the buildings in the distance where we got hit yesterday. Adrenaline kicks in. I'm sharp again, eyes scanning, 240 in my shoulder, ready for an encore. We pass by the field with shoulder high grass, where the enemy hid yesterday. McCormick shouts over the headset. There's too much wind from driving for me to make out what he's yelling, but it sounds like "Contact Left!" Here we go again.

I swing my turret left looking for the fight, ready to engage. I scan the field for motion or muzzle flashes. Nothing. I look at the roof tops where I saw men yesterday in fortified positions. Nothing. I look at the tree line where men in black were dropped off by trucks yesterday. Nothing. A voice comes over the headset from McCormick's team leader. A car got too close to their truck and McCormick overreacted. There was no enemy contact.

Stupid motherfucker. I call McCormick a list of names in my head, not sure if I'm pissed at him for freaking the hell out of me with that call, or because I'm just as scared as he is and now I have to face it. We continue driving down the highway, me trying to swallow my guts. God, I don't want to be out here anymore, but it's a long deployment, many months still in front of us.

2/4

I'm on the roof of a Police Headquarters in downtown Ar Ramadi, my machine gun pointed down the road adjacent my building. We got warning this morning of a car bomb coming our way, a black Opel sedan; it's always a black Opel sedan. I have good vantage from my position. Hopefully, I'll have time to identify the threat coming down the road.

So far, it's been a quiet day. A couple mortars hit near our convoy on the way here, but they were small explosions—probably 60s—and we were a good ten meters outside their blast radius. If they had been 81s, we would've been in trouble, but they weren't, so we pushed forward into the city before the mortar team could adjust fire and lob another volley.

There's a lot of foot traffic on the road below me right now. The people are mostly middle-aged men and women dressed in suit coats and nice robes. There must be a mosque nearby. The people seem relaxed. The way they mingle together reminds me of parishioners coming out of the Catholic church down the street from my house in Minnesota.

Though foot traffic is heavy, few cars drive down the road, and no black Opel sedans. I'm honestly more nervous about the Iraqi Policemen around me than any outside threat. This Police HQ is a fortress, high concrete perimeter wall, sandbagged fortified machine gun nests with two Iraqi Policemen on every corner. My roof is one story below them, a section jutting out toward the road, which gives me a good angle, but there are no fortifications. I'm uneasy having my back turned to a bunch of Iraqi Policemen with machine guns. Some of the guys staring down at me right now have probably been part of recent ambushes against American forces and would love to unload a belt of rounds in my back while I'm on this rooftop.

In the courtyard below, a handful of Iraqi Policemen laugh and joke. Most of them carry AKs, which doesn't bother me. Being an Iraqi Policeman is a dangerous job, and they need to defend themselves. But I can't help being uneasy when I see IPs walking around with RPGs slung on their backs. Four marines from 2/4 were killed yesterday by an RPG attack in the city, one of them blown in half. On the same day, Lima Battery got ambushed and said IPs near the action just stood by and laughed. I don't know these Iraqi men personally, and I try to keep my suspicion in check, but I can't help thinking I'm looking at weapons that are going to be used later against American patrols and convoys.

Gunfire erupts close by. It sounds like a 240 exchanging fire with some AKs on the next street over. This is probably a patrol from 2/4 and whoever decided to fight them today. These guys have about the shittiest job in Iraq. Day in and day out, they run contact patrols on the streets of Ramadi, looking to get attacked so that they can retaliate. They are basically just bait, trying to trigger ambushes. I can't imagine how that must wear on a guy. They have hundreds of casualties in the time I'm in Ramadi but kill thousands of enemies. They're the kind of Marines that make me feel like pussy.

When the gunfire starts, I get on my belly and scan the street and nearby buildings for threats. When I don't see anything, I look up at the Iraqi Policemen to see if they can give me any indication of where the fight is, but they aren't looking at the gunfire, they're looking down at me, laughing. The six Iraqi policemen I can see stand in a group outside their fortifications, smoking cigarettes and looking at me like I'm an idiot.

At first, I'm pissed off. Do your job, you lazy pricks. This is why you assholes keep getting overrun. Then I'm nervous. Seeing how these guys react to a nearby threat makes me realize I'm the only one up here on guard. These guys are supposed to be watching the other roads leading to the complex. If the car bomb comes from another direction than the one I'm watching, there's nothing I'll be able to do.

I put the IPs out of my mind and turn my attention to the people on the street below. I'm surprised by what I see. Not a single man or woman reacts to the gunfire. No one stops to see where it's coming from. No one speeds up to get out of the area. No one turns around to go the other direction. I think of what people in an American city would do if they heard a machine gun ripping off rounds a block away. I imagine their panic, their frenzy, their eyes going vacant as the flight instinct kicks in. But here, it's a matter of course, just another day in a city where people have nowhere to flee too anyway.

The whole area between Ramadi and Fallujah is fucked, and we expect to get hit every time we leave base. Civilian supply trucks have lost so many people, they quit making supply runs. Exploded fuel tankers smolder on the highways. Things are so dangerous we start getting air support on routine convoys. We are an MP company running non-priority missions, and we get F-16s and attack helicopters shadowing us on runs. It's nice having the massive fire power with us, especially the helos weaving in and out over our convoy, waiting to blow the holy hell out of anything that approaches us with aggression. But if we're getting air support taking a bunch of army mechs on routine supply runs, shit is bad.

The pressure is constant, rockets and mortars fired at our base, ambushes and skirmishes on the roads, IEDs. Our Humvees are soft targets. This is before up-armor kits and deflector shields. We do everything we can to try to fortify ourselves, but it's hard to tell if this helps or hurts. We scrounge shit off other vehicles, attach rusty old steel plating from God knows what. We sandbag the insides of our Humvees to help guard against shrapnel, but with all the extra weight, our Humvees top out at 30 miles per hour, which makes us much easier targets to line up for explosions.

A lot of guys in the area are losing arms and legs from hunks of shrapnel, especially turret gunners. We get sent bullshit fixes from America, Kevlar shoulder pads so chunks of shrapnel will just shatter our bones instead of slice our arms off, Kevlar thigh protectors, so at least we won't bleed out of our femoral arteries when we get blown in half. Guys riding inside the Humvees bitch about all the stupid strap-on protections, but I know how vulnerable I am up top, and I'm not proud. I take whatever they don't want and find an open part of my body to strap it to. As we drive down the highway, I look like a gypsy wagon, little pieces of Kevlar bullshit flapping in the breeze all over my body.

I've got a ritual every time we leave camp. Just before we go out the gate, I slap a belt of rounds in my 240 and say to myself, "Today you die. Just do your job." I say it over and over until I accept it. Once I acknowledge there is no tomorrow, no home, no future life, the panic in my chest dies, and I focus where I need to: scanning roadside garbage for IEDs and looking for potential ambush sites.

Our unit is chopped to hell. One platoon runs a detention facility on Camp Ar Ramadi for enemy prisoners. Another couple squads help train Iraqi Police. The rest of us, about twenty Marines, run security missions out on the roads for whoever needs to get from point A to point B. I love serving with these guys. Every one of them is tough and capable, and I've never had faith in anyone like I have faith in these men I work with every day, but I feel how small we are. It's clear to me every time we go out on the road. When the commanding general makes a rule for the region that we need at least double our men and gun trucks to keep running missions, I'm relieved. There is no way we can find the resources to make that happen, so Battalion pulls us off security missions and assigns us to the prison. The better fighters in my group are upset. They want to be out on the road; it makes them feel like Marines. But I'm okay at the brig. It's a job that needs doing, and it increases my odds of keeping my bits and pieces.

After I start at the prison, a massive operation kicks off in Ramadi. After the first battle of Fallujah winds down, Ramadi may be the worst place in the country. From the catwalk around the roof of the prison, I watch nearby artillery shoot illumination rounds over the river, intense magnesium orbs floating in the sky, turning the city from black to an eerie yellow-white. Bursts of gunfire come from multiple locations in the city, probably 2/4 again.

This is a housecleaning operation. People snatched during the fighting are ferried to us in the prison for processing and eventual interrogation. Late in the night, I rotate off the roof as two Marines from 2/4 bring in an Iraqi man and sit him on an open concrete slab near the front gate. He rocks back and forth, moaning, his hands tied behind his back.

"We can't take him like this," our Sergeant says, "He's got to go to the hospital."

The Sergeant from 2/4 looks unimpressed, like he wants to say, "I've got shit to do, you base-living faggots. Take this motherfucker off my hands so I can get back to work."

I walk behind the Iraqi man and see the problem. His hands don't look like hands anymore. The flexi-cuffs on his wrists are cinched so tight, his hands have ballooned up with fluid to about three times their normal size. They look like latex gloves filled with hose water to make water balloons. I cringe. The pain of this man is clear in the way he rocks and groans on the ground, and I'm furious at the Marines who brought him in.

I want to say, "What the fuck are you doing? You can't treat people this way."

But then the younger of the two Marines charges at the Iraqi man on the ground. "I'm going to kill that motherfucker!" he screams, kicking and swinging at the air, while his Sergeant holds him back.

This kid is nineteen or twenty years old like me, but I can see in his eyes that he's gone. His battalion has lost three times as many men as my company even has, and he's been eating and sleeping in the meat grinder for months. I don't know what this Iraqi did. Maybe he sprayed some AK rounds into the kid's friend. Maybe he planted a bomb that blew the kid's team into ragged meat chunks. Maybe he was just in the wrong place at the wrong time and is facing the wrath of an emotionally destroyed young man that only sees more grisly death in his foreseeable future. The wound done to this Iraqi man is egregious, but I've got nothing to say to these Marines.

The Iraqi man is taken to the base hospital. I hope he won't lose his hands. The 2/4 Marines drive back to the city, back to the fight.

WEAPONS OF MASS DESTRUCTION 5: IRAQI RESURGENCE

After the Husayn Kamel incident in 1995, Iraq disposed of most of its stockpiles of chemical and biological weapons, much of it in secret to avoid the further embarrassment of admitting what they'd been doing. At that point, with increased scrutiny from inspectors and with their economy devastated, Iraq simply had no ability to rescale WMD programs, but it didn't stay that way. 1995 to 1997 were survival years for the regime, but in 1998 with all the progress Iraq had made through smuggling and illicit revenue deals, Saddam decided it was time to remove international power from within his own borders. He threw UN inspectors out of Iraq and awaited a response from the US. The US dropped some bombs and said some tough words, but that was it. After absorbing a little bit of new damage, Saddam was freer than he'd been in years.

After 1991, one of Iraq's primary objectives was finding useful ways to stash its scientists. The regime knew that when the time came, Iraq could replace its equipment and materials, but the knowledge and expertise of its scientists would be much more difficult to recreate. If Iraq ever wanted to rebuild the arsenal that would again make it a formidable threat in the region, it was going to have to make sure its scientists stayed in top form. Iraq accomplished this by stashing scientists in places where they could practice related skills without generating hard evidence of wrongdoing.

Iraqi nuclear scientists were given jobs with the Military Industrial Commission, bio-weapons scientists worked in pesticide plants and vaccination centers, and chemical-weapons scientists worked everywhere. Chemical production became a nationwide priority across business, government, and academia. Chemical weapons were by far the most useful to the regime in the past, so it made sense they prioritized chemical knowledge as they were rebuilding.

Universities became particularly useful to the regime as places to stash talent and equipment. Collaborations between academics and the Military Industrial Commission became common. In 1997, the MIC funded just a handful of academic projects. By 2002, they funded over 3200 projects, and 700-800 academics worked regular hours each week at the MIC.

MIC missile experts worked closely with universities, teaching classes and supervising grad research. Long range missiles were a crucial part of Saddam's plans. There's not much point in rebuilding WMD programs if you don't have a delivery system. After Desert Storm, the UN put a distance cap on Iraqi missiles of 150km, which put most major cities of Iraq's enemies out of reach. In

1995, after Husayn Kamel defected, the regime paused work on long-range missiles in order to survive, but after 1998, with UN inspectors out of the country, Iraqi missile research and production ramped up quickly.

Saddam always cultivated multiple ways to reach an objective he wanted. That way if one thing got shut down, the regime's progress wouldn't be shut down. After 1998, Saddam implemented several plans for long-range missiles, including four plans for converting Surface-to-Air Missiles into Surface-to-Surface missiles and at least one plan for a 1000km cruise missile. With the help of technicians and engineers from Russia and several East-bloc countries, Iraq was well on its way to upgrading its missile tech.

Iraq had also begun missile infrastructure upgrades. With Indian help in 2002 and 2003 Iraq built production lines capable of creating 300 tons of solid rocket propellant per year. In 2002, Iraq got outside assistance on carbon fiber production to help decrease missile weight and increase range or payload capacity. The things Iraq wasn't able to produce locally it imported through its smuggling network. Iraq couldn't produce graphite of a quality necessary for missiles, so it imported 7.5 tons for missile plans in 2003 and 2004. Iraq also couldn't produce accelerometers or gyroscopes, so it cut secret deals with multiple sources abroad, including China.

Iraq was on a clear trajectory forward with its missile programs. Its inventory of missile parts in 2000 was 0 warheads, 7 motors, and 13 airframes. In 2002, it was 61 warheads, 57 motors, and 66 airframes. Outside of missiles, Iraq had also developed a long-range UAV that could deliver payloads of biological and chemical weapons at distances over 500 km. This drone was deconstructed and hidden in an aircraft scrapyard when UN inspectors returned to Iraq in early 2003.

So, what was the status of Iraq's WMD infrastructure prior to the US invasion in 2003? A lot has been said about the lack of WMD stockpiles found in Iraq, but very little has been said about the condition Iraq's WMD programs were actually in.

The program furthest away from being dangerous was Iraq's nuclear program. Iraq stopped all nuclear design in 1991, and after most of its nuclear infrastructure was blown up by US bombs or decommissioned by UN inspectors, it never attempted to reconstitute an active nuclear program, but it did make some choices that showed other intentions. After Desert Storm, Iraq's nuclear scientists were told to preserve their plans in their minds and were forbidden from leaving the country. Some nuclear scientists were ordered to hide necessary documents and equipment in their homes, some of which were discovered in 2003. Other scientists worked on secret projects that were hidden from the UN like the rail gun project which allowed scientists to practice skills in plasma physics, electrical engineering, motion physics, high-speed photography, and flash radiography.

In 1999, after Iraq began recovering financially, the regime started passing laws to increase the privileges of nuclear scientists. In 2000, Iraq's nuclear budget increased sharply, and Iraq also imported technology from Romania to establish magnet manufacturing that could be used for gas centrifuges. In 2001, Iraq began purchasing very precise machine tools, types that would eventually be necessary for a functioning nuclear program. In 2002, Saddam ordered the Iraq Atomic Energy Commission and the Military Industrial Commission to begin cooperative projects in physics, machining, and electronics. And from 2001 to 2003, the salaries of Iraq's nuclear scientists increased tenfold. None of this is to say Iraq had an active nuclear program. The war came before any demonstrable progress was made, but obviously, something was going on.

Iraq's biological program was more disturbing. From 1991 to 1996, scientists at the al Hakam biopesticide facility produced large quantities of anthrax that could be dried and used in aerosol distribution systems. This was discovered when Husayn Kamel fled to Jordan in 1995, so al Hakam was destroyed and TABRC became the primary facility for biopesticides. Unsurprisingly, one of Iraq's leading experts in anthrax production worked at TABRC until 2003, and secret fermentation vessels and bio production equipment were later found in an underground storage area.

Iraq used a lot of ingenuity to get around international constraints. Purchase of growth medium internationally was a huge red flag that would result in increased scrutiny of Iraq's bioprograms, so Iraq invented their own growth medium made from milk and corn byproduct. This new Iraqi growth medium had the added advantage of making testing for anthrax virtually impossible. This doesn't prove anything about bioweapons production in Iraq, but it clearly hints at some intent.

Small scale bioweapons research continued under Iraqi Intelligence all the way up until the war. Up to 5 of these bio-labs operated around the greater Baghdad area. Iraqi Intelligence sanitized these sites before US soldiers arrived in 2003, but some lab equipment was discovered hidden at a mosque nearby. Some of these labs likely focused on ricin testing. Ricin is a toxin derived from castor beans sometimes used for killing mice. Iraq maintained a castor oil processing plant they claimed was used for brake fluid, but the waste mash from the facility could also be used to produce ricin. Iraqi Intelligence reportedly used death row prisoners as test subjects. Prisoners were chained to beds, given ricin in various forms, and observed as their organs slowly shut down. Then autopsies were performed by medical staff to record results.

By 2003, most elements of Iraq's bioweapons infrastructure were larger and more advanced than they were before Desert Storm. Iraq maintained all of the necessary components for restarting a large-scale bioweapons program. It also maintained the ability to quickly convert vaccine and biopesticide plants into bio-weapon production. Samarra drug industries, for example, had the assets and personnel to convert from vaccine production to bioweapon production within 4 to 5 weeks. No research or development was necessary. Iraq may not have begun building stockpiles of bioweapons yet, but they were more than capable of making that transition at any time.

Iraq had big plans for its chemical infrastructure. Not only had the regime rebuilt a lot of what was destroyed, but the government had plans for gigantic new chemical production facilities, all of which would run through the Military Industrial Commission. This was an interesting choice for a country "not attempting" to produce chemical weapons.

Iraq had all the necessary basic chemicals on hand to produce sulfur mustard gas on a large scale. In 1999, Saddam asked lead officials how long it would take to rebuild a production line for sulfur mustard. The officials said six months if they weren't willing to sacrifice equipment, a few days if they were.

VX gas was a little more complicated. Iraq had plans to procure thiourea and nitrogen plants which were necessary for Iraq's method of VX production. Iraq had also expanded chlorine production well beyond pre-1991 levels. Chlorine was necessary for a variety of legitimate manufacturing purposes, but the type of chlorine Iraq chose to produce, Thionyl Chloride, was the compound they'd previously used in mass production of sulfur mustard and nerve gas. The former director of Iraq's VX program said the chemicals Iraq was producing showed unequivocally that they intended to produce nerve agents again.

In 1999, Iraqi officials told Saddam that mass producing nerve agent would take about two years. In 2000, Saddam began looking for scientists to open a new VX gas location. In September of 2002, Iraq purchased 900,000 nerve agent antidote auto injectors. This isn't definitive proof of anything, but it suggests a lot.

Iraq's capability to mass-produce munitions for chemical weapons ended with Desert Storm, but Iraq maintained the ability to retool existing factories quickly. It was just a matter of when they chose to do so. In January of 2003, just before the war, UN inspectors found a dozen empty 122mm chemical weapon rocket warheads. This isn't evidence of WMD in Iraq, but all of the component parts were there. It was just a matter of Saddam saying go.

(For more information on what was actually found in Iraq from the thousand plus people on the ground doing the investigation read *The Iraq Survey Group Report*)

WILD DOGS (5)

In Saddam Hussein's Iraq, there were few prohibitions on the upper class. A yellow sash was given to some members of government which granted them amnesty from almost any crime. Children of the rich and powerful did what they wanted, and no police officer would dare interfere. No one was a better example of this than Uday Hussein.

Uday made huge amounts of money from a variety of illicit sources, kickbacks on imports, sale of black-market whiskey and cigarettes, Asian prostitutes, theft—during the invasion of Kuwait he stole so much property he made 100 million dollars from selling looted cars alone. Much of his money came from exploitation of farmers. Uday owned land in all Iraq's most fertile regions, and his peasant farmers were required to buy all seed, fertilizer, and machinery from him at exorbitant prices and sell their crops to him at a fraction of their value, which Uday would then resell in Baghdad for ten times what he paid to merchants who were forced to buy because he was the President's son.

Uday's life was debauchery. He denied himself nothing. As the Iraqi people starved from heavy sanctions,

Uday had gaudy palaces and apartments staffed by butlers, drivers, pastry chefs, bakers, personal fishermen, personal shoppers, lion tamers, etc. He threw lavish parties with hundreds of exotic foods, cooks lined up like toy soldiers, tables twenty yards long of sauteed duck breast, turkey with poultry liver sauce, saddle of rabbit, three kinds of caviar, lobster tails, oysters on the half shell, French pate, duck with plums and kiwi, smoked salmon, salmon tartar, asparagus salad with plucked herbs and shrimp, Italian Parma ham, fine cuts of beef in luxurious sauces, and little carrot and radish twists cut to look like rosebuds.

Uday was notoriously jealous of anyone having anything he didn't and would fly into a rage over any perceived slight. If someone wore fine clothing or a watch Uday didn't have, he'd obsess about it all evening. Though he owned hundreds of Maseratis, Ferraris, Porches, Jaguars, and Mercedes, he had a law passed banning Ferrari imports so he could be the only person in the country to drive one. Uday always drove at high speeds. Once, when a man dared pass him, he had his guards blockade the road and pull the man out of his car. He threw him in prison and tortured him for six months. If anyone ever looked at a girl Uday was currently with, he risked being tortured and killed. He once sliced a girl's tongue up the center at a party and threw her out of a helicopter for claiming to be his girlfriend. He killed a girl in a club in front of dozens of people for daring to call his father old. He sold his girlfriend one night to pay a gambling debt then killed her later for having sex with another man.

Uday was meticulous about his grooming, spent hours in front of the mirror changing clothes, accessorizing, plucking the outline of his beard with tweezers. When Uday and his men took over a club at night, all rules were off. He'd throw out any man better dressed than him, beat men that dared dance in his presence, pull out a revolver and shoot up ceilings, wall panels, and chandeliers. He'd usually show up with eight to ten girls that his men procured for him and want the floor alone with them. First, he'd watch them move, leer at their swaying hips and breasts, and shout obscenities. Then like a graceless animal he'd throw himself onto them, pull them in, lick them, and grind and sway to the music.

Part of Uday's daily ritual was afternoon rape. Almost every afternoon, he'd hunt universities and hangouts for fresh young women. If he failed in his hunt, he'd get his men to intervene. If that didn't work, he'd just have girls kidnapped, sometimes three or four at a time, coercing them into group sex. After rapes, he insisted on paying women like whores.

Five nights a week, two dozen girls would be brought to Uday at the Baghdad Boat Club by his procurers. They'd dance and drink then he'd line them up and choose one or two to join him in his bedroom. Often friends bought favors from him by giving him female family members. He liked to have animals watch him having sex. He kept dozens of monkeys in a room at the boat club because he said he liked having them watch him deflower virgins.

Uday had many methods of punishing people that displeased him. He was a creature who loved pain and was always searching for new tortures and victims to try them on. Uday had private prisons in his palaces where he kept victims. He used welder's torches, pliers, scalpels, pillories, and iron maidens. He'd throw people in cages with his monkeys to be clawed and bitten. He'd throw people alive to tigers to be mauled and eaten. He'd peel skin, burn with acid, and leave people in tiny boxes in his walls for months. He liked tortures that were a process, like beating a person on one side of their body, stopping for medical tests, then continuing beating that side until kidney failure; or whipping a person bloody with electrical cords, letting the wounds fester, then whipping the pus-filled wounds again. A method he learned from his father was Thallium poisoning. Thallium is a soft metal used in rat poison that gives humans symptoms like Parkinson's. In the first 48 hours, the victim has bouts of diarrhea, nausea, and vomiting. Within a few days, they experience convulsions, muscle wasting, loss of reflexes, loss of control of sphincters, hair loss, numbness, disturbance of heart rhythm, headaches, dementia, psychosis, and eventually coma and death.

Uday's men were like extensions of himself, full of viciousness and perversion. Not only did they constantly procure and kidnap women, they'd often join in on rapes if a girl resisted. Uday made a point of sleeping with Iraqi beauty queens. One girl who was 15 and a virgin declined when Uday called her and said he wanted meet her, so Uday had his men abduct her. He and his men kept her in a room and took turns raping her for days. When they finally sent her back home, he and his men spread rumors about her, saying she slept with any man she saw and that she begged them for the opportunity to let her service them. The girl's father, outraged by the disgrace to his family, killed his own daughter, then went to find Saddam Hussein to complain. Uday intercepted him, and he was never seen again.

One of Uday's favorite sports was raping newlyweds. If a bride disappeared just after the ceremony, and the doors were blocked by armed men, there was a fair bet she was already pinned down somewhere with Uday sprawled on top of her. It was a good time for the groom to pull a pistol out of his waistband and shoot himself in the head.

In one instance, Uday's men dragged an eighteen-year-old bride to a guardhouse on his property where his men ripped off her wedding dress and locked her inside, sobbing. When Uday arrived, he was angry that she didn't come willingly, and the girl's sobs quickly turned into shrieks followed by silence and men carrying a body out of the room in a blood-soaked sheet. The maid who cleaned the room afterward said she found chunks of hair and skin all over the place. That's what happened to women who resisted.

One day, after duck hunting near Habbaniyah, Uday saw a couple of smitten newlyweds walking hand-in-hand near his hotel, a young woman and her husband who had been a Captain at the Iranian front during the Iran-Iraq war. Uday found the girl attractive, so he stopped his motorcycle and shouted at her. The couple attempted to run, but Uday caught the girl by her arm and pulled her from her husband. When the Captain lunged at Uday, he was overwhelmed by Uday's men, and beaten and restrained while Uday dragged his wife upstairs to the seventh floor of the hotel. Once inside the room, Uday offered the girl champagne. When she refused, he barked at her to undress. When she begged him not to dishonor her, Uday slapped his belt across her face, then cinched it tight around her neck. She gasped and fell to the floor. He released her throat and dragged her by her hair to the bed. She continued struggling, turning away as he forced her thighs apart. He beat her face until her cries got soft and blood poured from her nose. When the girl couldn't fight anymore, Uday slid inside her and gasped and groaned until completion. After Uday pulled up his pants and left the room, the new bride walked to the balcony door, slid it open, and threw herself to the street seven stories below.

The girl's husband screamed, "You murderers! You animals!" He was apprehended and later executed by firing squad for the crime of insulting the president. This was Saddam Hussein's Iraq.

It's always been strange to me back in The States when I hear people talk about Iraq like it was some prosperous, peaceful country that the US destroyed out of selfish evil. Maybe that was part of it, but Iraq was a depraved nightmare for a large portion of the population. It's true that some people did very well under the old regime, but what about everyone else? What about the nation of human cattle under absolute control and constant surveillance waiting to be cut up and devoured by perverts and psychos?

A little Palestinian refugee girl selling flowers walked into a hotel. Uday spotted her and her mother and led them to a back room, taking the girl for himself and giving the mother to his bodyguards. Both bodies were found in the street the next morning. A fifteen-year-old deaf girl walking down the street was pulled into a building where Uday raped her and warned her not to tell anyone what happened. When Uday's guards later saw her gesticulating in a hotel, sobbing, trying to get help, they grabbed her, dragged her to a forest, gang-raped her and buried her body. The list of victims goes on and on.

(For a deeper look at Uday Hussein from someone who knew him, check out *I Was Saddam's Son* or *The Devil's Double* by Latif Yahia)

RAMADI DETENTION FACILITY

"Take off your clothes," I say. The Iraqi man takes off his pants and shirt but leaves his underwear.

"All of it! Take it all off!" I say, motioning to his underwear.

"Please, mister."

"Take off your fucking clothes!"

The man takes off his underwear and stands in front of me.

I motion to him to turn around and stand against the wall.

He covers his penis with his hands, looks at the floor, and says, "Please, mister, no."

"What do you mean, no?" I grab his arm, turn him around and push him toward the wall.

He covers his ass with his hands and keeps begging.

"Wait. Do you think I'm going to rape you?"

He's a grimy forty-year-old man covered in body hair. It never occurred to me he'd fear me that way.

"Why the hell do you think I'm going to rape you?"

"He knows he's your type, dog." Garcia says, chuckling, from behind the desk.

"Fuck you," I say, starting to laugh.

I don't know Arabic for "I'm not going to rape you," so I ease up on commands and hand the guy an orange jumpsuit so he can cover himself up.

This isn't an isolated incident. Many Iraqi men expect us to rape them when we strip them down for processing into the prison. Our translator has lived in Baghdad his whole life, so I ask him if he can explain why this is happening. He tells me Saddam used to have male prisoners raped to make them more compliant, so these guys expect us to do the same thing.

It's a strange feeling having grown men afraid of us this way, and some guys don't handle it very well. One squad gets their biggest guy—6'5, 250lbs—to walk in the room after a prisoner is naked. The Marine looks the prisoner up and down, gives him dirty sort of chuckle, then orders him to turn around and put his hands on the wall. Sometimes, the big guy will snap on a pair of latex gloves while the prisoner watches for effect. That's where the joke ends. The team goes about their normal business of searching the prisoner's clothes and giving him a jumpsuit.

★★★

Power is a strange thing. It's a vital force that makes people believe they can accomplish things. The more powerful a person feels, the more they think about and pursue ambitions and desires. Feeling powerful is an important part of the process of accomplishment. But it's also very dark. The more powerful a person feels, the more consumed they get with themselves and their own lives. They start to lose the ability to think about other peoples' perspectives and how their actions might affect them. If power is enduring, it can warp a person's mind, inflating their sense of self-importance to a point of no return. The more reinforced and stable the power is, the stronger the warping becomes. With enough power over enough time, a person can become fully delusional, living a life so intently focused on their own desires and ambitions that they lose the ability to recognize the humanity of other people. People become nothing more than objects to be used, and their suffering becomes inconsequential. At the extreme end, the powerful person becomes so important in their own mind that the moral good of satisfying their own desire outweighs any pain or horror they might inflict on people surrounding them. This is how you end up with a guy like Saddam Hussein, and why a guy like Saddam at the end of his life could simply brush off the atrocities he committed like they were nothing. He legitimately believed they were nothing. There's a real darkness that comes with power. It's easy for people to get swallowed by it and do things that can't be undone.

In Ramadi Detention Facility, most of our abuses of power are petty. It's little things like telling prisoners "Eyes down" if they look at a guard or making them slurp down cold MREs for their meals. On shower day we take prisoners out of their cells two at a time and walk them to a plywood shower box outside the front gate. The prisoners strip down, step in the box, and a guard hits the water. If he thinks the prisoners are moving too slow, he'll yell at them to hurry up. If they're still moving too slow, he'll cut the water whether a prisoner is still covered in suds or not. Sometimes the prisoner will look at him with dejection, like "Come on, man. Don't do this to me," and the guard might have mercy and give a few more seconds of rinse time. Sometimes, he'll say, "Fuck you. Get dressed."

★★★

One aspect of power that makes it treacherous is disinhibition. People with power, especially stable power, are more likely to indulge themselves in things that are depraved because they don't have the same fear of what people will do or say to them in response.

Abu Ghraib was the central prison in Iraq, the place where we sent guys who were killing Americans, blowing up Iraqis, and conducting insurgent operations. I'm not sure what it is in human nature, but once we believe someone is our enemy, we start believing cruel uses of power are justified in dealing with them. Likewise, once we believe someone is guilty, we feel justified in exercising power to punish them for their actions. The men imprisoned at Abu Ghraib were both "enemy" and "guilty", and it didn't take long for Abu Ghraib to become a free-for-all of abuse—naked prisoners dragged around on leashes or attacked by military dogs in hallways, naked prisoners stacked on top of each other or forced to roll around in their own shit, prisoners blindfolded and beaten, prisoners hung against the walls by their hands tied behind their backs, prisoners tied up and sandwiched between military stretchers while guards sat on them or put weights on their backs, prisoners having their fingers or genitals attached to electrodes, prisoners forced to masturbate publicly in front of female American soldiers.

None of this is probably stuff these soldiers would've done at home with their buddies. But in Abu Ghraib, with the disinhibition that comes from having power and the dark pull that comes from feeling justified in abusing your enemy, this is what became normal.

★★★

Power affects different people in different ways. When power over other people is mixed with feelings of powerlessness in your own situation, you can get weird results. Murton is good Marine and a guy I like a lot, but he has a strange response to working at the prison. He learns two Arabic phrases—"Hello, my name is Doctor Satan," and "Are you pregnant?"—then walks around to fat prisoners introducing himself and pretending to rub their bellies and ask about their babies. He gets really into it, like he has deep concern for their unborn children. The first couple times I see it, I can't help laughing. It's such a strange thing to do, and he's so committed to it. Prisoners have no idea how to respond. They know he's making fun of them, but he's so earnest that they can't really be sure he's not just crazy. Usually, a couple skinny prisoners chuckle at the fat one, Murton walks away, and everyone goes about their day.

★★★

When you combine power factors like intense focus on self, seeing others as objects, disinhibition, and feeling justified in handing out punishment, you usually end up with very dark results. From a young age, Uday Hussein knew he had really no limits on his power. He could control peoples' pain, control their income, control their bodies, and control whether they lived or died. He became obsessed with using his power to indulge any perversion and became something beyond a predator, a man who whipped servants hundreds of times for serving food on the wrong type of tray, a man who abducted young mothers to suck from their nipples because he believed in the restorative powers of mother's milk, a man who kept people alive in tiny cramped boxes in the walls of his torture palace so he could experiment on them later, a man who would order hundreds of people at parties to take off their clothes and have orgies or face gang-rape and likely torture and death from his guards.

While Uday took corruption to the extreme, he wasn't a unique character in the world. Similar types of actions are frequently found among people with unfettered power. Pick a regime around the world that openly subjugates its people, and you'll find similar behavior among the ruling elite, their children, and probably the institutions of force that maintain the hierarchy.

★★★

Power doesn't always lead to corruption. People who have strong internalized moral identities sometimes aren't affected the same way. Mixon is one of those guys. Nothing changes who he is or how he treats people. He goes from cell to cell each day in his humble way talking and laughing with prisoners while he collects garbage or fills water bottles. Prisoners can feel right away he's different, that he genuinely doesn't hate them, and that no part of him wants to control or demean them. As he asks them questions in severely broken Arabic, they draw unto him like mayflies to a porchlight. They laugh and smile and help him pronounce words. He takes their corrections without any spite or hubris and asks more. I walk with Mixon a couple of shifts before he gets ordered to stop. His interactions with prisoners are unlike anything I experience in Ramadi. They feel totally human.

★★★

Our prison isn't Uday Hussein's torture palace, and it isn't Abu Ghraib, but it's plenty dark in its own way.

As summer wears on, more operations run in Ramadi, and more people are brought into our prison. What used to be one or two men per cell becomes seven or eight. The sleeping mats get so filthy from months of human grime and sweat they have to be thrown away. Prisoners spend all day and night on concrete floors.

Our prison was never meant to be this full. It was never meant to be a prison at all. It was a retrofitted Iraqi military building with no plumbing or running water, meaning none of the cells have toilets.

With the influx of prisoners, feeding, watering, and taking prisoners to interrogation, takes most of the day. We can only take each prisoner outside their cells to use the bathroom once a day. Showers are out of the question. Because prisoners can't go to the bathroom when they need to, they start pissing in their water bottles and shitting in MRE wrappers. The smell of unwashed bodies, MRE garbage, and human sewage in the summer heat is so thick it coats your lungs. We can't handle all these people, and there's a backlog with our interrogators. Some prisoners don't even get to talk to an interrogator for a month. They're stuck in these filthy cells without knowing why they're here or how long they're being held, and they beg and plead with guards to let them talk to anyone in power. But there's nothing we can do.

It's regularly 120 degrees outside and nothing is air conditioned, so the cells are sweltering hot. Some prisoners get so dehydrated they piss brown into their water bottles. I try to refill bottles as much as I can, but the more water guys drink, the more they have to piss. And since it's physically impossible to take everyone to the porta john when they need to go, they piss more in their water bottles. Our supply trucks keep getting blown up on the highways, so we can't always get more water bottles in, and with fewer and fewer bottles to refill, prisoners get more and more dehydrated, and their piss turns deeper and deeper shades of brown.

Any spare moment I have, I pass out food, pick up garbage, refill water from five-gallon jugs, or take men to the bathroom. Other Marines do the same. Day in and day out, we do what we can, but there's nothing for it. There are just too many of them.

★★★

I'm heading to Abu Ghraib tonight. Transporting prisoners is the only time I leave base now. Out front, prisoners walk up a ladder one by one into the back of a transport truck. After they're seated and packed tight, hands tied behind their backs and sandbags pulled over their heads, I sit in the center of the truck bed with my loaded rifle, and we roll out.

Most of these prison runs happen at night now. This gives the security team the advantage of night vision and thermals on their heavy weapons. I watch the machine gunners go through their preparations at the gate. Part of me misses it. There was an honor to being a machine gunner, preparing yourself mentally, loading your weapon, getting ready for the fight. I miss the wind blowing in my face and the feel of protecting other Marines. Now, I just manage human cargo.

As we start up the highway toward Abu Ghraib, the prisoner nearest me squirms, shaking his head back and forth to loosen the sandbag. I watch him for a while as he spits and thrashes. He's panicking a little, like the sandbag is suffocating him. Using his lips and jaw, he slowly works the bag up his face, first uncovering his chin, then his lower lip, then the bag rests on his upper lip. If he'd stop there, I'd let it slide. If he needs to breathe, he needs to breathe. But he doesn't stop. He keeps working the bag up his face, gets it up to his nostrils. I can't let it go any further, can't have the bag fly off in the wind and have this guy recognize our position. I lean over, grab the edge of the sandbag, and forcefully rip down. The Iraqi man whimpers.

"Shut the fuck up."

When he starts spitting and squirming again, working the bag up his face, I pull down harder than before.

"Kif. Stop moving."

He whimpers again but settles down. There's nothing he can do. Next stop Abu Ghraib.

★★★

Acres is an even-tempered dude, never raises his voice, always talks with a kind southern drawl. Taking a line of prisoners to the porta john one day, he snaps, throws one against the fence and then jumps on him. Kowalchek steps in, pulls Acres off, and tells him to go relax somewhere.

I don't know exactly why Acres loses it. I've never seen him act like that before. Maybe it's power. Maybe he's been lugging too many water jugs from cell to cell. Maybe it's the damn heat that never stops. Maybe it's making two dollars an hour in a place where shit goes boom so often you can set your watch by it. Maybe it's being trapped inside these walls for months, enemy in every direction, many months to go. Maybe it's the fermented-MRE-garbage-sweaty-unwashed-body-shit-in-wrappers-dehydrated-piss-smell of the prison. Maybe it's stripping down grown men and watching them beg not to be raped. Maybe it's listening to men plead every day for help and knowing there's nothing you can do for them. Maybe it's seeing a darkness in the world beyond anything you expected and knowing you can't unsee it, knowing you'll never be the same.

★★★

When extreme cases of abuse happen, like at Abu Ghraib, people wonder how all those soldiers could have just gone along with it. Why didn't anyone stop it? Here are a few reasons:

1) Grotesque things happen every day in a war zone. Over time, they just affect you less.
2) Soldiers frequently have to exercise power on other people. Eventually, that feeling of power feels normal and you lose inhibitions you'd normally have in a different environment.
3) People play roles. When you are assigned the role of prison guard, living up to the role influences your actions. You start to think about what a prison guard should do in this situation, not what a normal human should do. Prisons are places of punishment. The role of a prison guard is to enforce the role of the prison.
4) When you're dealing with enemy, you don't think of them as human beings similar to you. You think of them as evil savages whose only objective is to destroy you. If your fear or hatred grows strong enough, your perspective can warp to the point where you believe abusing your enemies is a positive good.
5) The power of conformity is strong and can cause people to engage in immoral behavior even if almost every member of the group privately disagrees. Military structure is particularly susceptible to this because of its strong hierarchy and pressure to obey. This can allow for dark

practices to take root with limited pushback from the group. Once these practices become normalized, they take on a life of their own. Group members will rationalize them, bend their wills toward them, and unconsciously enforce them. That's just how people are wired. Many large-scale atrocities can be traced back to this process of group normalization.

One of the interesting things about Abu Ghraib was the role of women in the abuse. Usually when we think about atrocities, we assume it's men. But at Abu Ghraib there were several female soldiers involved. The weird sexual humiliation stuff was done by female prison guards, and the person in charge of the whole operation was a female general.

I've never been sure what to make of this, but I think it has something to do with conformity. The culture of the military is toughness, and when you're in a war zone, that culture becomes even stronger. If you're a male in that situation, there is constant pressure to prove you are tough enough to do the job. If you're a female in that situation, the pressure to appear tough might be even stronger because the males in your unit will automatically doubt you. That's just the way it is. In a place like Abu Ghraib, where soldiers had tremendous power over prisoners, and where a culture of abuse had already been established, it might make sense that female soldiers would try to prove themselves to the group by showing they could be just as cruel or crueler than the men around them. Of course, they could have just been sociopaths.

★★★

It's strange looking back on Ramadi Detention Facility. It seems more dramatic now than it did then. I had grown so accustomed to the roughness of life, I'm not sure I even noticed a lot of it. And the stuff I did notice didn't seem that bad at the time. Many of us had been just as filthy as the prisoners at some point during our deployments. Many of us had experienced lack of food, water, and dignity. Many of us felt trapped, like our lives were completely out of our hands. I remember actually being jealous sometimes when rockets and mortars hit base. Our prisoners slept under concrete. We slept under canvas. I don't think we were the best judges of human suffering at the time.

The only part of the job that was somewhat uplifting was letting prisoners go, but even that was weirdly emotionless. When we released prisoners, we brought them to the gate of Camp Ramadi. Underneath the protection of machine gun nests pointing out toward the city, we'd cut their ties and uncover their eyes. I'd usually say, "Assalamu Alaikum" (peace be unto you), holding my hand over my heart. It was an empty gesture, but it was all I had. Even if we spoke the same language, I'm not sure what I'd say, "So, hey…uh…sorry we snatched you off the street and made you wallow like animals for a few weeks. The good news is we don't think you're terrorists anymore…so…good luck with the war. I hope you and your family don't die."

After cutting the men free, they'd usually hesitate for a few seconds, unsure of what to do and not wanting to make a wrong move. Not having the words in Arabic to tell them they were free to go, I'd motion toward the city until they got my meaning. They'd take a couple cautious steps and look back to make sure it wasn't a trick. I'd wave. They'd wave, and we'd all go about our day.

SHADOW MAN

There's a room of confiscated weapons at Ramadi prison from raids in the city, AKs, RPKs, AKMs, old WWII Russian rifles, RPGs, and stacks of land mines. None of that interests me, but I'm fascinated by the stuff that isn't factory made, PVC pipe rocket launchers, crude pistols chunked together in machine shops, oven timer and random machine part IED detonators. I'm a Marine. Our unofficial mantra is "adapt and overcome." This homemade shit is impressive.

I'm a decent fighter at this point, good enough that guys can trust me to do my part. I won't flinch, and I won't run. When I'm afraid, I'll choke my fear down deep in my gut so my brain can function, but I still need weapons, ammo, and a group of equally capable guys around me to be formidable. What am I without that?

A strange respect creeps into my heart for the guys we are fighting, respect for their ingenuity, respect for their ability to make do with what they have. If I wouldn't get my head sawn off or play the starring role in the next internet torture video, I wouldn't mind taking a class with them for a summer. It might be fun to learn their skillset, learn how to fight an enemy when you're technologically and logistically outmatched.

"Welcome to Club Jihad, sir, how many in your party?"

"Just one."

"And how long will you be staying?"

"Not sure yet, what kinds of courses do you offer?"

"Our most popular course is "America: That Great Whore!"

"Nah. Philosophy's not really my thing. You got any practical application courses?"

"How about 'Take Your Time, Record Their Screams.'"

"Eeegh, I don't know if I have the stomach for that. I grew up on Care Bears and Disney movies."

"Are you sure you're in the right place, sir?"

"What do you have on guerilla warfare?"

"Currently our biggest seller is 'BOOM! A Guide to Insurgency.'"

"That's more like what I'm looking for. Do you accept American currency?"

"How dare you ask me that! The suggestion sickens me."

"I'm sorry. I meant no offense."

"Just kidding. We take US dollars all the time. Here's your Club Jihad face shroud. Make sure you always wear it on campus, or you might get gutted on the way to your car."

What would I do if I had to fight a guerilla war? Sharpen sticks to poke at tanks? Stand beside my buddies waving our "Don't Tread on Me" flags hoping our love of freedom will stop hellfire missiles from attack helicopters? The only real option is to fight from the shadows, make your enemy feel unsafe every time he travels a back road. Make him bleed a little at a time until the prize is no longer worth the pain. That's what the insurgents are trying to do. I hate them for it. I hate IEDs. I hate rockets. I hate feeling unsafe on every stretch of road I ever travel, but I get the strategy. It's what they've got, so it's what they use.

I'm not an idealist. I don't foresee a world where Marines and Jihadists slurp ice cream cones together and feed baby otters at the zoo. And some of the men we're fighting are worse than animals, aiming to cause as much fear and suffering as possible, zero respect for human life or pain. But I will say this. The Marine part of me will always respect an underdog with the tenacity to fight off a superior enemy. If the situations were reversed, I'd fight just as hard and dirty as my conscience allowed.

LAST RIDE

Our replacements have come. Our time here is done. We load up in trucks and head for the gate. There's no fanfare, no goodbyes, no nostalgia. In a couple weeks, no one in camp will even remember we were here.

Our final convoy to Al Asad Air Base is an hour and a half northwest of Ramadi. We're the cargo of this convoy, guarded by Marines on trucks with machine guns. Maybe it's the warm air and diesel exhaust. Maybe it's being well protected by other Marines. Maybe it's just the last two years finally catching up with me, but as the city, the Euphrates, and the palm groves slowly fade into the desert, all sharpness leaves my body. I struggle for a few miles to keep my eyes open, but it's a futile battle. I fall into a deep sleep sitting upright in the back of a seven ton with my rifle in hand. No one says anything to me. They just let me sleep. My squad leader shakes me awake an hour and a half later at the gate of Al Asad.

When we go through customs, the guy searching me is someone I knew in MP school. He's gotten fat since I last saw him.

"How you been, man?" I say, as he kicks through my gear.

"Bored as fuck," he says.

"Not much happen around here?"

"We had a mortar hit a couple months ago."

"One mortar?"

"Yeah. And it wasn't close to anything, just way out in the desert."

"Hmm."

"How about you, man? How you been?"

"Ready to get out of here."

"I hear that, brother."

When our C130s to Kuwait land, we load up in their bellies, sandwiched around the sides of cargo pallets in the center. It's sweltering hot, so the crew leaves that back hatch open as long as possible for air flow. When the C130s take off, they don't fly in a straight line but circle higher and higher, avoiding potential rocket fire. As the plane rumbles its way into the sky and Western Iraq recedes below, Doc pukes into his helmet. I feel like doing the same but hold it in for now.

THE DEATH OF SADDAM

On March 16, 1988, waves of Iraqi warplanes flew low over Halabja, Iraq, a Kurdish town near the border of Iran. Instead of bombs, the planes dropped silver canisters, and yellow, white, and pink clouds wafted through the streets—VX, Sarin, and Mustard gas. In minutes, thousands of Kurds writhed in the streets, men, women, elders, children, almost all civilians. Five thousand people died that day in Halabja. Another ten thousand were injured with scorched lungs, blistered skin, blindness, swollen breasts and testicles, or bleeding kidneys. Before the bodies were even buried, Iraqi soldiers in chemical suits showed up with bulldozers and raised the city to the ground. This was part of Al-Anfal, Saddam's "solution" to the Kurdish problem in Iraq.

The Kurds are a fighting society, proud mountain people, fiercely attached to their homes, their values and traditions, and the idea of an independent Kurdish state. In 1975, the Kurds were crushed by the Baath Party and hundreds of thousands were rounded up and forced to relocate to desert concentration camps called "Victory Villages," but they didn't quit, they waited. When the Iran-Iraq war put Hussein's regime on its heels, the Kurds expanded their control in the North. In 1983, members of the Kurdistan Democratic Party led by Massoud Barzani, helped Iran capture Hajj Omran, an Iraqi border post. In response, the Iraqi army rounded up 8,000 Kurdish males and drove them to the southern desert never to be seen again. When loved ones inquired to the fate of their husbands and sons, the regime's reply was, "They were severely punished and went to hell."

With the Iran-Iraq war winding down in 1988, Saddam Hussein could finally deal with the Kurdish problem his way. He appointed his cousin, later nicknamed Chemical Ali, to sweep clean the North. Gas attacks were a cost-effective, low manpower method of accomplishing this goal. Sixty-seven towns and villages were hit with chemical weapons dropped from planes and helicopters. The results were severe.

Al-Anfal went well beyond chemical attacks. After the gas, 60,000 troops supported by tanks, swept north, soldiers arriving at night, rousting people from their beds, separating families, herding women, children, and elderly into camps, collecting males between twelve and fifty and trucking them to southern Iraq to be lined up and shot by firing squads then buried in mass graves. According to an old Kurdish proverb, "The male is born to be slaughtered." During Al-Anfal, 180,000 Kurds were killed. 70 percent were males between fifteen and fifty, primarily non-combatants.

Al-Anfal's objective was to completely destroy the Kurdish way of life. Thousands of villages were razed by bulldozers and explosives. Entire cities were leveled by napalm and bombs. Soldiers slaughtered livestock and sterilized fields and orchards with chemical defoliants. Ninety percent of Kurdish villages and more than twenty towns and cities were completely destroyed and left desolate. People were arrested, deported, summarily executed, or burned alive. Some surrendered and were killed anyway. Hundreds of thousands were forcibly relocated to appalling camps. Hundreds of thousands more fled to Turkey and Iran triggering a massive humanitarian crisis.

★★★

Saddam Hussein's list of accomplishments as leader of Iraq is long. He built massive monuments to his own glory while his people starved. He bankrupted one of the most oil-rich countries in the world through stupid wars. He threw away the lives of a million young men in those same wars and left millions more crippled and broken. He drained the greatest system of marshes in Western Asia, forcing hundreds of thousands of Marsh Arabs out of their ancestral homes, ending a civilization which had lasted thousands of years, and devasting a crucial ecosystem. He presided over state-sanctioned genocide of the Kurds. He oversaw constant terror campaigns to suppress the Shia, kept them like cattle crammed in cells, murdered their leaders, hung their boys from streetlamps and holy shrines. He created a police state that disappeared a million people and a military whose main job was suppressing its own population. He murdered, tortured, and raped at will. He brainwashed children, supported thugs, and somehow raised a son who was even worse than he was.

It's hard to quantify the amount of suffering inflicted on the Iraqi people by Saddam Hussein. It almost doesn't seem real that one man could do so much damage. What brought it home to me was a grey-bearded man two weeks into the invasion. I was standing in the middle of a city street at dusk when the old man shuffled toward my position. He stopped in front of me, grabbed my hand, and brought it to his cheek. I wasn't sure how to respond. I looked around for my team to help me, but they were busy with other civilians. I wanted to pull away, to get the old man off me, but there was such pain in his eyes.

When the old man spoke, his voice was strangled. He could barely get out the words. I had no idea what he was saying, but he kept holding my hand and started sobbing. A young Iraqi man who spoke English approached us.

"I'm sorry," I said to the young man, "I have no idea what he's saying."

"He says that many years ago, men from the government came to his house in the middle of the night. He had a son and a daughter then. They were the reason for his life. The men from the government tied up his children, put them in a truck, and drove into the night. There was nothing he could do to stop them. He never saw either of his children again."

The old man pulled my hand to the wetness of his cheek. How could I respond to this? I was a teenager barely out of bootcamp. This man's children were likely tortured and murdered then disposed of like trash in the desert, and he couldn't even grieve for them for fear that someone would see his grief as dissent and report him to the Mukhabarat. His government was so brutal, he had to seek comfort from a kid in an invading army who couldn't grow a beard yet.

Not knowing what I could possibly do to comfort this man, I let him sob against my hand and silently watched his boney frame shake until the young man gently grabbed his shoulders and led him away.

★★★

I watched an American scholar on TV say Saddam's regime was on its last legs, that revolution was inevitable if we hadn't intervened. I have no idea where he was getting this from. Saddam Hussein was like the boogeyman. He was everywhere, on every street corner, in every shadow, in every person you passed on the street. And he wasn't losing strength. He was gaining it. He had beaten the United States politically when he not only survived their sanctions but subverted the entire international system. He had turned the UN security council and most of its permanent members toward his will. He had survived insurrection and assassination attempts from his own people time and again and had crushed all resistance. Nothing could get rid of that man. At a certain point, when all your fighters are dead or in prison, who's left to rebel? Who's going to fight the man who has proven over and over that he sees and hears all and that no crime or brutality is beyond him? Who's going to fight the man who has rewritten history, programmed your kids, and turned your family members against you? Who's going to fight the man who makes people disappear, sheds blood with impunity on your streets and in your homes, humiliates your women, and uses the pain of your children as leverage against you? How do you fight when your enemy controls all force, all money, all information, all industry, and all means of governance, and you can't even run because you need an exit visa, and an exit visa is controlled by the man you're running from?

I wish I could've asked that scholar those questions. It frustrates me sometimes watching these people talk.

★★★

On July 22nd, 2003, Uday Hussein was killed in Mosul alongside his brother Qusay in a gunfight with the 101st Airborne and Task Force 20. When I read that the boys were dead, I was relieved. I was sitting on post under camo netting in 130-degree heat reading the Stars and Stripes. I set the paper down, put an extra fat wad of chew in my lip, and leaned back, thinking about how strange it was to feel grateful for the deaths of other human beings. I didn't know Uday Hussein, never had the misfortune of crossing him in my life, but I knew the world was a better place with him out of it.

★★★

Saddam Hussein was defiant to the end. At his trial, when a member of the audience jeered down at him from a balcony overlooking the proceedings, Saddam's attorney became outraged and requested the judge do something about the crowd.

Saddam's response to his lawyer: "A lion does not care if a monkey in a tree is laughing."

Even at his execution, rope around his neck, Saddam showed no fear, but sneered at the men in the crowd celebrating his impending death.

"You call yourself men?" Saddam said. "Is this the bravery of Arabs?'

"You have destroyed us," A man in the crowd shouted. "You have killed us!"

"I helped you survive," Saddam said. "Iraq is nothing without me."

The officiating officer at the proceedings begged Saddam to stop fighting the crowd and prepare for death.

Resolved as ever, still betraying no fear, Saddam said his final prayer, "I bear witness that there is no god but Allah, and Muhammad is his messenger."

The trap door opened beneath Saddam's feet. The rope jerked tight.

AMERICAN BARBECUE FLIES

It's a warm summer evening in my sister's back yard in Milwaukee, a good evening for a barbeque. I sit at a patio table with my parents, sisters, and brother-in-law sipping beers and talking about the normal shit people talk about: work, kids, types of fruit salads.

My sister's husband pulls a pile of meat off the grill and places it on a plate in the center of the table. Two flies land on the plate of meat and hop from hotdog to kabob to chicken breast. My heart rate rises as I watch the filthy bastards rub their forelegs together and drag their dirty feet all over our meat. My sister asks me a question. I don't hear her. She asks again.

"Oh, sorry. What did you say?" but I'm still not listening. My hands move slowly toward the meat plate, toward the flies.

Flies have a fatal flaw. They get spooked by quick moving objects even if those objects aren't going to hit them. I move my hands into position, one on each side of the fly about half an inch above the hotdog it rests on. When I clap my hands together, the fly will see the motion and spring upward to escape, right between my slapping hands. I've killed hundreds of flies this way, but right before I slap my hands together, I realize dead fly on the meat pile will probably gross everyone out, so instead of slapping, I kind of slap and kind of pull at the same time, trying direct the fly body away from the meat. The result is too slow. The fly jumps safely over to a kabob and rubs its filthy legs together without a care in the world.

Enjoy your victory. You won't get away from me again.

My focus increases. My eyes flit back and forth with the movement of the fly. My hands wait for the perfect moment.

Land on that hot dog again, I dare you. Some lazy American barbecue fly isn't getting away from me twice.

My brother-in-law brushes the fly away and covers the meat with a clear glass bowl. I look at him, somewhat perplexed, like "What the hell, man? I was going to kill that?"

"These flies are kind of annoying, huh?" he says.

The flies crawl through a crack beneath the glass bowl and crawl on the meat again.

Fuck.

I want to rip the bowl off the meat pile and give these flies the deaths they have coming. I want to feel their little bodies pop between my hands and scrape their yellow guts off my palms. But this isn't my house, so I force my eyes up at the people around the table. My sister stares at me like, "What the hell is wrong with you?" She doesn't understand.

I know they're just little creatures doing whatever they're programmed to do. I know they serve a valuable function breaking down dead bodies and other filth that spreads disease, but that's part of why I hate them, most of my memories of death and filth are accompanied by flies. They bred in gallons of diarrhea when Saddam's Revenge swept through our division. They swarmed on mountains of garbage in neighborhood alleys where smiling kids ran barefoot chasing our convoy. They laid their eggs on human limbs left rotting in the sun, left thousands of wriggling maggots on rigor-mortised cattle, sheep, and dogs. They crawled through seeping holes in men's brains, no consideration for anything, just eating and breeding, eating and breeding, eating and breeding.

This is what my sister doesn't understand. To her, they're just a couple of flies, easy to ignore. To me, they're something on the edge of everything I do, memories that look nothing like this grassy back yard under the canopy of a sprawling maple tree.

PTSD

We exit the bus at Fort Snelling, Minnesota, crowd cheering as our company forms up. Our Commanding Officer steps out front, dismisses us, and we disperse amongst our moms, dads, brothers, sisters, wives, children, and friends. The deployment is over.

My parents are somewhere in the crowd. When I find them, their eyes say how excited and relieved they are to see me. I try to mirror their emotions.

"You want to get a steak?" my dad says. I don't care if I eat or not.

"A steak sounds good," I say.

When we get to the steakhouse, the parking lot is full. All the cars look clean and in working order. There's no charred wreckage, no scattered gunfire in the distance. A middle-aged couple walks to the door of the restaurant. The way they move disturbs me. We park in the lot and exit the car. My parents move the same way as the other couple. Before I can place why it bothers me, I get distracted by a shiny black Hummer in the parking lot with a vanity license plate that says "T-man".

I've spent a good chunk of my life in the turret of a Humvee behind a machine gun. I've been through gunfire, mortars, rockets, improvised explosive devices. I've been on high-speed chases across the desert, pointed guns at kids, almost shit myself when Iraqi vehicles got too close, and I had to choose whether or not to shoot them and possibly slaughter an innocent family for making a driving mistake. Now here is this Hummer in the parking lot, no turret, no armored plating, glossy black paint. I don't why, but rage overwhelms me. I want to find the guy that owns this thing and tear out his throat with my teeth, feel his warm sticky blood gush down my chin. I want to look down at his body as the life drains out of him and say, "How do you feel now, T-man? Do you feel big lying in a pool of your own blood?"

★★★

Eleven years after I get back from Ramadi, I sit in a therapist's office in New Mexico. When I got home from Iraq in 2004, I was young, seemingly well adjusted, and ready for the next phase of life. This is a place I never expected to be.

Pam's office is small, about the size of a walk-in closet. Her desk faces the back wall and above it hangs a framed picture of a pink mountain at sunset. Wood flute plays at low volume, and the office smells like incense. The last three months have been one panic attack after another. My mind is broken. The walls are too close in this room. The incense makes my throat feel thick, like it's swelling shut. I fight to keep myself from running out.

Pam motions me to an open chair next to a fern and small rock garden. Her voice is low and calm.

"So tell me why you're here today?"

"I'm not sure where to start."

"Just tell me what's going on in your life right now."

A list of maladies pours out. "I got ambulanced to the emergency room last week because my throat and nose closed off. The nurse at the ER thought I was faking to try to get drugs, told me to pull myself up by my bootstraps, and sent me away. I can't sit or sleep longer than twenty minutes at a time because my back is jacked, and the pain is too intense. I gave myself heat exhaustion over the summer working out, now even a little sun makes me anxious. A girl I was seeing in my grad program started sleeping with another guy then making up rumors about me being a creep so people wouldn't think bad of her. Now other students give me dirty looks in the halls and walk the other direction. I've been sick for the last six months, throwing up nearly every day. I have no idea what's wrong with me, but I don't have medical insurance. I've got a full course load, and I'm teaching. I can't afford to drop classes or stop teaching, but I'm falling apart. That's why I'm here."

"That's a lot to have on your plate at one time," she says. "I saw in your paperwork that you served in Iraq. Have you ever been diagnosed with PTSD?"

"PTSD? No," I scoff.

"PTSD can manifest itself in some of the issues you brought up—chronic pain, problems with relationships, enhanced anxiety."

"I don't have PTSD."

★★★

"How many in your party?" the hostess says when we get inside the steakhouse.

"Three," my dad says, and the bouncy young girl leads us into the restaurant. As we walk past tables of chattering people, I realize what makes me uncomfortable. There's no fear here, no urgency. No one's eyes dart toward the door or scan cars pulling into the lot. No one is coiled, ready to move when explosives fall from the sky. No one jokes about dead babies, bodies splattered on the asphalt, or preferred methods of violent death.

"What can I get you to drink?" the hostess asks.

"You want a beer?" my dad says. His words sound wrong. I'm not old enough to order a beer yet, wait, I turned twenty-one in Ramadi a couple of months ago.

"Sure."

"Can I see your ID?" I pull out my military ID and hand it to the hostess, then remember that's probably not what she wants and grab my Minnesota license.

After I order my beer, I walk to the bathroom. There are too many voices in this place. I need to gather myself. At the bar, a pudgy red-faced man in a shirt and tie chats up the female bartender. There's a mountain of food in front of him—nachos, chicken wings, bruschetta—and two tall glasses of beer, one half empty. He laughs and gestures with his hands while telling a story. The slender chestnut-haired bartender laughs along.

While the man tears into a chicken wing, pleased with himself over the bartender's attention, my mind flips to an Iraqi man picking through garbage next to the Euphrates. There was nothing spectacular about the Iraqi man, no reason he should stick out in my mind.

He was thin with dirty robes, chorded arms, and hard eyes. He pretended like he didn't see me as my Humvee drove by a few feet away, but that could describe any of a thousand men I drove past on convoys. But here in this steak house, glancing over the red-faced man's shoulder, I can't think of anything else. Iraqi man picking through scraps, red-faced man and bartender laughing, Iraqi man picking through scraps, red-faced man stuffing food in his mouth. I push through the bathroom door and shake the image out of my head. I lean over the sink and splash cold water on my face. Running water, as easy as that, whatever temperature I want. I resist drying my face on my sleeve, wipe it on a paper towel instead, and walk back to my table, avoiding looking at the bartender and red-faced man again.

★★★

Jim once told me a story about a pack of wild dogs he saw crossing a highway in Iraq. The first few crossed without a problem. The last got clipped by a passing car and spun off the road yelping. Its pack mates, hearing the yelp, wheeled around. The injured dog looked up at its friends with big eyes, knowing what was coming next. Now that he was injured, he was an easy meal, and the pack charged at him to finish him off. He hopped up and sprinted away on three legs, pack nipping at his heels. No one saw how far the dog got before his brothers took him down. Probably not far.

The Marine Corps can be like that pack of dogs. When everyone is strong and healthy, the bond is tight.

But there's no mercy for weakness in the ranks. I've seen several young men torn apart, treated like garbage for having injuries not sustained in combat or being mentally or physically weaker than expected. "Therapist" is like a curse word in the Marine Corps, someone you go to when you're a broke-dick.

"I'm going to ask you a few questions, just to make sure you don't have PTSD," Pam says.

"I don't have PTSD," I say, "but go ahead."

"Do you ever feel sudden bouts of anxiety?"

"Just recently."

"Do you engage in reckless behavior—heavy drinking, driving too fast, looking for fights?"

Only when I want to feel alive. "Sometimes, I guess."

"Do you ever feel numb, like it's impossible to be happy? Have you struggled with feelings of depression? Do you keep very busy to avoid being alone with your thoughts? Do you feel apprehensive in crowds? When in public, do you sit with your back against the wall? Do you avoid talking about events from your past? Have you lost interest in activities you used to enjoy? Do sights, sounds, and smells trigger past events? Do you have nightmares or flashbacks that make you feel like you're reliving the past? Do you find it hard to have positive or loving feelings toward other people? Do you avoid forming relationships? Do you think the world is completely dangerous, that no one can be trusted? Are you jittery or always on alert? Do you have sudden flashes of uncontrollable anger?"

I can't answer no to a single question.

★★★

The steak comes out sizzling and juicy, the inside, a perfect medium pink. When I fork the first bite into my mouth, I barely taste it.

"How's the steak?" Mom asks.

"Really good. Perfectly cooked."

"It's nice to have a good steak now and again," she says.

"Yep, for sure."

I look down at my plate of food, meat bracketed by garlic mashed potatoes and string beans, a finer meal than I've seen in many months, but it doesn't make me hungry or grateful. It makes me think of my last night in Ramadi, playing Spades with our replacements when a couple mortars landed near our tent. The explosions barely registered to me, but our replacements looked like rabbits ready to bolt.

"What the hell?" I said, "Play your fucking cards!" but their brains had shut down. They were frozen, not knowing where to run. As I looked around the barracks, I saw all my guys were like me, going about their business like nothing happened. All their guys were frozen with that stupid look on their faces. That's when I realized how much we'd changed. Most everyone gets that rabbit look at some point, when you realize how little control you have and how the difference between life and death is often luck. With enough time and repetition, that rabbit fear becomes muted, something you push away, something you accept as a normal part of life.

"You guys'll get used to it," I said. "Let's keep playing," but they couldn't even hear me.

Now in the steakhouse, I see their eyes in my mind. That's where I should be, in Ramadi, helping those dickheads out.

Three middle-aged women and a grey-haired man sit at the table next to us.

"I just can't believe he's going to study Russian Literature," one woman says. "When I asked him what kind of job he's going to get with a degree in Russian Literature, he shrugged his shoulders and said, 'I don't really care, Mom. It's just what I want to do.'"

"No, he didn't," says another woman.

"Yes, he did. How do you like that? I tell you what, he's not going to get any sympathy from me in four years when he's unemployed sleeping on our couch."

The group nods along sympathetically.

My jaw clinches, and I stare down hard at my plate.

★★★

The PTSD workbook Pam gives me says there are two controlling systems in your brain—Executive and Default. The Executive System is what allows a functioning life. It fosters learning and growth by incorporating experiences then moving past them. The Default System takes control in someone with PTSD. It's like fight or flight but permanently switched on, turning every situation into a battle and every person into a prospective enemy. Thoughts get warped into storylines of fear, mistrust, anger, depression, anxiety, and violence, chipping away relationships, sense of well-being, and belief in the future. The person chokes daily on their view of reality. "No matter how hard I fight, things only get worse. The world is set against me. I can't win. I'm broken, unfixable; I'll never be worth anything again." They lose friends and family who don't understand. They shy away from new contacts, even healthy ones, because no one can be trusted. They have trouble focusing, being involved, staying employed, ever feeling okay. Strength and energy fade. Bodies break down. And eventually, if the cycle isn't halted, the person succumbs to their broken identity and drowns in it.

★★★

It's the goddamn whistling buzz that gets you, the second before detonation when your whole body wants to jump in every direction at once. The first time I heard an incoming rocket, I kind of liked it, the electric jolt of fear, the way I hummed with energy, senses sharpened, body tensed, ready to leap. But go through it enough times and it just wears you down, especially when you realize there's nothing you can do to stop it. You can't run because you don't know where it's going to land. You can't fight because you don't see the guy shooting you. You can't protect yourself because you spend your days roving out in the open. And you can't relax because you live life surrounded by enemy on all sides. So, what you do is live with the anticipation of the next attack and accept your reality that it's not worth thinking about life beyond today. You live minute by minute, day by day, until all the days disappear and you find yourself at an airfield waiting to fly home.

We wait in little huts along the airstrip at Al Asad air base for our C130 out of Iraq. Al Asad looks like Kuwait, flat brown in every direction, hard packed dirt covered with a thin layer of dust and loose rock. When we get word our plane won't come for several hours, we head across an open expanse of dirt to the chow hall. Other units rotating out of Ramadi and Fallujah do the same. A herd of three or four hundred Marines trudges out in the open.

Suddenly something huge whizzes overhead, and all four hundred Marines drop to their bellies in unison. This close to the end, this is how we die. We let our guard down for a moment, let ourselves group up and think we were safe. Now we pay for our carelessness.

But no explosion shakes the ground. There's no last hard lesson for us to learn. This is an F-16 pilot playing a joke. He knows there's a bunch of tweaked-out Jarheads coming from Ramadi and Fallujah. If he banks hard enough, his F-16 will sound exactly like incoming rockets, and we'll flop around on the ground like stupid fish. I imagine we look pretty funny from the sky.

I go with my dad to a golf course ten miles outside of my hometown. It's a warm day. The corn surrounding the course is tall and tasseled, almost ready for harvest. My dad and I played a lot of golf when I was in high school. It was the thing we did together, and being on the course brings me back. I always loved the feel of spongy fairway grass under my feet, walking across the neat, patterned mow lines. I love the breeze on my face, the swaying trees and tall grasses, the smells of each season—wet mud and crab apple blossoms in spring, fresh cut grass and sweat in summer, dried leaves and dirt aeration in autumn. I love carrying my bag as I walk to my ball, calculating distance, planning my next shot, never believing I'll shank it into the woods or dribble it into the river. I love the peacefulness out on the course, nothing but birds, padded footsteps, and the rattle of irons in my golf bag.

It's sunny and calm as my dad and I tee off on the eleventh hole, a dog leg par four I can reach in one with a perfect shot, though I never hit the perfect shot. Just as I tee off, a low flying private jet banks overhead, adjusting course to the local airport. I freeze. I have to stop myself from diving on the ground. You're in the middle of corn fields in Minnesota, asshole. That's not a rocket. Calm the fuck down. But I'm back in Ramadi now and won't release until the rocket explodes. My dad walks ahead, no idea what's happening to me.

When I came home from Iraq in 2003, I immediately jumped in my cherry-red Grand Am and zipped down the highway at a hundred miles per hour. 2004 was different. Roadside bombs had become a popular method of attacking American forces in Iraq. Now driving at home, down roads I've known my whole life, my eyes flit over every piece of trash, every dead animal carcass, every shredded retread tire, looking for anything out of the ordinary, detonation chord, radio transmitter, mobile phone, pager. If any trash is on the shoulder of the road, I swerve to the lane furthest away to distance myself from the blast.

I search for timing markers further off the road—tree stumps, billboards, old tractor tires—anything an insurgent could use to line me up for detonation. I scan ditches, corn fields, and tree lines for potential hides. All this stuff was part of my routine as a turret gunner, part of the hyperawareness and attention to detail that made me good. Now these qualities make me a lunatic. I'm not supposed to expect to get blown up or ambushed on the roads here. I'm not supposed to flinch every time an SUV speeds up behind me and moves over to pass, wondering if this is the ambush or car bomb that finally ends me. I'm not supposed to pull over on the side of the road until the cars pass and tell myself over and over, "This is Minnesota. People aren't trying to attack you. Quit losing your mind."

★★★

"I hate all this shit," I say. "I'm a U.S. Marine. I have a medal for valor in combat. When the fuck did I get so weak?"

"You're going to have to learn to think about things a little differently," Pam says. "You're not weak. I think you have incredible strength. But you need to understand that this isn't about strength. You've been living in fight or flight for ten plus years. Bodies aren't meant to function that way. They start to wear down."

"I just feel like I've lost myself. I've always met things head on. Fought whatever bullshit came my way."

"And this is where that got you. Your strength wore out. There's no shame in that. It's just the way bodies are. Eventually strength fails and you have to find another way."

But strength failing isn't all I'm worried about. I'm losing my mind. Normal things I see during the day make me think of rotting corpse flesh—the desktop some kid carved on with his pencil, pieces of gravel on what should be a clean sidewalk, insects crawling in the indents of tree bark. I have to stop myself from clawing at these things, from digging down with my fingernails and ripping out the impurities, scrubbing them until their festering skin is pink and raw and healthy. These things stick in my mind until I want to crack my skull against the ground, scrape out the insides with a spoon, and soak my brains in bleach.

★★★

A couple weeks after getting home from Ramadi, three Marine buddies and I took a road trip to the East Coast. A lot of the guys we served with were from big cities in the East—New York, Boston, Philadelphia, Baltimore—so we looked them up as we traveled. Some seemed to be readjusting well. Some not so much. Wexler was in full blown fuck off mode. We met up with him in Boston and before we even started drinking, he whipped out his dick on a downtown street corner and started peeing facing oncoming traffic while digging through a trash can with his free hand. A nicely dressed man and woman walking toward him scoffed in disgust. Wexler dropped the half-eaten doughnut he'd picked out of the trash, looked the man straight on and said, "What?! I'm peeing here!" The man and woman looked down and quickly shuffled past.

Later in the night, on the cab ride home, our driver was a young man from India. Wexler started in on him right away.

"Why aren't you working at the 7/11 tonight? What about all the people that need slurpies?" The cabbie looked at Wexler with disdain in the rearview mirror.

"Jesus, Wexler. Shut the fuck up," Tom said.

"Too good to answer me, turban boy? Running the Kwik-E mart going to your head?"

"For fuck's sake, Wexler," I said.

Wexler started with a fake Indian accent. "Hello, my name is Apunishad. I am from India. You want cookie? Two for a dollar?"

The three of us sandwiched in the back seat with Wexler all shouted "Shut the fuck up, man!"

"Abudabadabuda," Wexler continued, "Half price slurpies. Abudabadabuda. Hotdogs three for a dollar."

When we got out of the cab, each of us gave the driver a twenty plus cab fare and apologized for our drunken asshole friend. Looking at the cabdriver's face, money and apologies didn't do much. I was furious at Wexler for being such an asshole. But then I started thinking about myself a few weeks earlier, and I wasn't so sure that was it.

Most of my friends from high school went to college an hour away from my hometown. Walking to their dorm one night, I cut through a dark tree line onto an isolated walking path right as a student passed. The student wasn't even Arabic. He was probably from India or Bangledesh, but when I saw his brown skin, late at night unexpectedly on that dark path, something snapped, and I went after him.

This young man, probably eight inches shorter than me and seventy pounds lighter, stepped backward and curled over, ready to cover his vitals and hit the ground. His recoil stopped my immediate response, but I stared at him, rage blazing, fists clenched and ready. This is my home, motherfucker. Why are you here? My breath was erratic as I fought the impulse to jump on him and cave in his face.

In reality, this was his home. He was a student at the university. I was just some crazy fuck vet visiting friends. Eyes wide, like he'd come across some dangerous predator, the young man slowly backed toward the lights of the street. I watched him retreat a few steps, then tore myself away, continuing on to the dorms, wondering what the fuck just happened.

★★★

"I think it's working," I say, "I feel a little different sometimes."

"It's a good start," says Pam. "You're acknowledging things as they are."

"Sometimes I almost feel calm, like maybe I don't have to keep being this way."

"That's great, but try not to get too excited or too discouraged. This is going to be a long process. You had pretty much a total collapse."

"It's just nice to feel something different. It makes me want to push, really go for it, you know?"

"And that would be a mistake. You don't need to fix yourself. You need to heal."

"How would me pushing to get better get in the way of healing? It seems like the more effort I put in the better results I should get."

"Yes and no. It's good that you're open to the idea, but you've got to be careful not to fall back into old habits. Like you said before, you're used to dealing with things head on, but healing isn't something you can force. No matter how hard you push, you can't force a cut on your arm to heal. That happens naturally. The best you can do is provide optimal conditions for your body's healing systems to do their thing. The mind will heal itself just like the body if given the peace and space to do it. Force is the opposite of what your mind needs."

"Not every wound is a cut on the arm. A guy who had his legs blown off isn't just going to heal. He might scar over, but he's never going to be the same."

"Sure, but no amount of trying is going to change that. He'll still need to heal naturally as much as he can."

"I just wonder if mental wounds are the same? What if you're a thirteen-year-old girl and your dad brings different strangers home every night so he can watch them fuck you? What if you do a hot entry on a house you think is full of drugged up insurgents with RPGs, but find out it's really just a hideout for a dozen scared shitless kids, and the floor is sticky with their blood? Maybe some wounds are so devastating the mind can't be whole again."

"Maybe that's true. I don't know. But allowing the mind as much space to heal as possible will still put a person in the best place they can be."

★★★

Jim has a homecoming party in rural Wisconsin. He doesn't drink anymore, but he basically grew up in the town bar, so drinks are free all night for any Marine he served with, and I drive over. As the party ramps up and the liquor flows, I get more uncomfortable. I shotgun a beer, then chug another, but all that does is make things dull. It doesn't make me forget how I feel. As the night goes on, I get more and more restless. Finally, Jim's wife grabs me by the arm and leads me outside.

"Are you okay?" she says, standing out in the cool air. "You don't look like you're having much fun."

"I don't know what it is," I say. "This just doesn't fit me anymore."

Rebecca is beautiful. She doesn't drink, isn't vulgar, doesn't try to flirt with me when her husband's not around. She brought me outside because she could see that I was hurting.

"It doesn't fit me either," she laughs, "I would never even dress this way except Jim wanted me to."

I can see why he did—tight black leather pants, loose backless top, blonde hair teased up in a bun with a few loose strands perfectly framing her face. I've been jealous of Jim all night, and I'm sure the dipshits he grew up with are too.

Jim walks out of the bar and finds us. "I was wondering what happened to you guys."

"Just needed some air," I say.

"We were talking about how neither one of us really feels like we belong in there," Rebecca says.

"You know," Jim says, "I was just thinking the same thing. You guys want to get out of here?"

"Yeah," we say.

"Well fuck it. I'll go say some goodbyes, and we can take off."

It's late. Nothing in town is open but the bar, so we head to Jim and Rebecca's hotel room to talk. I feel at home with them in a way I never really have with my own family. We understand each other. But in the morning, they'll head off to Utah to start a life together, and I'll head off to the East Coast for more binge drinking with Marine buddies.

My road trip starts in Buffalo, New York. Tom has a friend that's an offensive lineman for the college football team. We meet at his house, slam a few beers, then go to get chicken wings before we start drinking for real.

The wing joint is packed, and behind the bar is a waitress that reminds me some of Rebecca. I've been thinking about Rebecca a lot, not because I'm interested in my friend's wife, I'd rather slit my own throat than betray a friend, but I could use some pretty and sweet in my life, if only to pull me out of my head for a day, so I sit at the bar. The offensive lineman sets a tall glass of beer in front of me. I don't know where he got it from, but I thank him and smile at the waitress.

I've never been charming. When people like me, it comes over time. Many people have told me I'm too intense or too quiet. I'm not flashy in any way. I dress plain, eat inexpensive food, and drink crappy beer. I'm only funny when I trust people, and my last deployment has made me even more distant than usual. I have no ability to pick up this girl right now, but I try anyway.

"How's your night going?" I ask the waitress. She smiles but doesn't say anything and walks away. While she waits on a table, I stay at the bar and pound my beer. When she returns, I wave her down and point at my glass.

"What can I get you?" she asks.

"Something cheap. Busy night, huh?"

"Yep." She sets my beer in front of me and turns away. My friends come and grab me. They've got a table and a pitcher. The waitress isn't interested in my weak attempts, so I leave the bar to sit with my buddies, but our table is in her section, and right after I sit, she comes to take our order.

Tom's friend orders wings for our table and mentions that we're Marines who just got back from Iraq. This is early enough in the war that that has an effect on people, and the waitress lightens up some. She smiles and laughs with us a little, letting her coolness toward me slip, then walks away and doesn't return. I polish off the rest of our pitcher and I'm drunk enough now that my judgment has slipped. I stand up, look around the crowded restaurant, find our waitress, and walk over to her.

In between tables I catch her, "Hey, can I talk to you for a second?"

"Look, I don't want to be rude, but I'm really busy right now."

"Oh yeah, it's just, when you get a sec, can we get another pitcher of beer?"

"Sure thing."

When I get back to our table, Tom says, "What was that?"

"Nothing. Just wanted another pitcher."

"Sure."

The waitress comes to our table with our next pitcher and our bill. Tom's friend pays.

"Thanks for coming in, guys," the waitress says and walks away. I get up again to follow her.

"What are you doing?" Tom says.

"Nothing. I just want to talk to her one more time."

"Come on, man, just sit down and finish your beer."

"Just a second."

I catch up to the waitress.

"Hey, hold up," I say.

"I can't hold up," she says, turning toward me.

"I know you're busy, but we're going downtown to the bars tonight, and I was wondering if you'd want to come hang out."

"I have to go. Have a good night." She turns to walk away.

"Hold on," I say, not registering that I grab her arm.

She rips her arm out of my hand and shouts, "Get away from me!" backing away until she bumps against the nearest table.

The look in her eyes isn't anger, it's fear. She's hunched over with her hands in front her like she's pushing me away. She reminds me of the Indian kid on the dark pathway a few days earlier. We're in the center of a packed restaurant, and the place goes silent, everyone staring at me. I just stand there stupidly trying to process what's happening.

A couple hands grab my arms. "It's time to go, buddy," Tom says, and my friends escort me to the door. The rest of the night is a blur. We meet football players downtown and they buy us shots and beers. I try to be friendly, but spend most of the night alone on a barstool thinking about the fear in that girl's eyes and wondering what's wrong with me.

★★★

The workbook says one of the most powerful things you can do to treat your PTSD is recognize your requirements. It's not what other people do that causes your distress but how you think they should act. You go up to a random girl at a bar and she looks at you like you're not worth her time, and quickly dismisses you. You leave feeling angry, thinking she shouldn't treat you that way, that no one should treat you that way. If you've got PTSD, this plays off all the stories you tell yourself and spirals into rage—Fucking stupid cunt. I ain't a human being to you? I'll show you how non-human I can be—followed by despondency—I'm a worthless piece of shit. That's what happened. She knew it. Everyone knows it.

All this rage and despondency started with one innocuous personal requirement—It's hard for me to talk to people. They should be nice when I try.

It's about lack of control. Getting tortured, blown up, raped, or being forced to kill someone are common events that result in PTSD. All are situations where a person has no control over what happens, but that doesn't stop them from maintaining the illusion of control, constantly thinking about what they should have done different, what they would have done different if only they were better. I got raped because I'm weak. I shot that kid because I didn't have the guts to say no. I deserve what I got or what I'm getting. The brain then creates an overcorrection, trying to force every little situation in life to fit your concept of how things should go. When reality falls outside of those attempts to control, which it always does, those small violations become a crisis the size of the original. Thus, the girl in the bar being a little unkind becomes some cunt in collusion with the rest of the world grinding their shit in your face. In reality, she's just some girl reacting for whatever reason she reacts.

★★★

I've been out of the Marine Corps for a couple of years, and I'm managing a Sunglass Hut in Redmond, WA. I don't mind the job, but there's no future in it. I don't feel like myself selling sunglasses; I lack the sense of purpose I used to have. I watch other managers, how anxious they get, how intimidated by our boss. Their lives and self-images are bound to things he says about their results, but for me it's all muted. I don't get flustered by lack of sales or elated when we surpass our goals. In neither case did someone try to blow up my crew, and no matter how mad my boss gets, he probably won't shoot me in the back of the head. I'm not cut out for this, but my job is all I have, so I try to make it important. On my days off, I go for long walks and consider walking into oncoming traffic.

For about three straight years, I wake up in the morning and pray God will kill me. What I really want is to take two pistols deep into the woods, put one in my mouth and one against the side of my head. I figure two bullets will make sure the job gets done. Maybe I should use a shotgun instead, but I like pistols; I've always been good with pistols.

The reason I don't shoot myself is my parents. I don't know how close I'd say we were. We didn't always talk much, and they didn't really know me—but they were decent people who kept me fed and safe and taught me to have integrity. If I shot myself, I think it would be bad for them. It wouldn't be fair of me to lay this shit on them.

I go for long walks at three or four in the morning, usually through places that make me nervous—warehouse districts, sketchy housing complexes, pitch dark trails along the Green River where twenty years ago Gary Ridgway dumped the bodies of his victims. I do this because the fear seems more honest than the life I'm trying to fit into. I want to get attacked. If someone has the balls to take me out, so be it. If he's some punk bitch, I'll make him pay. Strength on strength until death. The feeling is crisp, clear. As I walk through these areas, my senses heighten in the old ways, eyes flashing from potential threat to potential threat, ears straining for rustling in the tall grass or footsteps approaching from behind. My body buzzes with anticipation, ready for the struggle.

★★★

The workbook says to use your senses to interrupt the process. The next time your Default System turns something small into a meltdown, listen to the hum of the air conditioner or the wind in the Cedars. When a car cuts in front of you on the highway, focus on the whine of your tires on the asphalt. Feel the bumps on the steering wheel under your palms. Run your fingertips across each ridge of the air vents. When you go for a walk to get away, focus on the rope clanging against a flagpole or the train whistle on the other side of town. Feel the pressure of each step on the bottoms of your feet. Notice how your legs work, your thighs and hamstrings tensing and releasing as they propel you forward. When you're alone in your room thinking about being alone in your room, open the door, feel the mechanism of the knob turning. Step outside and place your hand on the metal railing along the second story walkway. Feel the imperfections against your fingers where the paint is chipped, the warmth of metal sitting in the sun. If it rains, let it sprinkle against your bare forearms, notice every prickle of sensation. Feel the cool drops roll down your forehead and cheeks. Listen to the storm crescendo, the wind whip through bowed treetops. Lay on the asphalt path along the stream rushing to empty itself. Watch the clouds roll past. Notice their swirling grays. Feel the hardness of the asphalt on the back of your head and elbows, the wetness of your shirt pressed against your shoulder blades.

It's then you might see him, just for a moment, while your mind is occupied not being occupied. You won't know what broke inside that let him out, but he'll be there, that other self, the one that smiles and means it. You'll be terrified he's not real, that if you notice him he'll evaporate like a desert cloud, so you'll focus on your palms passing over the grainy wet pathway, your hair matting slick against your forehead. You'll wiggle your toes in your shoes, marvel at how your body works, the electrical signals coming all the way down from your brain to accomplish a simple movement. And then it'll happen, wind whipping through the trees, sky crackling above, you'll look into the rain beating down on your face and laugh.

★★★

Lessons from Iraq

My first class back in college is Social Work. I'm in my upper twenties now, and everyone else is eighteen or nineteen. I'm not sure why I do this, but when we talk about state agencies coming into homes and taking peoples' children, I raise my hand and say I'm cautious of using government force as a solution for anything. I give an example of a massacre I was a part of during my first tour in Iraq. I never told this to anyone I hadn't served with in combat. Even then, I only brought it up sparingly.

A young blonde girl at the back of the class raises her hand. "How could you do that?" she says.

"Excuse me?"

"How could you let all those people die?"

"It's a lot more complicated than that."

"If it was me there, I would have stopped it."

"You have no idea what you are talking about."

"I just don't understand how you can be such a weak person."

If I was under better control, I might've said something like "Alright, you little cunt. The situation was confusing. We took fire from inside a building. When we returned fire, we couldn't see who we were shooting. And who the fuck are you? Do you know what the crazy fucks we're fighting would do to a little blonde girl like you? If you were lucky they'd rape you and cut off your head. More likely they'd throw you in some dungeon as a communal fuck toy for whatever animal felt like going balls deep while listening to you scream. After they got bored, they'd beat you until you were unrecognizable, throw acid on your face for being an adulterous whore, peel the skin and muscle off of your arms, slather your naked body in honey and feed you to their dogs. Then they'd sell the video of it all at the local market for a few dinars. But, by all means, tell me about how strong you are and how much you know about the world. Tell me about how you could extend your arm and stop a wall of bullets from killing those kids. Tell me how your years of being protected, well fed, and having your ego reinforced have made you so much wiser and stronger than me." But I'm not under control.

A rage has exploded inside of me that makes me shake. I'm concentrating everything in me on holding it down. I need to get out of here, go be alone until I can calm down. I know something about myself most people never will. I pull the trigger. Being female has bought this girl time. If she was a guy, I might already be beating a limp body down the back wall of the room, waiting for the cops to kill me or take me away. But I don't want that. I don't want to lose my shit like Parker, come home from Iraq just to kill someone and spend my life in prison.

"I'm just saying, I don't understand what kind of person you are," the girl continues. "If it was me in that situation there's no way I'd let something like that happen. I don't know how you live with yourself."

I press my hands on my desk, starting to push myself to my feet. A young man from Sudan speaks.

"You don't know what you'd do in that situation. You've never been through anything close to that. You have no idea what people have to do in war." I settle back into my chair.

"I know the difference between right and wrong," the girl says.

"But you can't judge him based on your life here. Soldiers live lives you can't possibly understand. You can't judge any of them."

My rage lightens a shade. The professor finally jumps in and changes the subject. When class breaks, I hurry out the door, not wanting to risk seeing the girl on the way out. I jump in my car, drive to the woods, and hike until the rage is gone.

★★★

A Jordanian friend shows me a video of a fighter pilot from his country being burned alive by ISIS. At the beginning of the video, the pilot stands in a metal cage, an Arabic melody playing in the background. As the string ensemble picks up intensity, a group of men draped in black from head to toe, enter the screen. One man grabs a jug and splashes a clear liquid on the pilot, then pours a trail leading away from the cage. The pilot doesn't flinch. He doesn't cry or beg, but stands erect, a picture of military bearing. The lead man in black pulls a lighter from off screen, shouts "Allah Akbar (God is greatest)" and lights the liquid trail. The flame spreads toward the cage and still the pilot doesn't flinch until the fire spreads up his legs, flares, and engulfs his whole body, then he contorts and spasms. He brings his flaming hands to his face, a useless instinctual attempt to shield his vital parts, he throws himself against the bars of the cage trying to escape the pain. But he's locked in his agony, an agony so intense he can't even scream. The group of men in black chant "Allah Akbar, Allah Akbar," as they watch. After about a minute, much longer than I'd hoped, the pilot quits fighting and falls to his knees. His body tips onto the ground and slowly curls together in the flames.

When I go to my therapy session that week, I'm not in the mood to mind my surroundings or recognize my triggers.

"Fucking thousands of people getting slaughtered like animals in Iraq, and no one gives a shit," I say.

"What makes you bring this up?" Pam says.

"ISIS just took Ramadi. They took it, and we did nothing. I'd go to Ramadi right fucking now to get it back, but no one will send me. They've already forgotten it. What about all the fuckers who died in those streets? Or the guys that lost legs and arms, had their faces burned off? What about the guys that came home stuttering retards from getting their brains bounced around inside their skulls, or all the other assholes whose lives will taste like chalk until they finally pack it in and shoot themselves in the head? All that these guys gave because they honored their obligations, and then we just quit. We let it all go. Let it mean nothing. And I have to listen to motherfuckers tell me 'Aren't you glad we finally got our soldiers out of there?' Fuck you! You don't give a shit about me. You pulled us out for you. The politicians pulled us out for them. If you gave a shit about us, you'd finish the fucking mission. All you did was make sure guys like me can never leave."

"Do you feel responsible for what's happening in Iraq?" Pam says.

"Of course, I feel responsible. I am responsible. Who's responsible if not me? A couple months ago, I saw a blurb on the internet about the curator of the Babylon Museum getting hung by ISIS. When I told my friends about it, they looked at me like 'What's one more dead Iraqi.' The thing is, I knew that fucking guy. It's not like we were close or anything, but at the end of my first tour, he showed me and my unit through the ruins. He didn't give a fuck that we were Americans. He was just excited to share the history of his country. I remember how thrilled I was that day. All I could think was 'Who gets this experience? Who gets to walk through the ruins of Babylon, to see the carved dragons on the restored walls? Who gets to see the four-thousand-year-old basalt lion across a dirt field from Saddam's sprawling palace?' And now this man is just another dead Iraqi."

"Are you responsible for his death?"

"Yeah, I am. I'm here talking to you, when I should be there. I'm a waste of space here, getting a degree in Creative Writing, worrying about some shallow slut who I don't even respect sleeping with some other dude. People are getting slaughtered, and this is how I'm spending my time."

"Did you kill the man from Babylon?"

"Of course not."

"Did you start the war?"

"Why are you asking me stupid questions?"

"Did you?"

"No."

"Did you fly a plane into the Twin Towers?"

"No."

"Did you order yourself to Iraq?"

"No."

"Did you order yourself home?"

"No."

"Did you command a unit while you were in Iraq?"

"No."

"This is going to be hard for you, and I'm not going to say I understand what you're feeling, but if you had no control over anything that happened and have no control over what's currently happening, how are you responsible?"

Silence.

"You've got all this turmoil inside that's going to be really hard to heal through. Taking responsibility for things you have no control over will make it impossible. You're here talking to me because you realized you need a change. Your body and mind are falling apart. Everything in you is rebelling, screaming at you to stop fighting and let yourself be. I know you want to take responsibility, to fight to make things right, but you can't. Nothing that happened was your choice. Nothing currently happening is your choice. The world is what it is. All you can do is try to heal and move on."

★★★

The rate of PTSD for vets is fifteen times higher than civilians. The rate of Intermittent Explosive Disorder which results in episodes of extreme and disproportionate anger is six times higher. The rate of depression is five times higher. One in four veterans abuses substances to make it through the day. Of the 1.7 million who served in Iraq and Afghanistan, over 300,000 have PTSD or depression.

According to the Substance Abuse and Mental Health Services Administration in 2014, only fifty percent of returning service members who need treatment for mental health seek it. Reasons why vets who need care don't seek it include, lack of understanding of what's happening to them, lack of shared values and experiences with mental health professionals, long wait times at care facilities, mistrust of the VA, and not knowing how to get help.

Over 30,000 military personnel who served after 9/11 have died by suicide, that's over four times the number who died in combat. Increased awareness of this problem isn't enough. We need a fundamental shift in the understanding of what PTSD is, and even then, treatment is complicated. Mental patterns aren't reversed overnight. Recovery is often long and full of pitfalls, and the person left standing at the end will not be the same as the person they once were, no matter how much they wish things were different.

OBAMA'S WAR

At some point back home, I started to realize that no news was good news. If Iraq wasn't being talked about on TV, it meant things were going better. After 2007 and before 2012, this was more and more often the case.

When Barack Obama took office in 2009, it became immediately clear that the new administration was going to treat Iraq differently. When Vice President Biden showed up in Iraq to talk to military leaders after the election, he told them Iraq was Bush's War, and Afghanistan would be Obama's war. And that's how the administration acted, like they wanted nothing to do with Iraq except get out of it at any cost.

Nouri al-Maliki was Prime Minister of Iraq when President Obama took office. Maliki was a political dissident who spent many years in exile in Iran during Saddam Hussein's regime. In 2006, when most of Sunni Iraq was in open insurgency and less than 3% of Sunnis across the country voted, Maliki was made Prime Minister. Under Saddam Hussein, the Sunnis brutally oppressed the Shia. Under Maliki, the Sunnis began to fear retribution, but George Bush had a good working relationship with

Maliki, so when he started acting with favoritism toward Shiites, Bush could step in and remind him that if he ever wanted peace, he couldn't favor his own people. He had to treat the Sunnis equitably or the fighting wouldn't stop. Barack Obama never had that same relationship.

By the time of the new Iraq elections in 2010, two years into the Obama administration, Maliki was showing strong authoritarian signs, using the military to enforce edicts, using the court systems to persecute political opposition, and using the security apparatus to have political rivals constantly monitored. More and more often he said things like "I am the only man who can save Iraq." And now, it wasn't just Sunnis who were worried about Maliki, but Kurds and even a large group of Shiites who didn't like Maliki's ties to Iran. None of these people wanted the future of Iraq to be the return of a sectarian despot, but Maliki's party was expected to win Parliament by a wide margin, granting him another term.

But then something unexpected happened. Despite Maliki's use of government power to keep political rivals out of the election. Despite a massive campaign by Iran to whip up fear among Shiites of the return of a Sunni government. Despite terrorist groups carrying out attacks across the country to keep Iraqis afraid and keep them from voting, the Iraqi people turned out a massive upset. Maliki's party was defeated by a coalition party of Sunnis, Shiites, Kurds, Turkmen, and Christians called Iraqiya. The Iraqi people had chosen the direction they wanted their country to go, and it wasn't Maliki.

Maliki was incensed. He claimed fraud and refused to give up power. In America, speeches from the White

House made it sound like Iraq was ready for American troop withdrawal, but the power dispute went on for months. Then something happened that as an American Marine I can't really wrap my head around. American military leaders were instructed by civilian leadership that Iraq's election wouldn't be honored. They claimed that Iraq needed a Shia strongman and Maliki was their guy. The military leaders were floored. They protested, said this was not what the Iraqi people wanted, but the politicians had made their decision.

Iraqis were outraged. Why was America choosing Iraq's Prime Minister? Why was it handing Iraq to Iran on a silver platter? After years of American promises of a free and stable Iraq, how could America ignore the will of the Iraqi people and subvert their election? An opinion poll conducted by the National Democratic Institute showed just 14 percent of Iraqis believed Maliki should be prime minister again, but that didn't matter. The Obama administration made their choice. And with that decision, everything we fought for in Iraq was destroyed.

The US withdrew its troops, and Maliki consolidated power. He made himself Commander-in-Chief, Minister of Defense, Minister of the Interior, Minister of National State Security, and National Security Advisor. He filled the judiciary with sycophants and purged the military of any officers that wouldn't blindly follow his edicts. He detained thousands of Sunnis without trial, accused leading Sunnis of terrorism, and reneged on payments to Sunnis who fought against al Qaeda. He allowed Iranian general Qasem Soleimani to embed Iranian officers within the Iraqi Army and personally direct operations in Iraq, and when protests began, Maliki cracked down and killed dozens of unarmed protesters.

In the US, President Obama called the end of the war in Iraq one of his greatest foreign policy successes. On November 1, 2013, he stood in front of the White House with Prime Minister Maliki and said, "We honor the lives that were lost, both American and Iraqi, to bring about a functioning democracy in a country that previously had been ruled by a vicious dictator. And we appreciate Prime Minister Maliki's commitment to honoring that sacrifice by ensuring a strong, prosperous, inclusive, and democratic Iraq."

That's what bullshit was fed to the American people. Meanwhile, the remnants of al Qaeda formed the backbone of a new organization called ISIS, and with Sunnis terrified of the new government, ISIS saw its opportunity. Sunnis needed protection. ISIS offered help. So Sunni leaders flipped again toward supporting lunatics, and ISIS rampaged across Iraq. They took cities, enslaved women and children, and burned and mutilated people. The Iraqi Army was fractured and routed, and ISIS took millions of dollars of American military equipment, making them even stronger. A new Sunni-Shia civil war began, enflamed by a conflict on Iraqi soil between ISIS and Iran. And the Iraqi people were once again thrust into a savage hell while men in finely tailored suits across the ocean made grand speeches about the nobility of their political accomplishments.

Between 2012 and 2016, roughly 70,000 Iraqi civilians were killed by sectarian violence. Many more were destroyed in other ways as groups like ISIS roved across the country cutting people apart, making women and little girls into sex slaves, making little boys into child soldiers. When we invaded Iraq in 2003, we invaded with the promise of freedom from tyranny. After bitter, brutal years of fighting, Iraqis finally had a chance to exercise that freedom, and instead of supporting them, we subverted their election, supported the claims of a false Prime Minister, left them defenseless, and served them up to be torn apart by animals.

(For more information on the collapse of Iraq from someone who was there watching it happen, read *The Unraveling* by Emma Sky.)

WEAPONS OF MASS DESTRUCTION 6: FAILURES

So why weren't stockpiles of WMD found in Iraq after the US invasion? Well, some were. About 5000 chemical weapons were discovered by coalition forces after 2003. These were weapons Saddam's regime previously said they destroyed to the UN. US officials didn't disclose their discovery because they weren't the weapons they were looking for. These were old stockpiles, not newly manufactured stockpiles, and many of the weapons were designed by US companies, which was embarrassing to the US government. So, while American soldiers were getting sick from exposure to chemicals. Government officials kept it covered up.

Stockpiles of new WMD weren't found in Iraq for one simple reason. Saddam hadn't started rebuilding them yet. Many things were in place, the scientists, the infrastructure, the precursors and bio stocks, but the regime was so close to accomplishing their worldwide economic goals, they didn't want to push too quickly and risk jeopardizing their position. They were within a hair of completely defeating the United States and the West by using their own corrupt institutions against them. They had withstood the giant and come out the other side potentially stronger than ever. And there were no signs of slowing down. On the contrary, with new investors from around the world ready to pour money into Iraq, it's more likely they were about to speed up.

Then 9/11 happened, and American policy changed almost overnight. Saddam thought American action would be like it had been for the last decade, a few tough words and some bombs. He didn't realize how much impact 9/11 had on the United States, and it wasn't just George Bush. 77 percent of the Senate and 70 percent of the US House voted for the War in Iraq. 53 percent of the US population supported American boots on the ground in direct kinetic war with Iraq to oust Saddam Hussein. By the time Saddam realized how much the situation had changed, it was too late.

So what happened with US intelligence? Was the whole Iraq War just a massive lie? The flaw with this idea is that a lot of intelligence gathered before the war actually turned out to be true. US intelligence was right about Iraq being resurgent and ramping up. They were right about Iraq smuggling goods into their country to rebuild WMD programs. They were right about Iraq using civilian industry to disguise WMD programs. And they were right about the widespread corruption of businesses and governments around the world. Though that turned out to be far worse than expected. But US intelligence was completely wrong about massive stockpiles of newly created WMD, and that needs more attention than just dismissing it as a lie. Here are a few factors that contributed to that result:

In 1998, Saddam grew tired of international interference and expelled UN inspectors from Iraq. At that point, the US essentially lost all ground intelligence and started relying on satellite images and information from Iraqi dissidents who proved less than reliable. The US also had no diplomatic contact with Iraq, and with America's history of extreme mistrust of anything Saddam said or did, with their lack of communication with anyone in Iraq, and with the panic from 9-11 and subsequent terrorist attacks like anthrax on Capitol Hill less than a month later, fear and bias began shaping information. George Bush was more involved with intelligence reports than many previous presidents. He wanted to be informed and got frequent briefings, but he also tended to go with his gut and had a clear bias toward information that validated his gut feeling. Despite their mystique, US intelligence is just humans attempting to piece together information to aid decision-making, and humans are susceptible to social pressure. Once it became clear what information was getting the best reception from the president, that information got front-lined while counter viewpoints got buried. With no one in the administration who had any real experience in Iraq, and no ground intelligence to validate or invalidate beliefs, the wobbly assumptions started piling up.

Saddam's paranoia didn't help matters. He had enemies all over Iraq. His own cooks conspired to kill him once, but the serving girl in on the plot lost her nerve and confessed before the poisoned food was delivered.

As attempts on his life and members of his regime piled up, Saddam became more withdrawn. After Uday got gunned down in the street and left crippled in 1996, Saddam could hardly be found anymore. Even his own ministers sometimes couldn't contact him for weeks to talk about important decisions. If they needed to meet with him, they'd be picked up and driven to undisclosed locations in vans with blacked out windows. The vans would drive in circles sometimes for forty minutes to disorient the passengers before arriving. These weren't strangers or enemies being treated this way, these were party and government officials, some of Saddam's closest confidants.

Saddam was also afraid of getting hit by US missiles. Years of precision strikes on Iraqi soil had shown Saddam what the US military was capable of, and they were only getting better with time. In response to that fear, Saddam constantly moved vehicles, equipment, and people around, anything he wanted protected from the US, even stuff not related to WMD. These movements got picked up by satellites and misinterpreted by analysts who hadn't spent time in Iraq and didn't understand the context of what they were seeing. This "evidence" was then given to the president who accepted it because it validated his biases. When enough "evidence" was gathered, it was combined with extremely speculative projections. (This might be where the lies came in. It was the projections that made Iraq sound like a truly pressing danger.) Then all of this information was packaged and presented to worldwide bureaucrats. That's how you get an American War on Iraq.

That said, the real question probably shouldn't be: Were there weapons of mass destruction in Iraq? The real question should be: Even with an arsenal of chemical and biological weapons would Iraq really have been a threat to the United States? The answer to that question is probably not, at least in the near term. Iraq would have been a major threat to some of our allies in the region and may have drawn us into a conflict anyway, but it's hard to see a scenario where Iraq would have threatened the United States itself. Saddam did have ties to terrorists, but he was much more calculated in his support of terrorism than the Taliban. If Bin Laden had fled to Iraq, it's a fair bet Saddam would have killed him to gain favor with the international community. Saddam preferred terrorism he could control, terrorism operated by his own agents against his own people. It's very unlikely he would have supplied chemical or biological weapons to anyone with ambitions to directly attack the United States. That's a fight he didn't want. It's just the fight he got.

So how do you account for what happened in Iraq? Who do you blame for the thousands of American soldiers dead, the hundreds of thousands of Iraqis dead, the people tortured or enslaved by ISIS, the mass slaughter of the innocent in a brutal civil war? How much blame do you assign to George Bush for seeing only what he wanted to see, to US congress for agreeing with him, to US intelligence for catering their information toward what the President wanted? How much blame do you assign to a short-sighted war plan, to off the cuff decisions that set up American soldiers for a brutal insurgency, to playing politics instead of securing Iraq and letting the

Iraqi people decide their own path forward? How much blame do you assign the corporate information peddlers for only showing half-truths, for twisting the story of Iraq at every turn in the ways they wanted the American people to see, for convincing the entire population of our country that Iraq was a lost cause even at the moment it had its best chance for a non-despotic future? How much blame do you assign Barack Obama for following through with his campaign promises no matter the cost, for taking something so many bled for and throwing it in their faces, for denying the votes of the Iraqi people and backing the man who lost Iraq's election, the man who was already handing Iraq over to the Mullahs of Iran?

What about Saddam Hussein's role, his lies, his delusions, his brutality, his constant pushing for power? What about Iraqi tribal leaders squabbling in the power vacuum, leading their people from bitter conflict to bitter conflict trying to get a larger piece of the new Iraq for themselves? What about Zarqawi and other foreign fighters swarming Iraq bringing blood and horror wherever they went, intentionally stoking the flames of the sectarian war that eventually came? What about Maliki opening the door to Iran, letting Iranian generals run operations inside Iraq, unleashing the terror that made a quarter of the country turn toward ISIS as a protector?

The list of people who played a role in the bloodletting of Iraq is long. It's a list filled with failure, greed, self-delusion, arrogance, and thirst for power. And the fallout landed on who it always lands on, the common people forced to endure the results.

(For more information on the failings of US intelligence from someone who saw it up close, check out *Hide and Seek* by Charles Duelfer.)

DARK-BRIGHT

When I got back from Ramadi, I used to pray every night before bed. Before the war, prayer meant nothing to me. Now, it was the only place I felt calm. I'd lie on my back for hours each night staring at the dark ceiling, talking to God. One night, in the middle of one of these long prayers, something dark fluttered across my vision, flying in a jerky irregular pattern like a bat or a giant flying beetle from Kuwait. I got off my bed, ducked my head, and walked to the light switch by the door. When I flipped on the light, there was no bat and no beetle. I searched all over the room, on top of the wooden bookshelves stretching from floor to ceiling, behind the white draftsman's desk in the corner and the dresser by the window. I kicked through a pile of dirty clothes at the foot of the bed, nothing. I decided I was seeing things, flipped off the light, hopped back in bed, and started praying again. Immediately, the fluttering began again. This time it was larger and more violent than before, like several bats were weaving past and through each other, but there was no sound, no flapping, no collisions, no squeals. Eager to figure out what was happening, I sprung out of bed again and stepped to the light switch, but when I flipped on the light, there was again nothing. The room was calm. I searched each individual bookshelf. I searched under the bed. I searched behind the collection of stuffed lions, dragons, and bears that used to protect me when I got scared as a little boy, but there was still nothing.

Now I was confused and uneasy. I flipped the light off and went back to bed. A thought came to my mind that I probably should have left alone. I hadn't been praying for much of my life, hadn't had any real faith beyond what had started to grow over the past year. Maybe something was trying to get in the way of that, trying to keep me from this new part of myself. I decided to talk to the thing.

"I know you're there," I said "And I know what you are trying to do. It's not going to work. Nothing you can do is going to stop me."

I started praying again.

The room erupted in total violence.

Everything around me began shaking like some massive earthquake without sound. I was like a hamster in a clear plastic ball, some huge being shaking me with all its strength just to let me know how much greater and stronger it was than me. My religious fervor was blasted to hell, and I leapt out of bed and ran to the light switch. When I flipped on the light, the room went still.

I stood frozen in terror, not daring to open my door and face the dark hallway, not daring to go back to the bed where this began. I stood in the corner by the light switch barely able to breathe. After fifteen or twenty minutes unable to move, I flipped on every light in my room, crawled into bed and pulled the covers tightly over my head, refusing to move from that position for the rest of the night, refusing even to peek outside of my covers at the fully lit room around me. It was like I was six years old again.

For the next couple weeks, I lived in absolute terror, each day dreading the setting of the sun, each night trembling in fully lit rooms waiting for the unknown thing to come for me again. I couldn't tell anyone. Being a guy just home from war, telling stories about dark forces shaking his bedroom didn't sound like the kind of attention I wanted, so I just added it to the list of things I didn't talk about. The thought of prayer made me physically ill for fear.

Around this time, I was supposed go on a trip to Utah to visit my friend Jim. Though I was frozen by fear, friendship eventually broke through the chill in my heart enough for me to get on the road. And right away, starting down the highway with a full sun overhead, I felt a little better. I had never been on a road trip that far west, and I felt a little thrill every time I pulled out the road atlas to navigate through a new city, or every time I saw a piece of land that was different than I was used to. I enjoyed the hours of rolling-hill farmland as I passed through Iowa, and the flat endless open of Nebraska. I was having fun stopping at little cities I had never heard of for gas. But after a long day of driving, sun sinking on the horizon, my anxiety started back up. I dreaded stopping at some crappy roadside motel, being alone in an unfamiliar place, waiting for the thing to come for me. I pulled off the highway in Laramie, Wyoming and got a room. As night came on full-force, I sat huddled in my blankets, every possible light on: overhead lights, bathroom lights, vanity lights, desk lights, TV. I spent most of the night wide awake in primal terror, willing myself to keep it together, cringing at every sound and feeling like something was there with me, watching, waiting for me to drift off so it could make its move. Late into the morning, as the sky started to lighten, I let myself drift into an uneasy sleep. A couple hours later I was back on the road.

The next day started heavy. I was worn out and somber, and as I drove through the miles of hilly sagebrush in southern Wyoming, the emptiness of the land seemed to mirror my feelings. But as I neared Utah, and the mountains became more prominent, the beauty of the land worked its way through me. I veered off I-80 onto a winding canyon road. I drove past waterfalls cascading down rocky cliff faces and cities nestled in foothills. I stopped briefly at a lake of mountain runoff and stared into a perfect reflection of white capped mountains and blue sky. I fell in love with the land, and for the first time since being back in the states, I felt really good, like I was in a place where I should be. When I finally met up with Jim in Provo, the darkness had gone.

On the last full day of my visit in Utah, Jim and I hiked up a mule deer trail in the canyon near his house. Winding up the narrow trail through scrub oak and pine, we hit a clearing, and I noticed a lone tree some distance up the mountain in front of us. It was scraggly, dead, and unremarkable, but it was the only tree on that part of the mountain, and I felt a pulsing need to get to it.

Forty minutes later, when we reached the tree, heavy snow began to fall. I wondered if we should start back down before the snow became unmanageable, but I couldn't bring myself to leave; the scene was too perfect. From our vantage point on the mountain, I watched the snow fall like I felt God must watch the snow, slowly drifting from a precipice on high to the valley below, not sleek pelting snow, but luscious fat snow, almost obese, lazily meandering down...down...down into the valley until it melded into the white blanket below. And then, as soon as I'd had my fill of watching, it stopped. Jim and I took a moment, breathed in the last remnants of peace, then started back down the mountain.

The sun peeked out behind me. Its warmth fell over my shoulders, flowed almost through me. I turned toward the sun, looked up and thanked God for the warmth.

"Mike, you've gotta look at this," Jim said from behind me.

Just as I turned back, the sky exploded with color. A huge thick rainbow streaked over the neighboring mountain, completely encompassing it. Everything below the arc was bathed in gold, from white-capped peak to scrub brush foothills, everything outside the arc was deep stormy grey. The rainbow cut a perfect line between snow clouds and sunshine, and the contrast made each the more stark. Jim and I watched, unable to speak.

For the second time in half an hour, a spectacular beauty struck us dumb, and for the second time, we soaked it in until we'd had our fill, and then it gently faded away. But where the serenity of the snowstorm left us calm and contemplative, the fierce color in the rainbow and golden mountain left us brimming over with energy, and we bounded down the mountainside, finding a supple trail of peat moss that allowed us to run and jump at almost full speed. Our hearts were so full we couldn't have stopped our feet if we wanted to, and in what seemed like minutes, we reached the bottom of the trail, washed our faces in clear mountain runoff and felt totally refreshed, like we hadn't been climbing at all.

As we drove away, I didn't know what it all meant, but I was grateful. I had been so full of terror and emptiness. I needed beauty to show me the world was not all darkness, pain, and fear. The world I'd been living in was brutal, untamable, and frankly beyond me, but in that moment, I didn't feel the need to carry it with me. In that moment, I was free.

★★★

Part of how I feel about the Iraq War will always be linked to my experience as a Marine. In some ways, Iraq raised me. I was a timid, doughy kid when I got there, a liability on the battlefield, but through insane moments, chaos, and pain, I became something else, and the men I served with showed me how.

Patterson and Chilcot taught me about consistency, about giving the same effort day in and day out, no matter how you feel or what's happening around you. Adler taught me about always learning, about applying yourself every minute of every day until you're the best at what you do. Kowalcek taught me about trust, about how special a team can be when each Marine knows he can count on the Marine next to him, and each Marine knows he can rely on the integrity of his team leader. Frank taught me how to survive in the dark, how to be the same straightforward asshole no matter who's watching. Mixon showed me that decency can exist anywhere. No matter how dark the situation, a man still has a choice.

Some Marines cracked under pressure. Some Marines were revealed by it. Some Marines showed fearlessness. Some Marines showed that even tough men have breaking points. All Marines taught me something.

I wasn't the toughest Marine in the Corps, the most battle-tested, or the bravest. I didn't suffer or lose the most—not even close. I joined the Marine Corps because I didn't like the person I was. I hoped they could teach me to stand like a man. I paid a heavy price for my lessons, but I got what I asked for. I learned to run in a pack. I learned to hold my own, and after all the horror, all the brutality, all the fighting with myself and the world around me, I found a place, and I was counted as one of them.

But all these years later, my feelings are still complicated. I've never regretted my small role in ridding Iraq of Saddam Hussein. I've never felt bad that his sons were gunned down or that his police state was broken. Given the opportunity to fight and break another regime like Saddam's, I'd probably take it if I had even a minor amount of trust in the decency of the US government, which I don't. I'm filled with memories of those early days of the war, people celebrating in the streets, people shouting praises and weeping with relief, men grinning, waiving their hands, passing out endless cigarettes in celebration. That euphoria was real, and the warmth in my heart from those memories will always be a part of how I feel about Iraq. But I also have memories of tremendous failures—failures in myself, and failures in Marines around me.

How I feel about our country's leaders is something else. Their values are so different from the men and women who actually fight. They make decisions based on power. The men on the ground make decisions based on life and death and the courage to face whatever hell comes. The politicians treat war like it's a game. They give orders and press buttons and hold rallies and people die. The men on the ground spend their blood protecting their brothers and trying to help a people they don't even know. The politicians make plans with powerful friends around the globe. They carve up economic interests and figure out which young men to use in order to get what they want. The men on the ground make two bucks an hour and think about not letting the Marine or Soldier next them down. The men I served with in Iraq were imperfect creatures, but I've never again in my life seen a group of people give so much of themselves in a cause that benefitted them nothing. Every drop of Marine blood was worth a thousand bureaucrats in Washington DC. I still can't believe how much damage those people did from offices across the ocean. Over a 150,000 Iraqis died from sectarian violence between 2003 and 2016. That's 150,000 people dying not from conflict with Soldiers and Marines but from the chaos largely caused by policy decisions made by the Bush and Obama administrations. Many hundreds of thousands more suffered other physical and psychological wounds that will likely never heal. And in the end, we abandoned the people of Iraq to their fate, left them with their broken country to try to pick up the pieces.

Mike Kubista

A couple of years after my last deployment to Iraq, when I was a missionary in Holland, I met an older Indonesian woman at a local congregation. Most of the time, I avoided talking about my military background when I was in Europe, but somehow the topic came up, and as soon as she heard I was a US Marine, her eyes lit up, and she bubbled over with enthusiasm and invited me over for dinner. When I arrived at the woman's house later that day, we sat down and started talking, and I understood why she was so excited.

During World War II, she was a little girl in a Japanese prison camp where Japanese soldiers were worse than animals. Her mother was the house matron for a building of girls and young women.

A Japanese officer came into the women's quarters one day and informed the mother that all the girls would now serve the Imperial Army as sex companions for officers, and that her job was to make them clean and pretty to begin their purpose that evening. A woman of immense faith and conscience, the mother knew she couldn't aid the soldiers in the rape of those girls, so as the girls sobbed hysterically around her, she took matters into her own hands. Instead of cleaning them and prepping them for use by the soldiers, she shaved each girl bald to make them less appealing to the soldiers and awaited her fate.

When the Japanese officer returned, he was beyond wrath and beat the mother mercilessly then threw her into pit of water and human waste where he made her stand for days while the putrid liquid ate away her flesh. According to the daughter, the mother bore it all with grace and dignity, barely staying alive, but succeeding, at least for a time, in protecting the virtue of the young girls from the soldiers.

Suddenly, the woman telling me her story looked at me and started to cry.

"US Marines took our camp from the Japanese. Young men like you came all the way around the world to people you didn't know and set us free. I will always remember the US Marines."

Helping people that desperately needed our help, freeing people that couldn't free themselves, ending a nightmare that for so many seemed like it would never end. That's how Iraq could have been. That's how Iraq should have been. But it's not how Iraq was.

Made in United States
Orlando, FL
01 March 2024